10p

UNREASONABLE BEHAVIOUR

Also by Jim Parton
and available from Simon & Schuster

The Bucks Stop Here

UNREASONABLE BEHAVIOUR

DIARY OF A DIVORCED MAN
BY JIM PARTON

SIMON & SCHUSTER
A VIACOM COMPANY

First published in Great Britain by Simon & Schuster, 1997
A Viacom Company

Simon & Schuster
West Garden Place
Kendal Street
London W2 2AQ

Simon & Schuster of Australia Pty Ltd Sydney

A CIP catalogue record for this book is available
from the British Library.

0-684-816 92-X

Printed and bound in Great Britain by
Butler & Tanner Ltd, Frome and London

ACKNOWLEDGEMENTS

Tessa Hilton for starting this project off. Jessica Davies for close involvement with early drafts. For later drafts, Jacquie Clare, my editor. Thanks to Martin and Mathilda Thompson of Abercrombie and Kent for setting up my discussions in Uganda. For helping me through an unpleasant divorce, Lisa Adamczewski (hope I've spelt that right), Eile Gibson, Kathleen Haskard, Mary Clare Jerram, The London Japanese Rugby Football Club, Katie Matthews, Lewis McCormack, Rupert Otten, Nick and Kerry Parton, Stephen Soghoian, Steve Stephenson, Teresa and Bernard Stillwell, Lucy Stuart, my parents. As a rule it is better to represent yourself in a divorce but there are some family lawyers who I would recommend in some circumstances, including Caroline Attwood, Martha Cover, Karen Davies and Hilary Pennington-Mellor. Various friends thought it would be fun to be acknowledged at the front of a book. I can indulge them in that. Jane Eastell, Anne Peach, Deborah Walter, Jane Ward.

DEDICATION

For the Memory of Bruce Lidington, Chairman of Families
Need Fathers for far too short a time. You didn't half leave
us in a mess by dying. Where did you put the bloody bank
statements?

INTRODUCTION

My ex-wife and I are friends now, thank goodness, but for too long our lives were very much as described in the pages that follow. *Unreasonable Behaviour* is a story that any separated parent will recognize, except that I wouldn't for a moment make out that my own sex life is anything like as complicated as that of the hero of this narrative, Michael Henry. That would be boasting.

I must emphasize that for legal reasons this is not my own story retold. I have been threatened with libel writs three times in my life and although I have seen off all three without apologizing, it really was most vexing at the time. Proceedings in Family Law are conducted 'In Chambers' which means 'In Secret'. This is designed to protect the children involved. But secrecy corrodes natural justice – it makes the whole system unaccountable. If a judge is so out of touch he or she comes out with the equivalent of 'Who are the Beatles?' their inadequacy is not properly exposed. And if they are overbearing or rude, as many are, no one will know.

Legal professionals can bully or be plain lazy if they like. There are few checks. The Inner London Probation Service, for example, which has the responsibility for producing all the welfare reports deciding the futures of countless children, has no formal complaints procedure. Other regions are no better. The officer himself assesses his own work and lo! discovers he's done a fine job. If the complaint is continued up to the next level, the officer's superior will state (in writing) that he does not need to look at the case file to assess the work. No complaints procedure means no quality control.

The Solicitors' Family Law Association has an excellent Code of Conduct, but no sanctions. They have never upheld a complaint against a member in their history. Solicitors join because the promise of membership looks good on their note-paper. The SFLA employs a PR company to keep us all thinking that they are a good thing. But no complaints procedure means no quality control. Scandal or what?

I sought help from the campaigning charity Families Need Fathers during my divorce. I'm not sure how, but I've ended up as national chairman.* I stumbled over a layer of society, of angry, embittered men (mainly) with an acute sense of injustice arising from the fact that the will does not seem to exist to help them stay in touch with their children.

Fatherlessness affects nearly 50% of the child population. That's a million kids, probably. Tragedy or what? To me, it's the main social issue of the age.

Jim Parton.
March 1997

*For more information about Families Need Fathers call 0171 613 5060, or write to:
134 Curtain Rd
London EC2

IT was as we attacked the *foie gras* that she said, 'I'm going to leave you.' I wasn't too worried, because this particular bad patch was not especially worse than any other bad patch as far as I could see. It was nearing Christmas, a time of high stress in any family, and I surmised that Marie-Sophie was probably suffering from a bout of SAD, or Seasonal Affective Disorder (the syndrome that afflicts some people as the days draw in and sunlight becomes scarce). If my wife was Finnish or Swedish, more concern might have been warranted, because it was the time of year when Finns and Swedes disappear off into the forest on their cross country skis and top themselves. But Marie-Sophie is French, and I felt sure that if the *entente* was less *cordiale* than it might be, it was only a temporary set-back.

'Good pâté, this,' I said, feeling that perhaps I had not complimented her enough on her unusually lavish culinary efforts. 'Where did you get it?'

'Harrods. Michael, I just said that I am going to leave you, and I am going to take Pierre with me. I want to get him accustomed to the idea of our living apart before I take him back to France. I can't stand this country any more.'

Now, Pierre is the apple of my eye so, cool as I am, I didn't have the self control to let this remark pass. 'You wouldn't win custody,' I said, as I spread a bit of pâté on some thinly cut toast. My mouth had gone slightly dry

1

so I took a slug of the champagne she'd bought.

'Women always get custody, my solicitor says so.'

'Not these days,' I replied. 'You work, I work, but I spend more time at home. Anyway, this is where Pierre lives, this is where his school is. You wouldn't have a chance of winning custody.'

'That's not what my *solicitor* says,' she repeated, emphasis on the word solicitor.

I didn't bother asking 'What solicitor?'. We have all got a friend of a friend who is a solicitor but not for a moment did I think my wife had actually been to see one. So she was picking a fight, and what better way to get at me than by threatening to take Pierre away from me?

I decided it was prudent not to expand on the leanings of the long arm of the law and made a few carefully chosen comments to the effect that I really was enjoying my meal. But when we got on to the salmon she said, 'Michael, I don't love you any more. In fact, I think I never did.' The whole evening had started to go quite badly and she had more than succeeded in putting me off my food. By now, it wasn't just that my mouth was dry, I felt as if I had been socked in the stomach, too.

I thought it was a bit unnecessary to say such a thing. A husband and a wife can have a few scraps during which hurtful comments get aired, that's all part of it, but some things not only shouldn't be said – they are taboo. When Marie-Sophie told me she didn't and never had loved me, I didn't believe her. 'Don't be silly, of course you do, dear,' I said. 'We're married.' Which to me explained everything: marriage is 'till death do us part' and not until one party gets bored and wants to go back to France.

You are allowed various weapons in a domestic tiff: a good sulk, the withholding of conjugal rights for a day or two, even a month or two. My speciality with Marie-Sophie was a gratuitous insult directed at the mother-in-law's taste in floral curtains. Marie-Sophie's was to rail at me down the phone at the stockbroker's office where I did translations, knowing full well that, although I was on a reasonably lucrative contract which paid me by the 1,000 words, personal conversations on the company telephones by menial, non-commission earners like me, were strongly disapproved of.

There is a sort of Geneva convention of domestic quarrels whereby she is free to throw saucepan lids, or indeed plates at you, provided she always misses. If she chooses wedding presents given by your friends or family as missiles, then that represents a marked escalation in hostilities. The mass destruction of a dinner service given to you by your own mother would be pretty serious, the equivalent of carpet-bombing Dresden. Saying 'I don't love you any more' or 'I don't think I ever really loved you' on the other hand, is like dropping an atom bomb on Hiroshima.

So when she said that, I'd finally had enough and lost my temper. I didn't throw plates at her, as she would have at me, but did something far more stupid. I took the cut glass bowl containing an attractive and delicious *tricolore* salad and upturned it with considerable force on the table. The bowl shattered, depositing mozzarella, tomato and avocado everywhere. For good measure I then hurled a china candlestick (cheap one from a distant relative of mine) at the wall, where some of the melted wax left an agreeable splat. *Rage over, player one.* Nintendo should develop a game called 'Wedded Bliss', I thought.

I immediately felt very silly. Also, my forefinger hurt rather a lot, and when I looked at the many colours mingling on the table, splatters of blood added a certain *je ne sais quoi* to the slightly pallid winter hot house tomatoes and mustard dressing. I extracted a shard of broken glass from the base of my forefinger, which then bled profusely.

I said 'sorry', but Marie-Sophie burst into tears and without saying anything went upstairs to her *'boudoir'*. *Boudoir* is about the right word for it: she used it as a dressing-room, a study and for bouding (in French the verb *bouder* implies quite an intense sulk). I heard her lifting the telephone. Her solicitor? Naah, that was just a bluff. Anyway, who would call their solicitor at ten in the evening?

I decided to try and make amends by clearing away the mess and doing the washing-up, which is not the easiest task one-handed, left-handed at that (my damaged finger continued to bleed quite badly). The salad was a gonner, but the salmon would do for my lunch the next day since I was planning to skip going to the office and work from home.

Afterwards, I took some of the remaining champagne up to Marie-Sophie. She was still on the phone and gestured me away. 'Shut the door,' she said. I guessed she was on to her friend Tiffany, which was a bad sign. I quite liked Tiffany then, probably for no better reason than that she was blonde with great legs – very attractive for a feminist, I used to think. Tiffany, for her part, had never approved of me. This could be because I worked for the City, albeit in an ancillary non-capitalist-pig-dog role. But it was probably just to do with the fact that I am a man. Where I had a problem with Tiff was that Marie-Sophie would frequently ring her of an evening, usually just as I was serving supper. British Telecom run advertising campaigns about the importance of maintaining communication, with slogans like 'It's good to talk' and 'Make that call'. I think they should add a rider: 'But NOT during supper time'.

Marie-Sophie did, and still does, a busy, unsociable-hours job as a roving TV reporter and researcher for a French TV station. At this time, I worked sometimes at my office in the City and sometimes at home, so it often, usually even, fell to me to cook and tend to Pierre. If Marie-Sophie fancied a 'girly chat' (*girly* being the wrong word for anything to do with Tiff) it could go on for an hour or more, by the end of which I had given up waiting and eaten my food, while hers had gone cold. I felt that if there was now a breakdown in communications between Marie-Sophie and myself, a good part of the cause was her enslavement to the bloody telephone and the person on the other end of it.

Marie-Sophie was obviously still upset so I closed the door as requested and let her be. But I did put my ear to the door to try and overhear the extent to which I was in the doghouse. I couldn't hear much except that I was obviously the topic of conversation: 'And you know what he did next . . .' and so on, all delivered in sympathy-inviting tones. I didn't much enjoy the feeling Marie-Sophie gave me that I was a permanent subject of discussion amongst her friends. In my darkest hours I would imagine myself being tried and found guilty by unmarried and childless women like Tiff, who would say brightly, 'Why don't you leave him if he is so awful? You'd be much happier on your own.'

THAT night Marie-Sophie slept on the sofa-bed in her boudoir while I occupied the matrimonial bed. 'Wedlock the deep, deep peace of the double bed after the hurly burly of the *chaise-longue*' as the actress Mrs Patrick Campbell once said, except that I couldn't sleep. Marie-Sophie had put the wind up me. It wasn't the first time she had threatened to leave me, to the extent that it had become like the little boy crying wolf. This time it seemed different, though, even if I couldn't quite put my finger on why other than the fact that she hadn't thrown anything at me.

I'd long been accustomed to dodging flying saucepan lids, although they had not really presented any particular danger. I put it down to Marie-Sophie being French. The French play neither cricket nor baseball, and thus have no culture of throwing things accurately. The only exception to this deficiency in hand – eye co-ordination comes in the gentle game of *pétanque*, or boules, which is no preparation for doing damage to a husband. Even so, being pragmatic people, the French sensibly don't allow their wives to play *pétanque* either. So, although Marie-Sophie had the habit of displaying displeasure by throwing saucepan lids, or crockery, I was never in any physical danger. Nonetheless, Le Creuset is heavy stuff, and it is better to get out of the way just in case. My policy was definitely to let the kitchen units take the brunt of any attack.

It was a surprise and a shock when, quite early on in the marriage, the first lid came my way, but I soon learnt from conferring with my married colleagues at the office that mine was not a particularly unusual case. There is a whole world out there of ratty women who slam doors, chuck crockery, or have prolonged sulks. Call me complacent but, in spite of such goings on, I had never previously considered our marriage to be seriously at risk. You expect ups and downs.

When I got married, my old Aunt Winifred wrote me a letter with various bits of advice in it, one of which was that you must never go to sleep on an argument. That was how she and Uncle Hubert, God rest his soul, had stayed happily married for 53 years, although I think that if I had endeavoured to follow this piece of advice I would never have got any sleep at all: Marie-Sophie could never let an argument go. If you ever admitted to one shortcoming she'd be flushed with success and demand that you admit to more. After a while the only defence was to admit to nothing except being perfect. It was the basis for quite a few arguments.

As it was, I lay awake and pondered the unusual display of fine fare that Marie-Sophie had chosen for dinner. I was somewhat unpleasantly reminded of the observations of a guy at work some weeks before. He wasn't a close friend but we'd gone for a lunch-time pint and had begun discussing wives and how to manage them. He told me that his wife would express her displeasure by dispensing with the usual pre-cooked professional girl's supper from Marks and Spencer and cooking him a fantastic meal. She chooses a day when she knows he has had a huge business lunch, then repeats one of the menus she originally seduced him with. She portrays the occasion as a treat, the point being that because of its symbolism of happier times he cannot refuse it. A huge steak (*saignant*, with a mass of vegetables including *gratin dauphinois* laden with cream and cheese) is followed by a pudding, outwardly light, like lemon syllabub, but built with double cream and impossible to digest. The couple then go through a charade in which she works out her anger by pretending she loves him more than anything in the world, while he pretends that he is thrilled at the spread placed before him. He is bloated, but for the sake of a quiet life has to eat the lot. If he is really in the doghouse she can make him suffer further·

'Darling, I can't manage the rest of this steak, would you eat it?' she coos.

'I'm a bit full, why don't you . . .' *give it to the cat*, he'd like to say, but obviously he can't say that, he'd end up in even deeper trouble, so the sentence is left in the air.

'Oh you are sweet, don't worry about me, I'm not hungry,' she says and plonks a large lump of her steak on his plate which he then has to eat.

Marie-Sophie had clearly gone for a variation of torture by steak. She had taken a great deal of trouble to 'put together a very nice supper with expensive ingredients. *Foie gras* followed by salmon? Candles? Best silver? Champagne? Was her idea to soften the blow? As Last Suppers go, it was ruinously miscalculated.

Still, things always seem their worst late at night. I say tomato, you say *tomate*, I say potato, you say *pomme de terre*, but no need to call the whole thing off. She'd be fine in the morning and so, as usual, I went to sleep on the argument.

<< >> << >>

A few days later, we were still sleeping on it but I lived in hope of my wife coming to her senses before Christmas. It was the day of my firm's Christmas party and I'd had enough of the doldrums, I wanted to get festive. In the morning I took Pierre to school as I usually did, while the trouble and strife lay in. I was particularly attentive to his morning babble as I knew I would be coming back home both late and drunk. There would have been an argument for dropping the party and rushing home from the office with a big bunch of flowers clutched in my wounded hand, but I didn't see why I should miss an occasion which would be fun just because my wife was miffed.

The firm party was generally quite lavish. There were serious tasks to be accomplished, like collaring people in high places once they'd got drunk and making sure that your job was not about to be written out of your department's business plan. But the main aim, for me anyway, was to drink too much then flirt disgracefully with Annie from personnel.

As yet, I had never come close to committing adultery. I

have wondered since whether this was a matter for self-congratulation or not. I would like to think that I was a man of such probity and moral fibre that I would never even have considered it; after all, it is wrong and disgusting and unfair to all parties involved: husband, wife, mistress, dependants. There is also the small matter that I loved my wife so much that I would never have thought of such a betrayal.

Anyway, sex isn't everything. After a few years of being married you don't feel the need to perform against the latest mid-market tabloid survey on how many times the average couple does it a week: in my experience once or twice a month is about right – less is frustrating, more a chore (excepting, of course, the possibility of thrice-a-night rekindling of activity on holiday).

So I would like to believe.

The reality was, as Jimmy Carter once put it, 'I've looked on a lot of women with lust, I've committed adultery in my heart many times . . .' (assuming that this is not an admission from the ex-president of the United States that he spends a lot of time in private with filthy magazines). But I had never even contemplated starting an affair. Perhaps this was because I managed to exude such an aura of saintly impenetrability that no woman dared make a play for me. Maybe I am so very unworldly that hordes of women were constantly trying to get me into bed but I didn't notice. Or it could be that I am so unattractive that no woman ever considered it.

Discount the last possibility. It isn't true. No one is that unattractive. King Henry VIII had no trouble pulling even when his face was at its most volcanically bilious, and Lady Caroline Lamb was keen on Byron despite his club foot. Probably kissed its toes even. Besides, Marie-Sophie fancied me lots to begin with. The truth is that I was never exposed either to the opportunity or the temptation, and so my views on adultery (I am definitely against it on paper at least) had not at this point in time been put to the test. Would I have had the will power to resist? I don't know. Marie-Sophie had once come back from a month away in France and accused me of having an affair, but I hadn't had one. If I had, she would have wrung the confession out of me in minutes, because I am the world's worst liar.

It should be emphasized of course, that chatting up Annie had nothing at all to do with adultery – rather it was enacting some pathetic male fantasy about being fancied by someone young and attractive, and by someone who everyone else in the office fancied. However, as I walked over to her, the thought did cross my mind that if I was going to be divorced I might as well be hanged for a sheep as a lamb. I ought to do something really wicked like sleep with Annie.

Unfortunately, at that moment I was intercepted by a jocular prat called Roger. Actually, he was a good friend of mine and, whilst I considered him to be arrogant, boorish, thoroughly superficial, and disapproved of the way he led a succession of women up the garden path, he was quite a laugh and I liked him. He was a French equity salesman, giving investment institutions like Clerical and Medical or Mercury Asset Management advice on what to buy and sell for the French portion of their share portfolios.

Technically, he was my senior, because he decided which bits of language research should make their way into English to help his sales effort. Roger wasn't that senior to me but there was something about occasions like the Christmas party which made him show off his responsibilities as a caring, sharing boss. He'd come over all pastoral and try to catch up with the well-being of his staff, a mood which never seemed to afflict him at any other time and one which profoundly irritated me.

'How's that beautiful wife of yours, still giving you the run around then?' was his greeting to me. He knew better than to start pulling rank on me and anyway, he was always asking about Marie-Sophie. 'Her-not-indoors' he called her. It was a bit double-edged because what he usually meant was 'Buggering off to get child from child-minder again?' Or 'Unavailable for overtime or a beer after work?' Bad for team spirit and end of year bonus. Roger's bonus that is.

'The run around?' I now countered. 'She says she is going to leave me.' I said this with a smile, the intention being to make him feel as bad as possible about asking after Marie-Sophie. Even so, I didn't quite expect him to look at me as if I'd just told him I'd got a brain tumour and only three months to live.

'Sorry. Put my foot in a bit, didn't I?' he said with, for him, unusual awkwardness.

It was fun to embarrass Roger, hard-nosed stockbroker extraordinaire, not known for his sensitivity. I'd succeeded where others had failed miserably. It bothered me however that he was taking me so seriously. Could he possibly know something I didn't?

'My misfortunes are not anybody else's, you weren't to know,' I said with a show of bravery I thought would embarrass him further.

Roger just didn't seem to know how to react. He usually found it amusing to say something along the lines of 'I fancy that bird of yours. When you've finished with her send her my way.' To add extra piquancy to the joke he even used to say it in front of Marie-Sophie. 'I'll have to ask her permission,' I would reply, to which she would say, 'That's fine, he's more attractive than you, Michael.' She didn't mean it; at least, I hope not because, despite being a little bit younger than me, Roger was balding, paunchy and prematurely grey without being distinguished.

'Come on Roger, can't let my worries spoil the Christmas *joie de vivre*,' I said. 'Snap out of it. If I look sad and self-pitying, quite apart from being exhausting, it will be very dull for other people. My marriage is on the rocks, so what? So are the marriages of three hundred thousand other Britons. It beats being Bosnian. A few drinks inside me, and I'll be back to my normal self. Don't worry about me. Anyway stress is good for you. It's supported by scientific study you know.'

I began to explain to him about a famous experiment in which a test group of hamsters had been put in a 'stimulating environment' while a control group had been left to contend with the boring insides of a dull old cage. Both groups were fed the same food and kept at the same temperature. The 'stimulated' group were then subjected, over a set period of weeks to loud rap music, a cat scratching at the bars, a mad scientist with wild hair injecting hamsters with morphine nearby, that sort of thing, while the unstressed group were let be. Following this period, identical for both groups, the hamsters were marched out of their quarters and they too were assassinated with a shot of morphine. Dissection and extraction of brains followed. These were then weighed on high precision scales. On average, the stressed-out hamsters had heavier brains than the unstressed ones who'd had the quiet life in a boring cage.

'Thus Roger,' I rambled, 'I rejoice in the hard time my darling wife is giving me. It's life on the edge, it's fun, it's good for me, it's making me more intelligent by the minute.'

Roger had several problems with this conversation, I could see. One was dealing with someone who has just told you he has a major personal disaster looming in his private life. Another was that, as my supposed friend, he had completely failed to notice anything untoward (mind you, so had I). The third was that I was apparently cheerful, when I should be distraught. This obviously puzzled him, although he would probably have run a mile if I'd blubbed all over him. He probably thought that I had taken leave of my senses and with hindsight he might have been right to think so.

Roger got out of it lightly in the end: 'Women huh. Can't do with 'em, can't do without 'em.'

Well, things could only get better and they were already doing so: Annie was coming our way. Her face lit up when she saw us – at the sight of Roger. Annie was a nice girl from Romford, in Essex, as it happened. No matter that Essex girl jokes were *passé*, Roger couldn't resist them.

'What's the difference between an Essex man and an Essex girl?' he had time to ask me.

'Dunno.'

'An Essex girl has a higher sperm count.'

Dear me. Most unfair really. On the other hand, that very day, Annie had probably entered Roger's bonus into the payroll system. She knew which side her bread was buttered on all right. I was making about 25 grand as a humble translator; I could have earned considerably more because it was a well paid position, but I didn't work quite as hard as I ought. Domestic duties for one prevented me from doing so and, well, I have to admit that I wasn't driven in the same way as Roger. Annie had obviously sized me up and passed. In the final analysis what counts is not Linford's lunchbox but Lloyd-Webber's wad.

I got home and into the matrimonial bed at about half past one in the morning. I was quite surprised and relieved to find Marie-Sophie in it, rather than sulking next door. *Rage Over, Player Two*?

I tried to put my arms around her, but she pushed me away.

'Don't touch me,' she said. *'Tu es degoutant!'*

This was undoubtedly fair because I am sure that I smelt of both cigarettes (passively smoked) and booze (actively drunk). She obviously had not forgiven me, which was a pity because she was quite provocatively apparelled (in other words silkily naked). *In vino veritas.* Whatever the upsets of the nights before I still fancied her, and even given that she was naked and I was drunk, it amounted to more than lust.

I gave up and lay awake musing before going to sleep. It was not just me who found her attractive, lots of men seemed to. She was permanently being opportuned on the Tube and people like Roger went on about her all the time. Perhaps she was the one having an affair.

When we had first fallen in love – or I had fallen in love – I was a lodger in a cheap room belonging to her parents in Paris. I had been an impoverished English teacher on an exchange. In Parisian apartment blocks these rooms are often several stories above the actual apartment, and are where the domestics lived back when people could afford them. They are very basic, with a wash basin, if you are lucky. I used to have to pretend I was a member of the squash club in Montparnasse to shower.

Marie-Sophie's parents were quite chuffed at having an in-house English teacher, and I was frequently invited to spend evenings with them. Marie-Sophie used to sneak up to my quarters or we would go off into the Parisian night for romantic escapes. Her parents were quite small 'c' conservative and large 'C' Catholic and would have been horrified if they had found out that their daughter was carrying on with the Englishman upstairs. I marvelled at the range of subterfuges employed by my girlfriend to keep them in the dark. If you live with ultra-strict parents then the ability to wield guile is a skill you learn at an early age. We were careful never to leave, or arrive at the apartment block at the same time, and if we were going away together

I had to meet her several streets away in a café.

She once bought her parents an SNCF five-day break in a Château-Hôtel with a famous restaurant, somewhere in the Jura, as a thirtieth wedding anniversary present. This gave me the opportunity to move in downstairs while they were away, where we enjoyed several days of orgiastic excess. We got the time of their return wrong: they arrived early one morning (well, about half past eleven) and I found myself trapped in Marie-Sophie's room while her parents gushed over their daughter and told her what a fantastic time they had had, and how sweet it had been of her to send them away like that. Marie-Sophie failed completely to get her mother out for some fresh air (*'Je suis trop fatiguée cherie'*).

I was obliged to enact a real-life French bedroom farce, spending until about four that afternoon under her bed. The family's Irish setter discovered me very quickly and started barking, but fortunately this did not amount to a security risk. The dog was in-bred and mad and thus taken no notice of. I had the opportunity, too, to kiss Marie-Sophie's feet as she made her bed, and to relieve an aching bladder into her wash-basin while the family were in the kitchen having lunch.

It was all dead romantic, but it did cross my mind that if Marie-Sophie were ever to employ any of this armoury of deception against me for any reason (such as having an affair) I would be the last to find out.

<< >> << >>

THE next day we had breakfast together with Pierre. We didn't exchange many words beyond 'More coffee?'. There was nothing to read into this – it was less likely to be a symptom of the *froideur* than of the time of the morning. Pierre was on good form, and made a big fuss of us both, as he always did when we ate *en famille*, possibly because our differing schedules made such occasions relatively rare.

Children are often attributed with great instinctive insights into problems between parents, picking up on atmospheres and becoming disturbed. I would be very surprised if he had the faintest inkling that there were any difficulties between us, and on this morning he was very happy. This child was virtually bomb-proof, nearly always placid and good natured; if we ever had a *pas devant l'enfant* argument it seemed to wash over him completely. It surprised me because my own parents very rarely had arguments in front of their children. If they did I felt very uncomfortable. I suppose it's what you are used to and Pierre was used to seeing us fight.

At six, he was a lively, sociable child, with a complete lack of shyness arising, I think, from a policy of bringing him up like a Mediterranean child, where children join in social occasions and are not packed off to bed while the adults enjoy themselves. His dark good looks were inherited not from me, I modestly admit, but from his mother; the Mediterranean genes giving him something of the appearance of an infant Omar Sharif. Being a bit of a mixture he also had what they would describe on *Gardener's Question Time* as 'hybrid vigour'. Slightly less euphemistically, his teachers sometimes complained that he was 'a bit of a handful'. When we took him to school that morning we were due to hear his teacher give her Christmas report on his progress, and find out if he had become more of a handful than in the previous year.

At his birth I had to fight off suggestions that he be called Yannick (after the tennis-playing Noah) which just sounds silly in English (probably in French, too). I think the idea of Yannick sprung from a penchant Marie-Sophie had for annoying her parents. She went through a phase of dressing in African styles and telling people she was black. She has the distinct dark skin common amongst Corsicans. Her family had a great, or a great-great, grandparent who spent time in colonial Mauritius, so who knows what blood Marie-Sophie has in her veins.

As a family, they always seemed to be a bit defensive on the subject, which I found odd because at other times they wouldn't lose the opportunity to remind you that Napoleon was Corsican and that, according to them, most of the higher echelons of France remain peopled by Corsicans.

Speaking as someone who is so English he doesn't even have a Scottish antecedent that he knows of (although my pork-pie manufacturing grandfather used to tease my grandmother that her Germanic surname came from distant Jewish roots), it is not for me to comment. But still, why should they not be proud of the Mauritian bit? It is boring being pure-blooded English (in other words a mixture of Celt, Roman, Viking, Pict, Angle or Saxon). The pedigree Irish setter was beautiful to look at, but profoundly stupid. If you pointed out of the window and said *lapin*, it would get very excited and look to jump out for a good chase. If it had leapt, I think it would have been a merciful release. Who wants to be pure-blooded anything?

I had always thought that our particular mix of French and Englishness had turned out very well. Obviously I was wrong, but I still maintain that it certainly did in Pierre. Most parents are full of the achievements of their children and I am no exception, so during this next bit indulge me and refrain from throwing up if it is too gushing. Apart from being good-looking and lively, Pierre (now eight) is bright (well, I think so). That he is behind with his reading is a disappointment, given that he mastered the alphabet at three. Marie-Sophie thinks it's just an attention thing because as long as he can't read, someone is obliged to read to him. It could also be to do with the fact that he has two languages to learn. Marie-Sophie has taken great care to ensure, with my heavily-accented support, that he is bilingual. Pierre is constantly correcting my genders, although I am still slightly better than him at tenses. At eight and thirty-eight respectively, neither of us can do the subjunctive.

Pierre has a complete fascination with anything mechanical. He may not have fulfilled early promise with regard to reading but he can follow complex instructions to make sophisticated models from Lego Technics (a sort of advanced Lego with cogs and drive shafts and tiny fiddly bits). Lego is a great toy – possibly the best thing ever to have come out of Denmark – but the composition of the sets, is clearly accountant-led because each packet is supplied with only exactly the right number of fiddly bits. Thus, when the fiddliest bit disappears down the back of the sofa you have a major crisis on your hands. It is always the crucial link which drives the helicopter's rotor blades. On top of this, Lego designers have taken great pains to ensure that no dad can devise or improvise a replacement. There is nothing for it but to go out and buy another set, and Lego Technics is bloody expensive.

On the packets of the models Pierre currently constructs it says 'For ages 10+', so Pierre must be clever, although there is a form of inflation in the labelling of products aimed at children. No parent of an eight-year-old would buy a T-shirt marked 'Age 8' for example. You want an 'Age 10' one so that it lasts a couple of years. The manufacturers respond to this by making the ones labelled 'Age 10' deliberately small. The parent who wants a T-shirt to last an eight-year-old for two years thus has to buy an 'Age 12' one. Every parent likes the idea that their child is not small for its age, and so sales are good of T-shirts marked 'Age 12', despite the fact that these are appreciably dearer than the ones labelled 'Age 8'.

He asks questions non-stop. There are plenty of 'How Things Work' books on the market but, though I've swotted up on them, they never seem to cover Pierre's current obsession. As Marie-Sophie and I sat eating breakfast on that morning of marital discord, it was gasometers. A couple of weeks before, we had driven past the gasometer next to Chelsea Bridge and on this occasion Pierre said that it was lower than usual. Having never consciously observed the thing, I was in no position to contradict him. 'That's interesting Pierre,' I said, and thought that the matter had been laid to rest, childish curiosity satisfied.

So there we were, at breakfast: Marie-Sophie and I trying not to talk, me with head buried in newspaper, when he asked, 'Why did the gasometer get lower, Daddy?'

I was tempted to answer 'to reach the other side' but Pierre was already familiar with the chicken crossing the road joke and wouldn't have found it funny.

'Because people have been using a lot of gas.'

'Why?'

The dreaded *Why*. My head was thumping from the effects of the previous evening but I did my best.

'For cooking and heating.'

'Why?'

'Because it's cold.'

'Why don't they fill it up again?'

'I don't know, ask British Gas.'

I pretended to be deeply engrossed in the paper. Accounts of who was divorcing whom, murdering whom, libelling whom. Strangely nothing about gasometers or even British Gas.

'How does it get into your house?'

'Through pipes.'

'What makes it go through the pipes? Is there a kind of propeller inside?'

'I don't think so.' I tried to imagine whether it was pumped or what. It was something I had never thought about before. 'I think it works by pressure.' I knew this was the wrong thing to say the moment I'd said it. It introduced a new concept to be explained.

'What's pressure?'

'Er . . . the gasometer is very heavy, and it squashes the gas, that's called pressure, and it squeezes it down the pipes into our homes.'

We both paused for thought, while I reunited myself with the story of the younger son of a peer who had been sent down for two weeks for dealing in cannabis at his Oxford college and Pierre had a mouthful of Coco Pops.

'Why does gas burn?' he asked dribbling milk and Coco Pops down his clean school sweatshirt.

'*Manges comme il faut,*' said Marie-Sophie angrily.

'Quite right,' I added in a moment of parental unity.

'*Oui, Maman.*' He pretended to swat at the spreading stain with his napkin but was not to be diverted. 'Daddy, why?'

'It burns when it is mixed with air and lighted.'

'Which burns, the gas or the air?'

It was a completely logical question about cause and effect, or chickens and eggs, of the kind that exercises philosophers for years of their academic lives. It was way beyond me at breakfast time, and should have been way beyond my six-year-old, too.

'Pierre, get on with your bloody cornflakes otherwise we are going to be late for school. We've got to meet your teacher today,' I growled.

'They're Coco Pops, Daddy . . .'

The joys of parenthood are not always obvious in the early morning; from the happy moment when the child first bounces on its parent's head at 6 a.m. until being shuttled off to school, they are sometimes difficult to identify.

Morning is when children are at their sunniest, most alert and most cheerful and you are at your least.

After breakfast we walked the two minutes or so round the corner to the school. The teacher, Miss Jardine, said that Pierre was doing very well, 'But he is a bit lively at times . . .' So that was fine. Then Marie-Sophie suddenly said, 'He's going to a new school next term, because my husband and I are separating.'

Blimey! I'd heard this one before but I must have missed the bit where it was agreed upon. All right, darling, I promise to take all your most ridiculous threats seriously from now on, but on the condition you make them in private, OK? Bringing innocent third parties like the school teacher into our argument was a marked escalation in hostilities. Thermonuclear war.

I said, 'That is not quite yet decided.' I didn't want the meeting to degenerate into a 'I'm going and I'm taking Pierre', 'Oh no you're not', 'Oh yes I am' session. Not in front of the teacher.

Matrimonial rows, like sex, should be between consenting adults in private. Now I heard the teacher say, 'I'm very sorry to hear that. He is such a nice, well-adjusted boy, I never dreamt that there might be problems at home. Some of our children, you know . . .' Then she added, 'It can be best for children to have the stability of continuity, and the school can help to provide that. Mr Henry, when you leave your wife, perhaps it might be as well to bear that in mind.'

'I'm not leaving,' I said. The teacher looked confused, but the whole topic was not one of my raising.

We left Pierre at the school and on our way back home had some cross words. Soccer or snooker stars if guilty of a crime like head-butting a spectator get hauled before committees and accused of 'bringing their sport into disrepute'. I now accused Marie-Sophie of bringing our marriage into disrepute. 'Can't you keep our problems to ourselves. Nothing is decided yet,' I said.

'I'm not joking, Michael. In fact, I am looking for a flat. I think I may have found one.' She went on that she needed to think things over, she needed her own space, being with me was making her ill. It isn't pleasant to be told by your wife that you make her ill. But then she switched to reassuring mode. 'Look. After a while I might even come back.'

'In that case, why do you need to involve Pierre, embarrass us both in front of his bloody teacher? Move out yourself, tackle your problems yourself, but leave the boy in his home, near his school with all his friends.'

I was obvious (to me) that Pierre should remain with me, particularly if she was saying that she might change her mind and come back, and especially as I reckoned that her busy TV reporting job meant that I'd end up having him dumped on me at short notice more than half the time anyway. Why uproot him? She repeated to me that her solicitor had advised her that women always win custody, so I might as well let her and him go.

'What solicitor?' I asked this time.

'She is called Rachel Bonham-Lee, of Bonham-Lee and Baldinelli. I advise you to get a solicitor, too.'

'You seriously think that you're going to win custody working your hours,' I mocked.

'Does Dolly Parton sleep on her back?'

Not a bad joke for a French woman.

<< >> << >>

CHRISTMAS came and went, and she didn't leave. We spent Christmas with my parents before crossing to Paris for the New Year with hers. There wasn't even much of an argument about it, because it happened to fit in with her work schedule.

We didn't row, but my parents are quite astute and asked me if anything was wrong between us. My father offered to have a word with Marie-Sophie, in fact he tried, but didn't get very far. I think she may have been already fighting the divorce in her head, and didn't want to compromise herself, because, as I was to discover, she had indeed been to see a solicitor.

She said to me, 'Your dad is sweet' though, which was quite a breakthrough, because Marie-Sophie had never forgiven them for opposing our marriage. Our marriage had got off on the wrong foot for various reasons. When you go and live in another country the risk is that you fall in love with the country first, then find the lover, and my parents were concerned that this was what had happened with me. Who knows? I did love France, no question, still do, but I was also in love with Marie-Sophie.

We had a little slip-up in our *chambre de bonne* and so my parents were understandably upset when I presented them with my new fiancée. They had to cope with two things: one, my bride to be was pregnant, and two, she was French. The problem wasn't xenophobia, but shock. In short, although I had expected them to advise me to do the decent thing, my parents tried to dissuade me from my marriage. When he met her, my father said that he thought that I was more in love with Marie-Sophie than she with me. Afterwards, they realized that they had made a mistake in opposing a marriage that was going to take place anyway and tried to make amends, but Marie-Sophie never forgave them. I didn't for a while either.

As for her parents, I had got on very well with them while I remained the resident English teacher in the *chambre de bonne*, but when we presented them with our marriage plans, and explained that they were to become grandparents a little earlier than the script required, they were a bit put out. Papa was so enraged that he chased me around the little Parisian apartment kitchen with a small Sabatier knife, at which point the idiot dog got very excited, joined in the fun and tripped Papa over.

I doubt that I have the dog to thank for my life; if I had presented my shoulder blades to my future father-in-law I do not believe that he would have plunged the Sabatier between them. It was more an exercise in Corsican melodrama. While he picked himself off the floor, however, I didn't hang around to find out. I hurtled down the stairs and past a startled concierge, followed by Marie-Sophie, who was not only in tears but fighting off an attack of morning sickness.

Marie-Sophie was only 22, and had only ever lived with her parents, so she was a young 22 at that. Her father must have felt a deep sense of betrayal that I had abused his hospitality by sleeping with his daughter. The room he had agreed to let me lodge in was virtually free and that was how I repaid him.

Her mother, Hortense, was quite calm at the time, but whereas Papa got all his anger out in one go and we soon became the best of friends, she was a different kettle of fish. I don't know if this is classic mother-in-law syndrome or not (she is still my only case) but she was what the French call *rancunière*. She bore grudges. She was never overtly hostile but had other ways of getting at me.

For example, one summer she came to stay in London. It was an evening when Marie-Sophie was late back and Hortense announced that she was tired and was taking to her bed early. (Actually, our bed, the only one she said she could sleep on. This left Marie-Sophie in her boudoir and me downstairs on the sofa-bed.) I set about cutting the lawn with an old push mower in the gathering gloom. It rattled a bit but had no motor so was not outrageously noisy. However, before long, Hortense stuck her head out of the window and complained that I was keeping her awake. Fair enough, so I stopped.

About an hour later I was watching television, when she came down. It was Rowan Atkinson as Mr Bean. I offered her a glass of wine, delighted at the opportunity to share a bit of English humour with her, particularly as it was entirely visual, no dialogue to test her limited English. But no, Hortense now informed me that I knew she hadn't been able to sleep, and that I had been mowing deliberately with the intention of keeping her awake. I apologized, but she warmed to her theme. She moved on from accusing me of keeping her awake deliberately to her belief that I wished to ruin her health and drive her to an early grave so I could inherit her money. At that moment, I had begun to understand how perfectly normal, well brought-up people from good homes sometimes commit murder.

The French as a people are hypochondriac – they consume more medicine per capita than any nation on earth except the Japanese – and Hortense made a profession out of being slightly off colour, never happier than when having to administer fistfuls of suppositories. You need a mother-in-law like Hortense like you need a hole in the head. I think the reason I got on well with my father-in-law was partly because I used to tell Hortense what to do and how to do it in a way that he would never dare. On this occasion, her outburst was the culmination of various things – like sniping at how I brought up Pierre – so I told her either to go back to bed, or to get on a Eurostar Express and go home.

Marie-Sophie had spent long periods of her life in full rebellion with Hortense but, watching the pair of them gossiping that tense Christmas set me wondering if I should have taken more notice of a certain old adage: how a man considering matrimony should case his future mother-in-law beforehand – because that's how your wife is going to turn out, mate. Marie-Sophie at 29 was a far cry from the doe-eyed 22-year-old who seven years before had played a sort of Juliet to my (admittedly rather feeble) Romeo.

Anyway, I believe in 'for better, for worse' and at this point in time I still very much wanted to stay married to my wife. So far, she had neither left, nor had she brought up the subject again. Her parents, while effusive in their New Year's welcome of her and Pierre had given me no indication whatsoever that they expected their daughter to be coming home for good. I felt it was safe to relax a little, I stopped holding my breath.

<< >> << >>

I don't believe in New Year's resolutions, particularly not hair-shirted ones like giving up alcohol for a month. I did, however, decide that I would try to be as nice as possible to Marie-Sophie. I also considered that I was getting fed up with her periodic patches of being fed up with me. The gaps between them were getting shorter again, like mild seismic activity before a major volcanic eruption. Whereas in the past I would have suffered her slings and arrows, by then, frankly, I was battle weary. I finally made up my mind that if things came to a head I wouldn't fight to keep her. I would let her go. But Pierre stayed: 'You lay off the boy, the boy stays.'

School resumed, we both got back to work, things were more normal again. Still, the uncharacteristic calm was worrying; not a saucepan lid in my direction, nor anything to provoke me into upturning more salad.

Marie-Sophie had already gone off to work one day in mid-January, and I was half way through a translation I was finishing off at home on my lap-top when my worries were justified. I received a polite letter from a solicitor. Her solicitor, the famous one threatened in previous arguments.

Bonham-Lee & Baldinelli
Solicitors
Michael Henry esq.,
28 Dunwenchin Road,
London SW4

STRICTLY PRIVATE AND CONFIDENTIAL

Dear Sir,

Your Matrimonial Affairs

We have been consulted by your wife, Ms Marie-Sophie Dufour, in relation to your matrimonial affairs.

We understand from your wife that she feels that the marriage is at an end, and that she intends to seperate from you, with a view to applying for an annulment of the marriage. It is your wife's intention to apply for a residence order in favour of Pierre, but she intends that you should have reasonable contact with him.

She has asked us to inform you that she does not currently intend to take Pierre to live in France at the present time and we are instructed that if she does intend to do so that she will give you at least 72 hours written notice. If you have instructed a solicitor or you intend to consult a solicitor please would you pass a copy of this to him or her asking them to telephone this firm to discuss this matter further.

Yours faithfully,

Rachel Bonham-Lee (Miss)
Solicitor

(At least lawyers themselves don't go in for any of this 'Ms' crap, I thought, but you would think, given her line of business, that she would be able to spell 'separate'.)

Serious stuff. My marriage was in tatters, or flames, or ruins, past its sell-by date, superannuated, dissolving before my very eyes, withering on the vine, taking French leave. Any metaphor would do, but the bottom line was that I, too, would have to get a solicitor. Being middle class and conventional it never entered my head that I should or could do otherwise – it is what one does in the circumstances.

A solicitor – weird. Here we were, living together and she was sending me messages through a perfect stranger. Why not say it to my face? I suppose she had tried, but I hadn't taken her seriously. OK, Marie-Sophie, you've shown me your armies massing on the borders of Poland, you're serious and I believe you, but don't just throw away seven years of marriage. Actually I still couldn't believe she was serious. I couldn't see what I'd done wrong. No affairs, no violence, my chief crime seemed to be that she found me a bit dull these days. I could see that her TV station was more exciting than my stockbroker's office, but still.

I am not as dull as I used to be. When I was eighteen and should have been listening to Pink Floyd, I was in fact a somewhat nerdish square, rather keener on Brahms. The idea that by the time my age had doubled I would not only be the father of a half-French child, but getting divorced, was too absurdly racy for words. By nature I am the kind of person who remains happily married for 63 years then dies, leaving two point three kids and five point two nine grandchildren.

I'd been brought up to believe that the whole idea of marriage is that you give and receive unconditional love, just as you do with your children, when they arrive. The theory is that although you might not be each other's actual flesh and blood, and you might go through difficult patches (sometimes continuing like a soap opera for months), you always kiss and make up. Or snog and make up, because sometimes the recovery process involves the rekindling of unbridled passion for a couple of weeks, to make you feel that you've got a decent pay off for the preceding weeks or months of angst. Moreover, I am probably typical of my generation in that there is little divorce in my background; a godparent, a distant cousin. Some school friends had divorced parents, but they were unusual.

I got married at the very respectable age of 29 which put me in the vanguard of getting permanently hitched amongst my contemporaries. I never planned to conform to the statistics and be in the divorce vanguard too at 36. Divorce, like death, was something which happened to other people and was completely outside my experience, notwithstanding well-publicized statistics to the effect that a third of all marriages end in divorce.

The words from the Frank Sinatra song – 'Love and marriage, love and marriage, Go together like a horse and carriage' – were, as far as I was concerned, bang up to date.

How to get myself a solicitor? Uncharted territory for me; I hadn't even used one to do the conveyancing on the house, I'd done it myself. The best way to find one must be through personal recommendation – a specialist. My instincts told me to avoid ones in the high street promising 'Probate, Conveyancing, Housing, Planning, Personal Injury, and Matrimonial'. They were obviously spreading themselves too thinly. But, I found that I had no friends to ask, being the first among my male contemporaries to reach this stage of the life cycle. In fact, at this moment in time, most of my friends were either not yet married or just married.

Even if I had had any friends of the right specification – newly-divorced, divorcing or deeply satisfied with the performance of their legal adviser – I was still not sure that I wanted to share the information that my marriage was on the rocks with all and sundry. It had seemed OK at the office party to make a bad joke of it when I still didn't believe it was for real. That was one thing. Now, the fact that I had somehow failed as a husband began to hit me, and it was certainly no laughing matter.

When Marie-Sophie came home that evening, I said to her, 'What do you mean by this letter?'

'I tried to tell you, Michael,' she said.

True, she had.

'You should get yourself a solicitor.'

Should I? 'Why can't we just talk?'

'I've tried Michael, I've tried. It's too late, you wouldn't listen. You just throw food around the place.'

True, too, but only once, and not at her. 'You're right, it was a waste of a nice salad. But it's the way you tell them. So who's this Bonham-Carter person, then?'

'Bonham-Lee. I got her because she is very good.'

'Good' sounded threatening. In this context the word 'good' could mean all sorts of things: efficient, kind, sharp, nasty.

'Look Michael, she is very nice. We can do this amicably. I don't want an acrimonial divorce.'

What a sweety. How can you hate a woman who mangles English so nicely. 'But why can't we go to mediation?'

'We can, but I suggested it before and you said "no".'

Did she? Did I? Maybe. I couldn't remember. It is quite likely that I would have said No given my dislike of unburdening myself to complete strangers. 'Mediation' inspired in my mind a vague picture of some crabby, interfering psychiatrist/psychoanalyst/psychologist or do-gooding therapist telling me how to run my life. Therapy – not my scene. Nutcases telling other nutcases how not to be nuts – I thought. Who counsels the counsellors? that's what I wanted to know.

Another thing worried me. As part of her dowry, Marie-Sophie came to me fully equipped with her mother's suppository-inserting hypochondriac streak. I could easily see her becoming dependent on an a counsellor and I didn't like that idea one little bit – hours of moaning on about Michael, with the possibility of a nice bill at the end of it which, no doubt, I'd be expected to pay.

Still, if my marriage was worth hanging on to, it was worth a shot.

<< >> << >>

MEANWHILE, get myself a solicitor. I telephoned Roger at work. 'Not feeling very well,' I said, which was true in its way. 'I'm going to work from home.' Which was untrue, because that afternoon I was planning to go and get some legal advice.

The local delicatessen might not seem an obvious place to start, but I live in a villagey part of London where you talk to your neighbours. The deli is run by Hank Stevens, a slightly eccentric black American. I think I am entitled to describe him thus – it is unusual for a black American to run a deli in South London. I didn't know him well then, but he is one of these slightly larger than life characters who everyone thinks they know well. I decided to get some lunch there.

'Hi, Hank.'

'One death-by-chocolate to go! Hi – with you in a moment.'

At the back of the deli is a place where you can sit and eat. Hank has an American attitude to food, so portions are generous, and the best things there are the cakes. Hank is mad on New Orleans jazz, so the music is good too. If I have a quarrel with the way he manages the place, it is that he allows local artists to hang their pictures on the wall with a view to selling them. It would be a worthy gesture if the artists themselves were any good. Sometimes you see paintings jocularly referred to as 'daubs' . . . these are splurges. Against all the odds an occasional sticker goes on them marked 'Sold', but this may be an example of china-egg syndrome. My grandmother used to put a china egg in the chicken coop to encourage them to lay, and this apparently works.

The reason I now sought out Hank was that I knew from the Clapham gossip mill which revolved around Pierre's school that he had been going through a protracted access battle over his own son.

'Hank, I'm getting divorced, need to pick your brain.'

'Not another one. One capuccino in the corner coming right up. What are you going to have?'

I was off my food, so I just ordered coffee.

'No cake today?'

'No Hank, no cake today. I've lost my appetite.'

The grill pinged and Hank shot off to rescue the contents. 'Baked potato with cheese for the lady in the corner!' A few minutes later he joined me. 'What's up?'

'Marie-Sophie says she is leaving, and she is going to take Pierre,' I started to explain, then burst into tears. 'Pull yourself together and act like a man,' I said sardonically.

'Take your time, mate, take your time,' said Hank.

I found myself wondering why he didn't say 'man' or 'dude'. Black Americans don't say 'mate'. When I'd pulled myself together I explained the situation, then asked if he knew a good solicitor.

'They're useless, do it yourself.'

'Myself? You have to have a solicitor don't you?'

'No.'

'I can't do it myself, I don't know any law.'

'It's not about law. It's about what's best for a child. Two parents good, one parent unfortunate. It's about common sense. Listen, you're intelligent, you're articulate, you can do it. All lawyers are interested in is your money, they'll clean you out, mate.'

'So do you do it yourself?'

'Sure.'

'But you've been to court lots of times and you don't get to see your kid . . .'

'Right – about eighty times, and no, I don't get to see my kid. Not officially anyway. Christopher and I meet in secret. But I'm still fighting – I will.'

'Eighty, what seriously eighty? Well, you're not much of a walking advertisement for doing it yourself, are you?'

'Hey, I didn't always represent myself. I had lawyers. I also had three Cajun restaurants. Now I've got no Cajun restaurants. She's got three Cajun restaurants. I started again, and I've got a delicatessen in Clapham. Those guys cleaned me out.'

We were talking bitter – I'd have to be careful not to end up like him. But Hank is American, so I reasoned it was natural for him to hate lawyers. But British justice is the best in the world, everyone knows that . . .

'Look, if you really want a solicitor, I think they are a waste of time, but talk to Toby. Toby thinks they are hip, cool and groovy.'

He introduced me to Toby, who was sitting at another table. Toby duly gave me the name of a solicitor: 'A specialist. Understands fathers, not all of them do. Did a neat job for me.' Which sounded like a surgeon specializing in vasectomy. Then he added, 'Hank's a good guy, but he doesn't know everything.' Uncontroversial, because we all know Hank is a good guy, and that no one knows everything, but I too backed the solicitors to know more. I mean there's all that law, they spend years learning it. Anyone would agree with him that lawyers were to be avoided if at all possible, but the matter was already out of my hands. I had to meet fire with fire.

I rang the recommended solicitor immediately I got home, and spoke to his secretary. 'I am afraid Mr Howles has rather a lot of cases to look after at the moment,' she explained. 'Perhaps you would like to speak to his assistant, Miss Oldcastle?'

The firm is a small one, with just four solicitors, all specializing in family law, situated in the upstairs of a terraced house just off Balham High Road. I liked the informality of it. I put Miss Oldcastle at 27 or 28: not too tall, not too fat, not too thin. No 'stunna', but not unattractive either. She was a little pale and pasty, but then what Londoner isn't in midwinter? She had straight, fair hair all the same length, circumnavigating her head at earlobe height, with a gap for her face. It fell slightly short of a fashion statement and didn't quite work for her. She said she liked to keep formality to a minimum and that I should call her Sally.

There was a well-behaved, semi-asleep red setter curled up in a basket in the corner. I said *lapin* to it and it gave me the briefest and most pitying of looks before closing its eyes again.

Sally asked how I had heard of the firm.

'Ummm, you were recommended to me.'

'May I ask by whom?'

'Toby something in Clapham,' I said uncertainly.

Personal recommendations must be the way to go if one must choose a solicitor, I thought, but looking for one in the local deli was only slightly less random than looking in the Yellow Pages (they cover eighteen of the London South edition). Still, the firm of Howles and Easby could be gratified at its customer loyalty rating, if not its brand-name. There are prestige brand-names in family law: Farrar and Co (the Queen), Mishcon de Reya (Princess Di), and Charles Russell (Camilla Parker-Bowles).

Mention of Toby of Clapham did not seem to strike any chords with Sally. 'Perhaps one of Mr Howles's clients,' she said. She told me a little of how she worked. She asked me a few questions about my income, and quickly came to the conclusion that I would not qualify for legal aid. 'Has anybody explained to you how horribly expensive we are?' she asked, before adding, 'Even so I think you may find that we cost considerably less than some of the firms in the centre of town.'

I wondered if the egg-timer was already on, but it somehow seemed indecent to ask. Money was not an issue against my child. I had read in newspapers of super-QCs on three quarters of a million a year, so I was not sure whether to be relieved or shocked when she explained that she was not a partner and thus cost only £90 an hour. She said that if things got really hairy then she could consult her boss, Mr Howles, who had many years of experience so he was quite dear (£150 an hour). Does that mean that if you consult him, I am paying for both of you at £90 + £150 an hour? was a question that passed through my mind, but I was too polite to ask. The answer one discovers later is, of course, yes.

But, as I said, money was the last thing I was thinking of. If she cost that much then she presumably got a lot done within each hour, and this was a straightforward case which she could clear up quite quickly. The nub of it was that I was at home more than Marie-Sophie, my timetable was both more predictable and flexible, plus there would be more stability for Pierre if he carried on in the same school and in the same house. Obvious, innit.

Sally seemed rather nice, reassuring, with almost a bedside manner – sympathetic, like a doctor brandishing a syringe, who, being a realist, would admit that it would hurt a bit, but – look the other way, please – not too much. Yes, doctors, lawyers, professionals, they inspired trust, although I did recall reading somewhere that when doctors went on strike in Jerusalem, the death-rate actually fell.

In different circumstances, I might have quite fancied Sally, although at this particular moment, lust was not on the agenda. My sex drive was in remission. I was off women, pure and simple. The emotional buffeting I was getting at the hands of Marie-Sophie had left my willy as shrivelled as a rugby player's. (Note for puzzled female readers who can easily see what Princess Di saw in Will Carling: crashing around a rugby pitch shrivels willies.) So, temporarily but, I hoped, not terminally, I was off sex. I checked Sally's wedding ring finger (empty) but only as an inquiry into her level of personal experience. Since she seemed too young to be divorced, I made the assumption that she must be both unmarried and childless. I kept an open mind as to whether one wants one's divorce lawyer married, unmarried, or in some state of transition.

We discussed my problems.

Sally said, 'Oh yes, I've heard of Miss Bonham-Lee.' Both Sally and Rachel were members of the SFLA. She showed me a cutting from the *Daily Mail* about the organization headlined something like 'Divorce – The Gentler Way'. To me the SFLA sounded more like a central-African guerrilla force, but no, it is the Solicitors' Family Law Association, and they have a code of conduct which commits members to a conciliatory approach to separation. 'Although of course,' continued Sally, 'we can be firm if we need to be.' The way things were escalating I felt that I might be in need of that 'firm if we need to be'.

All the Royal family divorce lawyers are SFLA members. Perhaps they should have a Royal warrant. By appointment to almost everyone except the Queen Mother. Many family lawyers have a file with HRH on it: an abbreviation for HuRraH, more fees!

No divorce lawyer worth his (or more likely in this field, her) salt is not a member of this association (I was told). I was lucky, it would make things much easier because Rachel was too. The two of them would be on the same wavelength.

'What chance do you think I have of winning custody?' I asked.

'Lesson number one in children's cases is that there are no winners. It's like a war, there are no winners in war, all are losers.'

Neville Chamberlain said something like that, I thought to myself.

'We look for solutions. I think there is a good chance that you would be successful in obtaining a residence order in your favour.'

'A residence order?'

'The old law was repealed a few years ago and there is a new one called the Children Act. Nowadays the term custody has gone out of the window and it is called residence.'

'What's the difference?' This, I supposed, was what you paid your lawyer for. To know the difference between 'residence' and 'custody' although both terms seemed to mean 'where the child lives'.

'There is a narrow legal difference which pleases lawyers, but basically it is the same thing. You will have to apply for a residence order for your child. Custody makes it sound too much like a criminal enjoying the hospitality of the police, and we don't talk about access either. You are both equal as parents before the law, and if one of you wins custody, sorry a residence order, then the other will have "contact" with the child. Contact is the right of the child and not of the parent. Mothers do not automatically win residence orders these days, and so you have a good chance, because you are often at home, and you have played a full part in bringing up the child.'

'Custody' versus 'residence'. 'Contact' versus 'access'. 'Winning' versus 'being successful'. I suppose this is lawyers' politically correct speak. Still, I had a lawyer and I might get 'residence'. On top of that, I liked Sally, she was reassuring. I hadn't wanted to talk to anyone but now it was good to know that someone was on my side. I felt better already.

>> << >> << >>

THE next day, still feeling relieved and reassured, I returned to work. Over a pint at lunch-time I decided it wouldn't hurt to recruit some more members to the Michael camp and updated Roger on some of my dilemmas.

'It did cross my mind that you weren't ill yesterday,' he said. 'My advice is, whatever you do, don't let the lawyers get involved. Just let Marie-Sophie have the child, she'll get custody anyway; it's not natural for fathers to have custody, children need their mothers.'

This wasn't the kind of manly support I had in mind. I found myself a bit irritated by Roger, but then, what could I expect from the worst kind of marauding bachelor? What do you know mate? I wanted to say. If you ever get into the reproductive way, it will be with a woman who does not make you go near a nappy. Strange in a way, because Roger was the hunting and fishing type who could grulloch a slain stag at the drop of a deerstalker. But dealing with the business end of a baby, no way. I have often wondered why a surprising number of women seem to find this masterly approach attractive. I suppose it makes them feel secure, knowing where they stand. Roger was a master of the on-off relationship – usually with some nice girl who was willing to both cook for him and administer amazing blow jobs (so he claimed).

I said, 'Of course children need their mothers, but they need their fathers, too, and we live in an emancipated age in which the roles of men and women are equal. What if I just let her have custody, and she decides to go off to France?'

'If she decides to go off to France, they will let her. I wouldn't wind her up if I were you, otherwise she might. Keep the lawyers out of it. They are interested in only one thing. A bit like me. Your best chance is to get her to fall in love with an Englishman, then she will stay here. I'll volunteer. I'll give Marie-Sophie a good seeing to. But you keep out of the way of the lawyers.'

Sensitive and tactful as ever. And already too late. Anyway, I didn't subscribe to this cynicism about lawyers.

'How do you tell the difference between a run over skunk and a run over lawyer?' asked Roger. 'There are skid marks in front of the skunk . . . How do you tell the difference between a run over skunk and a run over lawyer?'

'Roger, you're losing it, once was enough.'

'Nope, the lawyer smells worse. What do you call one lawyer at the bottom of the sea with concrete anklets? A start.'

'Roger, people who recite jokes do so as a substitute for wit.'

As I had done when talking to Hank, I comforted myself that Roger's jokes had originated in America where things had got out of control on the litigation front. But I was British. I believed in experts and professionals.

'Let me give you a further bit of advice, Michael, since your wife's French. General de Gaulle once said –' (I have been unable to track this down in any dictionary of quotations since so Roger's version will have to suffice) – '"There are three ways to ruin: One – through women, which is the most enjoyable; Two – by gambling, which is the quickest; Three – by believing experts, which is the most certain."' Of course Roger was a stockbroker. He'd know.

I was getting too much conflicting advice from different

quarters. Love and marriage, horse and carriage . . . I had to admit that no rhyme presented itself in quite the same way. Divorce and solicitor, horse and . . . ? But still, there were lives and futures at stake and I was not going to mess around. Marie-Sophie had a solicitor, so it followed that I should have one to counter her. It took up to five years of study and training to get to where Sally was. I liked her. She inspired confidence. I was keeping her.

<< >> << >>

BACK home, over the next few weeks, a kind of normality reigned. It was a phoney war. We were trying on gas masks, digging slit trenches, practising air raid drill. The two solicitors seemed to be handling things smoothly. Sally told me that we needed some 'Assurances'. She wrote to Rachel Bonham-Lee, who gave the 'Assurances', the gist of which was that Marie-Sophie intended nothing precipitate. There would be certain demands, but an effort would be made to keep the temperature down. In between, life went on.

Normality could perhaps best be characterized by breakfast, though even this was strangely *à trois* since the solicitors had entered our lives. We didn't talk to each other in the morning exactly, but when we did it was to the effect of 'If you're making some coffee, put enough in the machine for me, would you, dear.' Putting in extra coffee and extra water implies extra effort and, given our state of near-estrangement, something along the lines of 'Make it yourself' might have been expected, even justified. But no, each meekly made the other's coffee. Solicitous behaviour for the solicitors.

At around 8.30 a.m. there would be the thud of mail on the doormat: joint bank statement (leave unopened), bumf from Visa (bin), a mutual invitation (mantelpiece), postcard notifying of start of sale at a frock shop called *Raffinee* offering additional 10% discount for early arrivals (hand to Marie-Sophie), the *Economist* (no wonder she is leaving me – pass to me). We quickly got to know whose envelope was whose without reading the addressee's name on the front.

It was slightly surreal to be sitting in the same kitchen as your wife reading opposite ends of the same correspondence. His and hers hate mail. Her letter from Rachel Bonham-Lee forwarded Sally's letter containing my transcribed thoughts on life, the universe and everything (re Pierre and her at least). Mine, from Sally, forwarded Rachel Bonham-Lee's transcript of Marie-Sophie's *pensées sur la vie, l'universe et tout*. Sally and Rachel had become regular pen-friends, all because we had become incapable of addressing anything except impolite words to each other.

'Milk, darling?' I asked as I opened my envelope and read in my letter from Sally that Bonham-Lee was 'seeking instructions' from her client as to whether or not to proceed with our suggestion of a mediation appointment. Sally thought it was definitely the way to go, but her enthusiasm for it had failed to raise my spirits, particularly as we were not guaranteed a slot for three months.

Pierre's best friend Jake's mum, Michele, is a divorcee. She told me how she went to see a shrink who told her that her problems in relating to men were down to a separation she had experienced from her mother at the age of three months when her mother had gone off for two weeks to her father's funeral in Italy. What a load of bollocks.

She had also been to mediation. The mediator had told her that, in times of anger, she should choose a chair in one corner of her living-room, which was to be her 'angry chair'. Whenever she felt anger coming on she should work out her frustrations by sitting on this chair. Her husband would have one, too. At the end of the process there would be a ceremonial immolation of 'angry chairs' and the couple would live happily ever after. Surprisingly, Jake's mum and Jake's dad still separated.

Even so, Sally had persuaded me that there was no harm in trying these things out. She said that Marie-Sophie and I ought to go to Relate or similar, and see if we couldn't sort out our problems there. 'Something good may come out of it. Ninety per cent of cases don't go to court and that has to be the aim. But if we do have to go to court, then you won't look good before the judge if you have refused mediation.' A cynical approach to mediation but pragmatic.

'More coffee?'

'Yes, please. If there's enough.'

'Mediation?'

No, I didn't say that. She was bound to have agreed to mediation, because Rachel would have told her, just as Sally had told me, that whatever happened, refusal would look bad.

It was funny how we were both in the kitchen at least ten minutes before 8.30 and remained for as long as the post took to arrive, making sure the other didn't nick the mail. There was always an excuse for another coffee, even if it made Pierre late for school. I'd have liked to have steamed open her mail and discovered what the enemy was up to. I even thought about slipping a recording device on to her telephone to catch her unburdening herself to Tiff. With the benefit of hindsight I rather wish I had. Certainly the advice I would give to anyone else whose divorce has gathered any momentum is to do so.

Such were the preoccupations of breakfast-time. Positively puts you off your Weetabix, I can tell you. Supper-time was an altogether more puzzling affair. Quite often Pierre went to Jake's house after school. Jake was a classmate and fellow winsome urchin. Michele didn't mind looking after Pierre in an emergency nanny capacity as the two together kept each other amused and largely out of trouble. I picked up Pierre from Jake's house more often than did Marie-Sophie and I gave him his supper if he had not already had it. When we were both in, given that we were heading for divorce, it might have been natural to occupy the kitchen separately. But no, we cooked for both of us, or all three if Pierre had not been fed.

Quite often Marie-Sophie would work till late at night, and come home after I had gone to bed. If so, she would get up for the arrival of the post and then go back to bed if she didn't have to get out on a job. Hence, I continued to process Pierre for school, thinking all the while that it would be an amazing injustice if this pleasure – a chore for some – were taken away from me.

The pattern was not new, although it certainly became more pronounced around this time. If her news station was busy or she was involved in some documentary, the nearest I would come to seeing my wife would be a dim awareness of a warm body arriving in the bed next to me in the small hours. We were like ships passing in the night. Or battleships perhaps – each trying to give the other the slip while guessing at the opponent's tactical manoeuvres.

Still, I got used to things being like this, and if Marie-Sophie did come home early it upset my routine. I would have just got Pierre to bed, story read, lights off, sleep tight don't let the bed bugs bite and all that ritual out of the way, child nearly asleep. The doorbell would go and Pierre would leap from his bed, shouting excitedly 'Mummy, Mummy'. The process would then have to be gone through again. 'School tomorrow, Pierre. Bed.' Finally I'd get him off to sleep.

One area of parenthood where I am weak is that I don't much enjoy reading to children. However, you learn to do it on complete autopilot (well I have), putting inflection into the story, making it lively, while the rest of your mind is absolutely elsewhere. I had got used to thinking quite complex thoughts, almost as if I had two brains, but with divorce looming my mind was racing and I was making a mess of bedtime stories. 'So what did Charley the dragon say, then, Daddy?' Pierre would ask me and I'd realize that I hadn't even noticed the story had a dragon in it. This was one particular reason why I found having to repeat the bedtime process irritating.

Ironically, in the silence of the long evenings when Pierre did sleep and Marie-Sophie stayed away, I missed the plaintive ring of the telephone. I even missed Tiffany. I wished someone would call, not to ask how things were between us, but just about anything. Even a telesales vendor would have been welcome. However, an embarrassed silence seemed to be held by all. Perhaps the word was getting around. No one wanted to put their foot in it. No one wanted to ask for Marie-Sophie if she was no longer resident. On the other hand, it was more likely that she took all her personal calls at work. If so, her receptionist must know Tiffany quite well by now.

There was something else which seemed strange and which I still fail to completely comprehend. Unnecessarily (she had her sofa-bed in her study) Marie-Sophie continued to sleep in the matrimonial bed, and if she did make it home at a reasonable hour, she appeared to want to seduce me and not necessarily in bed either. I found it confusing when she sidled up to me naked, after a bath, say. It was odd given that on other occasions she was telling me that she found me physically repulsive. Perhaps she hadn't quite made her mind up. On several occasions she declared, 'You wouldn't even dare rape me.' A strange thing to say. And she was right, I wouldn't. Not only did I not want to, the thought was strong in my mind that matrimonial rape is a crime and these days consent is a very grey area indeed, legally speaking. Paranoia, perhaps? But during divorce you are so out of your depth when it comes to understanding norms of behaviour that it would not have surprised me if some ghastly trap had been cooked up.

I mention this because much later I was telling a similarly divorced man this story and he said that exactly the same thing had happened to him. He couldn't remember the last time they'd made love, but as soon as his wife filed for divorce, she started pouncing on him. Weird. I wonder if there is some uninvestigated behaviour pattern which psychologists haven't got their teeth into yet? I'd love to know.

Anyway, I didn't feel libidinous at all. She could perhaps have tried to take me against my will. It's been done – not rape it has to be said. It was a little before I got seriously involved with Marie-Sophie in Paris that I got to know an American missionary called Sherryl. She was an English teacher like me, but had been dispatched by some organization which hoped that she might win over the odd convert on the way. She had not made any converts amongst the French but I am not completely convinced that her heart was in it either. In being sent by the missionary society she had seen a risk free way of going to Paris for an adventure at somebody else's expense.

We used to go and see films together, which she knew a lot about and I little. I like the latest Bond movie the same as the next guy, but for her sake I was prepared to endure the arty French ones and I'd get the odd surprise – some are quite good. Paris is a film buff's paradise, with more cinemas per capita than almost anywhere. Cinemas in Britain went into decline as television improved. This never happened in France, despite Marie-Sophie's contribution.

Afterwards we would go for a bite to eat. I think Sherryl was a little bit lonely. She was 23 and not unattractive, but not quite my type. Besides which she was a missionary and off limits. One evening she missed her last metro home, and so I offered her the floor of my *chambre de bonne*. The offer was not as ungentlemanly as it sounds because it included an air-bed and a sleeping-bag. Besides, missionaries are supposed to eschew worldly pleasures – she'd appreciate the asceticism of my floor. I lent her an outsized T-shirt for the sake of modesty, didn't peek as she undressed, turned out the light and we set off for sleep.

For some reason I couldn't quite go to sleep, there was something intangible in the air, and I sensed that she was lying awake as well. An hour or so later I heard Sherryl getting up, and so I said 'It's down the corridor'. She seemed uninterested in this intelligence and, before I knew what she was about, she was getting into my bed and fumbling with the buttons of my pyjamas. The wearing of pyjamas is a quaint habit of mine that persists to this day. Although the proceedings were slightly against my better instincts – not for moral reasons, I just didn't fancy her – I found myself being eased on top of her. As I eased, she whispered 'I am on the pill'. Ah, those were the days. Life was so uncomplicated. I remember a flurry of worry about Herpes, but while AIDS was in the headlines it was still perceived as the 'gay plague' and no heterosexual took it seriously.

I confess to having been a little overwhelmed by being with the missionary in the missionary position, so events came to a head pretty rapidly. Poor Sherryl. I might have been able to summon the energy for another go, which would have been gentlemanly in the circumstances, but I didn't have the passion for her that the situation called for.

Sherryl and I never went to see another film together. It bothers me a bit that she might still think that my subsequent avoidance of her was in shame at not quite having risen to the occasion in the way she'd have liked. I felt used, inadequate and slightly ashamed. Being a decent sort of fellow, I didn't want to lead her up the garden path with repeat performances. To equate this with rape would bring the feminist thought-police down on me like a ton of bricks, but still, I did feel as though I wasn't given a choice in the matter. The spirit was unwilling but the flesh had proven surprisingly strong.

But I'd learnt my lesson. I wasn't going to make a similar mistake and sleep with Marie-Sophie in the current circumstances when it didn't feel right.

<< >> << >>

IN the last week of February I opened a letter over breakfast to find that the opposition had agreed to mediation. There had been a cancellation at Relate and there was a take it or leave it opportunity to meet in two days' time. Sally's letter told me that we were very lucky given the three-month waiting list.

'Feeling lucky?' I asked Marie-Sophie in my best Clint Eastwood voice, as I filled up her cup with coffee. I think she realized that I was having an obscure joke at her expense because she didn't answer.

The day before this, Marie-Sophie had announced that she had found a flat in Knightsbridge, and that she was going to move out with Pierre imminently. Who did she think was going to pay for that? Shopping at Harrods was one thing, but living next door? We were struggling enough with our mortgage in Clapham. One understood that she found South London a little beneath her dignity, but Knightsbridge? I supposed it would remind her of Paris where everyone accepts being cooped up in little apartments, emerging only occasionally to get a baguette, buy another handbag and give their dogs the opportunity to foul the pavements. She had even asked me if I would help her move her stuff, to which I had said no. I considered this to be like asking a condemned man to press the button on his own electric chair.

She said, 'I will be taking Pierre with me.'

'On no you won't.'

'Oh yes I will.'

'Oh no you won't.'

'My solictor will get me permission to.'

'My solicitor will stop you. She's better than yours.'

'Mine helps Princess Di.'

'Now there's a woman who is happy and fulfilled.' She'd got it wrong anyway. Princess Di uses Mischcon de Reya. A silly conversation really.

Go off, darling, to your expensive new accommodation in Knightsbridge, sort yourself out. Pop back at weekends, or whenever you feel like it, but leave Pierre. I was frightened. I couldn't bear to be separated from him. I was still pretty gutted to be separating from Marie-Sophie, difficult though she was. She still had the qualities I first went for: intelligence, good humour (currently in suspension), and that 'plus alpha' which no one can explain.

Maybe I'd find the internal resources to get over her, although I hadn't begun to call on them, but Pierre was a different matter. Every stage of a child's development is exciting to a parent and I wanted to be there, not getting little snapshots every other weekend. I remember the little bundle that was Pierre when he was no bigger than, and roughly the same shape as, a rugby ball. I used to bounce him up and down on my knee. He used to gurgle and slobber contentedly, which marked him out from a rugby ball, but was otherwise similarly inert (apart from when he cried). I had been doing this for a few minutes one day (he may have been three months old, not much more) when suddenly, in mid-bounce, his whole face lit up and he let out a first yelp of joy, the meaning of which I think it was fair to interpret as 'Daddy, this is fun. Do it some more'. It was a fantastic moment of bonding and I began to treat him with even more affection than I used to reserve for rugby balls before marriage put paid to it.

When he was about seven months Marie-Sophie took him off to her parents' holiday house in Corsica for a couple of months. I was a little concerned that if I didn't see him for that length of time at that tender age he would not recognize me, but because my relationship with the in-laws was still not all it might have been, I thought it was politic to let *Grandmaman* have an extended go with her new grandson.

When I joined them two months later, meeting them at Bastia airport my worst fears seemed confirmed. He'd certainly grown bigger. Still a blob, but showing signs of looking like a human being. He had been born with a thick tuft of black hair which stood up exactly like the hairs projecting from the end of a coconut. He no longer looked like a coconut, which was pleasing, but I was disappointed that he took no notice of me whatsoever. It was about fifteen minutes before he suddenly spotted me, his little face lit up, his arms shot out, and he lurched out of his mother's arms into mine. Another supreme moment of bonding. I think Marie-Sophie always had problems with this. I've always been good at engaging Pierre's attention or entertaining him. People used to remark that it would be me he'd run to if he grazed a knee, say. For my wife I think that hurt.

This flat in Knightsbridge was a worry. If she upped and offed taking Pierre, there would be nothing I could do to stop her. I could scarcely ban her from taking him out for a walk. I could hardly manacle her to the kitchen sink. If she went when I was at work, there would be nothing I could do. If she went openly when I was around all I could do was make a scene in the street, but that would give no more than temporary reprieve. There had to be a legal remedy.

I phoned Sally. She said that if I was really worried we

could apply for a Prohibited Steps Order which should be enough to stop her until the thing was heard in a full hearing. If it looked like she might be thinking of a serious attempt to whisk him off permanently to France then we could consider applying to have Pierre made into a Ward of Court. If he were a Ward of Court he would get his own representation, somebody called a Guardian *ad litem*, who would make recommendations in line with what was in 'the best interests of the child'. As a course of action it would be a bit drastic unless I really did think she might be considering going as she sometimes threatened. 'The trick in these things,' Sally said, 'is to keep the whole thing away from a court. That just serves to raise the temperature. Don't forget that the other side has agreed to mediation,' she added. 'Rachel Bonham-Lee is a member of the Solicitors' Family Law Association. We do have a code of conduct. I don't think that they would be planning any kind of snatch when there is mediation set up.'

Sally was getting a lot of phone calls from me, one way and another. It did occur to me that every time I rang her on would go the egg-timer. Every minute was the equivalent of two cans of Boddingtons' and she told me she was cheap – or rather 'good value'. Ten minutes' chat costs a bottle of Bolly. Which would I prefer to have? If a child is at stake the question answers itself. I've always thought champagne an over-hyped pleasure anyway.

<< >> << >>

At work Roger was being most understanding. His advice was 'let her take the child, she'll get him anyway because that's the natural thing' but he gave me a long translation to do which I could take home. This also enabled me to manage my time so that I could go for the mediation session.

Logically, Marie-Sophie and I should have driven together to the therapy centre, but this somehow seemed more perverse than eating breakfast at the same table. If we were going to go before a marriage guidance counsellor, and tell him or her that our love for each other had changed to hate, surely the form was that you arrived separately. At least that way we wouldn't have a fight in the car on the way there and another on the way back. When I arrived Marie-Sophie was waiting by the front door having pressed the intercom bell.

'Fancy meeting you here,' I didn't say. I didn't know what to say, so I said 'Have you pressed the bell?'

She looked at me as if I was stupid.

'Sorry darling, I was only making conversation.'

The atmosphere was established as we went up the stairs to the first floor mediation centre, passing a stony faced couple on the way out of their session. One would have liked to have seen a happy couple, beaming from ear to ear, embracing their counsellor whose contented face reflected a job well done, another marriage saved.

Probably these places ought to have separate entrances marked 'Boys' and 'Girls' as in a Victorian primary school. Separate waiting-rooms should also be provided. But they are run by charities, and charities are strapped for cash. A receptionist asks you to help with this cash shortfall (Sally had warned me to bring a cheque book). You are given an envelope in which you find a sheet of paper detailing the level of contribution the organization feels it would be appropriate for you to make. This varies from zero for the one hour session if you are impoverished, to over £100 if you are on stockbroker wages.

I would liked to have known what sum Marie-Sophie settled on. Her earnings were a bit of a mystery to me, because she was freelance, working for a French company, and took the attitude that Britain was not her country (so

51

why should she pay tax?). Most of her pay was in cash, and whenever I asked what happened to this cash she would always say that she was very junior, worked for a pittance, and certainly couldn't contribute towards the mortgage. 'Who do you think bought Pierre his new shoes?' she'd say. She may have been to the shop but I, we, paid for them. My only bank account was a joint one, ditto my Visa card.

There was another couple in the waiting-room. They were sitting in opposite corners at the greatest geographical distance attainable. Whereas dental waiting-rooms have posters about caries and plaque, in a marriage guidance waiting-room the walls are pretty bare. 'Divorce is bad for your health.' They should have big posters saying that. I read somewhere that being unmarried knocks nine years off a man's life expectancy (none for women). That's nearly as bad as smoking. Thirteen years (for both I think).

A pile of old magazines lay on a table in the middle of the room including some quite appropriate titles. *Country Life* – obviously useful for richer couples when mediation fails and they are forced to sell the estate. *Cosmopolitan* – for rediscovering sex. *Time Out* – lots of that on the horizon, and it has comprehensive dating columns. Marie-Sophie picked up a copy of *The Lady*, the magazine in which au pairs advertise.

The other couple were in their late forties or early fifties, which made me feel a compete failure. At 36, I was far too young to be getting divorced. The trouble with sitting in the corner of a room is that you are forced to face out into it, and I could see that the wife was uncomfortable with this: her body was angled, sullen, angry, so that her husband would get a view mainly of (cold) shoulder. The man looked bemused and out of place, rather as I felt. Talking problems through is something women love and men find awkward. The bloke then made a ruinously misjudged attempt at breaking the ice by saying superciliously, 'You're looking lovely today dear.'

There was quite a complicated bit of needle going on of a kind I did not fully understand. It was all getting a bit tense. I sat fiddling with my fingernails. With two couples occupying opposite corners I found myself wondering where a third would sit.

When the other husband got no reaction he said, 'Where did you get that hat?' This made me want to laugh because his wife had a rather grand bouffant lady-mayoress hair-do, held together with quite a lot of lacquer. This gave her the chance to snort, flick her hair, and employ even more rejectional body language, turning her shoulder even more to the centre of the room.

Having been rejected, the man couldn't just leave it at that, but rolled his eyes theatrically, looked at me knowingly, and said out loud, 'Women. I see you've got that problem, too. Don't yer love 'em.'

I have to say that my sympathies lay with the wife. If the other couple were like us, his wife was wondering how he could be so thick-skinned, so insensitive as not to understand why she was angry with him. During their mediation session she was going to spell out to him in detail all his faults. He, on the other hand, had only come along because, like me, she'd made him do so in response to some ultimatum such as 'I'll leave you if you don't'. I expect he hadn't a clue what he'd done wrong, although it was obvious to me. I wonder of it was obvious to him why Marie-Sophie didn't like me.

Then a man came in asking for 'Mr Henry, Muzz Dufour?' We were on. I don't like this Dufour stuff, I thought. The counsellor led us into the counselling chamber. One wall was taken up with a huge mirror, and the place was wired for sound. Before he started the session he explained that the mirror was in fact a piece of one-way glass, and that behind it were video cameras, and conceivably a bevy of researchers taking notes. He opened a door and showed us the room, which I was relieved to find was empty, otherwise I think I would have got stage fright.

I couldn't say which school of thought our therapist had emerged from, whether he was a loony Freudian or merely a guy who didn't want to leave this planet without improving it first. He seemed like the latter, a nice enough bloke with a standard issue caring and sharing, compassionate voice. I slightly wanted to pick him up, shake him and say, 'Listen, is this how you talk to your friends in the pub? Why can't you talk normally?' But it was not an occasion for humour. Compassion isn't very funny. Or very helpful in our case.

Our counsellor wouldn't take sides, or give any advice. His technique seemed to be to get us to start to tell him our grievances, I suppose on the principle of 'a problem aired is a problem shared'. But as soon as one of us embarked on a narrative he would interrupt and say, 'Well Michael, do you mind if I call you Michael, what do you say to that?' 'Well Marie-Sophie, can you understand what Michael is trying to say?' I found the whole experience rather frustrating. I think Marie-Sophie did, too. I think she had expected an opportunity to give me an ear bashing, imagining that the man would act as referee while she got off her chest all the things she had wanted to say but which I used to run out of the room to avoid.

I would have liked him to have been more robust, and to have given us some advice to save our marriage. To tell us what is normal in these situations, explain to us how it is that two people who loved each other enough to have a child together could get into this state. On a scale of one to ten, was our divorce very acrimonious or really quite mild and soon we'd recover? As you go into this whole thing there seemed very little guidance available. Should I, for example, let Marie-Sophie go, as Roger advised, or should I battle for my rights, or Pierre's rights, as Hank put it?

Marie-Sophie seemed to be saying that it couldn't be saved. 'It's too late, I tried to discuss this with you a year ago,' she said. The counsellor just seemed to accept that it was too late, which was jumping the gun as far as I was concerned. He was more like a divorce counsellor than a marriage one. What I thought we needed was some advice. 'Michael, you've got to start doing more washing-up', or 'Marie-Sophie, you've got to work less hard and spend a little more time around the home. Wear some sexy lingerie and seduce Michael. Otherwise he'll get grumpy', or 'If you do split up, do you realize that that will be very bad for Pierre? Perhaps you should both think more about your child and less about yourselves.'

Still it was a first session, and we agreed to come back a week later. I went away with a feeling of dissatisfaction and anger, partly because Marie-Sophie was insistent that the marriage was done for, and partly because the counsellor seemed to accept this and didn't want to offer any guidance about anything. He was too studiedly neutral.

'Will you give me a lift home?' Marie-Sophie said. Because I was cross, I did a foolish thing. I said, 'You must be joking. You came by yourself, go home by yourself.' I got in the car and, tyres scorching, squealed the vehicle round the corner. Once round it I was stricken through with remorse and drove round the block in search of Marie-Sophie, but she had gone.

I decided to stay at home again. I was not making great progress with the previous day's translation so I felt there was no point going to the office to discuss other pieces of work.

'Why aren't you going to work?' asked Marie-Sophie suspiciously on her way out. With no reason not to, I told her the truth. I rang up Sally to tell her how the mediation had gone.

'Persevere,' she said. 'It can take a long time.'

Quite a lot of domestic bits and bobs had started to disappear. Marie-Sophie's room had always been more or less out of bounds to me, but now when she left the house she made sure the door was shut and told me I must not go in. She couldn't lock it because the previous owner lost all the room keys and I had not seen the point of buying new locks. No matter that I was forbidden, like Bluebeard's wife, I waited until my spouse was out of the way and sneaked in.

Normally, Marie-Sophie's boudoir was like Sarajevo after a good day's shelling, but it seemed a little more ordered than usual. She is not tidy. This is not a criticism, because neither am I. Should an untidy person marry another untidy person? One thousand words, discuss. The stuff of a marriage guidance waiting-room's magazine feature. If a tidy woman marries an untidy man, does she succeed in changing him? Or does she sink to his standards? If two untidy people marry each other, do they wallow in filth happily every after? If a tidy man marries an untidy woman, does he end up thinking his wife is a slut? Or does the fact that he is tidy merely point to the fact that he is a repressed gay, and hasten him into infidelity (with a man)?

Let's face it, men are usually untidier than women. It is slightly unnatural, for example, for a man to fold his pyjamas. Me, I assert my masculinity by throwing them in a gungy heap on the floor. It occurred to me that I should perhaps photograph the crime scene just in case we went to court. She would want to allege that I was a hopeless housekeeper, but I would counter this with a series of photos of Marie-Sophie's 'personal space'.

The office section of the room had long print-outs of filming schedules (usual), piles of expenses receipts (usual, too), copies of our joint account statements (unusual, but not unreasonable if she was totting up what she would actually have to earn to support herself in the future). I moved over to the dresser and opened the top drawer. An unedifying sight of jumbled underwear greeted me. I can't understand why some men get excited about women's underwear, but there we go. I rummaged through to the bottom. The drawer was lined with some of our excess wallpaper which was loosely glued into place. Should I peel it off? I guess I could have conducted a search of several hours in the hope of coming across a library of secret correspondence with Rachel Bonham-Lee or a lover. Catching my reflection in the mirror I looked liked a burglar caught in the act. Daft. If Marie-Sophie did have anything to hide from me it would no doubt be too well concealed for my detective skills.

On top of this, were she to catch me, how would this level of suspicion look? Rachel Bonham-Lee would have a field day making things up about my general paranoia. For my own well-being, I decided I had to believe that my marriage still operated on a level of trust. I closed the drawer again, took a last look around the room, shut the door and wandered downstairs.

At lunch-time I went down to the deli for a bowl of Hank's excellent home-made soup and a chat. I toyed with it while I waited for the other lunchers to pay up. When Hank had a moment to cool off, I offered to buy him a coffee.

'Call mine on the house.' He grinned as he squeezed his bulk into the chair opposite me.

'Hank, Sally says maybe make Pierre a Ward of Court.'

'Who's Sally?'

'My solicitor.'

'So you got yourself a solicitor. I knew you would. Listen, Christopher was made a Ward of Court, that's one of the reasons I don't get to see him any more. Christopher wants to live with me. He is eleven, he knows his mind. But he is a Ward of Court so the Official Solicitor looks after his best interests.'

'Why has he got an official solicitor? Isn't my solicitor official?'

'He's got *the* Official Solicitor. He's called Peter Harris. He works under the Lord Chancellor and he has a bunch of wankers working with him. The people at the Official Solicitor's office do not like fathers, repeat do *not* like fathers. *Period*. It's "A child needs to be with his mother . . . his mother this, his mother that . . . ." Then when you get before a judge he says "What do you want to see the little blighter for anyway?" Different generation. They can't understand hands-on dads.

'Whatever, it all still goes through the Official Solicitor. He's like my wife's proxy. I spend more time fighting him to see Christopher than I do fighting her. Christopher fights him too. He's eleven and he knows his mind. He gets on a bus and turns up in Peter Harris's office and says "Why can't I see my dad?" You know that Peter Harris. He's the one that sold the film rights to all Fred West's papers. Only doing his job but he seems to me more like a concentration camp guard. I think he's loathsome. Then he only sold it for £7,000. That's not much money so could be he's incompetent too.

'I'm warning you, Michael, if you get your child warded don't you come crying on my shoulder when it all goes wrong for you. It won't be warm soup you're needing.'

'Hank, calm down, nothing's decided.' I'd gone to the

deli for him to calm me down.

'You don't understand. These people have the job of interfering in other people's lives. I have been banned from seeing Christopher. It was supposed to last three months, but can I see him now? No. Six months on I can still go to prison if I try to see my son. Prison. I'm his father for Christ's sake. I'm banned from any contact with him. Even my letters to him have to go via the Official Solicitor for censorship.

'We have to meet in secret at a café near his school. Also he's fully computer literate, I taught him. I managed to get the Official Solicitor to let him have a computer I got for him. I slipped him a modem and some software so we send e-mails to each other. Access by e-mail, we must be the first. Fortunately his mother doesn't know where the "on" switch on a computer is. She thinks he just plays games and does school projects on it.'

Angry man, Hank, and with reason, but then I was only hearing one side of the story. Danger, keep clear, I thought. They didn't stop you seeing your child unless you'd done something really serious. Did they?

'Look Hank, thanks for the advice. I'll think about it.'

I fumbled for my wallet and clanked some pound coins on to the table. Hank pushed it back at me. 'It's on me. See you around then, Buddy, huh. You take care of yourself.'

<< >> << >>

BACK at home the telephone rang.
'Could I speak to Marie-Sophie Dufour?' asked a polite female voice.

'I'm afraid Mrs Henry is not in,' I answered.

There was a pause at the other end of the line as this intelligence was digested.

'Oh . . . she said she would be in.' The tone of voice somehow suggested that it was my fault.

59

'Am I my wife's keeper?' I wanted to say. I asked instead, 'To whom am I speaking? Can I take a message?'

There was another pause, before the voice said, 'Rachel Bonham-Lee.'

What excitement. Once we had got over the niceties of introducing ourselves to each other over the phone, she softened, actually sounded really nice. She said she was sure everything would be all right, that it was very rare for these things to go to court, 'ninety per cent don't'. She reassured me that she was a member of the SFLA, 'we advocate mediation'. She was telling me all the things Sally had told me.

'Don't worry Mr Henry, I am sure we can resolve your marital difficulties amicably.'

I asked her what Marie-Sophie's plans were, whether she really planned to leave the country in the near future.

'I'm afraid I am not at liberty to disclose what instructions Mrs Henry has given me, Mr Henry,' she said rather more formally. 'In fact really I shouldn't be talking to you at all, but to Miss Oldcastle. It was just that you answered the telephone. I am sure that together we can come up with satisfactory arrangements for you, your wife and above all your child. We are very sensitive that in cases involving children it is most important not to raise the temperature unnecessarily. We will sort something out. I'll try calling your wife at work.'

And at that the phone call came to a polite but firm end. I wasn't sure how I felt. I'd made contact with the enemy and had been given nothing to hate her for. This I decided could be a good thing. After all, I didn't want to end up bitter and twisted like Hank.

I went to bed that night and dreamt of e-mail messages that I couldn't open.

I T was around five o'clock on a Friday, one of those bleak, late-February afternoons when although the days have begun to get longer, darkness still begins to gather rather too early. If you are British you go through a phase of asking yourself why on earth you bother carrying on being British, and dream of emigrating to somewhere warm and sunny like California or the South of France.

I was sitting at my desk at home again, trying to catch up on another overdue translation. I was not really concentrating, but thinking about my disintegrating private life. Thus my mind was not wholly on the problem of how to render into acceptable English the phrase 'Sewage to out-perform manufacturing sector'. Silly me: I had always imagined that sewage was part of the manufacturing sector. Could sewage be in the service sector? I didn't know. I had started the translation not having an understanding in English, let alone French, of what a 'box culvert' is. Neither had I been aware how a lead in box culvert know-how was going to be crucial in sorting out metropolitan Paris's turds from its used condoms and its recyclable water, so boosting the profits of certain French companies and hence throwing up investment opportunities for the likes of Scottish Widows or Clerical and General. My life was now enriched with a thin understanding of all these issues in both languages, an awe-inspiring if transient achievement. I would be unlikely to retain this knowledge until the next day.

It was nearly a week since the last mediation session, and I was trying to think of ways in which it might be possible to make session number two more effective. The counsellor had been so doggedly neutral, that I could come up with nothing.

Marie-Sophie had the afternoon off so she'd taken Pierre shopping after school. He was cross about it at first because, like any six-year-old, he hated being dragged round the shops, but he perked up when she said he could have a new Lego model if he was good. She hadn't asked me if I wanted to come, too. I surmised that this was because she was glad to see that I was getting down to earning the money to pay for her purchases, but actually, she knew I hated shopping. Along with the telephone, shopping is up at the top of the list of those things which come between men and women: a chore verging on torture for him, a pleasure greater even than sex (with me anyway) for her.

I couldn't bear to watch Marie-Sophie shelling out another two hundred quid on a snappy outfit, when I managed to make three suits last five years. I didn't doubt the necessity for these outfits – she worked in telly, after all – it was just that I couldn't bear to watch. The shopping process is also desperately dull. There is a brand of man who enjoys a trip to Joseph or Issey Miyake to watch his woman parading various outfits. I have nothing in common with such men and do not begin to understand them. I take scant notice of what women wear. Eyes, hair other assets, yes, but clothes to me are just practical accessories. Marie-Sophie always complained about this.

'Do I look better in the black, or the navy blue?'

'You look gorgeous in both.'

'But I wore black at Tiff's last night.'

'You did?'

'You never notice what I wear, I don't know why I bother.'

'But, darling, you look gorgeous in anything.' And she did. She could make a paint splattered overall attractive as far as I was concerned.

It is not just that I didn't notice: part of the attraction of women to men is achieved by a certain mysterious distance. Whether a bra is seamless, or lift-and-separate, or padded is a technical issue a man shouldn't have to confront. As

Roger would probably say (not me of course) the key thing is that they are put together with sufficient skill to create in a man the desire to rip 'em off the moment he is allowed to. Whether a woman is wearing black or navy blue to do so, is not a choice he wishes to make. His role is taking off not putting on.

I was shaken from my musings by the sound of the front doorbell. My first guess was that it was probably Marie-Sophie needing help to bring the shopping bags in from the car. Or maybe she had forgotten her keys. Marie-Sophie's scattiness was, I thought, both her most endearing and her most enraging quality. The year before she'd had three handbags stolen, all Gucci. She would do things like leave the bag at her feet in Harrods' canteen from where some sharp-witted thief would hook it with an umbrella or other appropriate tool. Or she'd just forget it altogether. Plastic money companies are remarkably tolerant provided you get on to them quickly, and if there wasn't too much cash involved in each heist, it didn't seem to matter too much. Certainly, I could never bring myself to grieve over the actual piece of leather. Most designer handbags look like some variation of a cow's vagina.

The enraging part came when she forgot to inform the credit card company, or when the duty devolved to me to have the locks on the front door changed. Women's handbags are also things which I cannot come to terms with: I somehow manage with a nice slim wallet with a few credit cards, a bit of cash in one pocket and a mini Filofax as an address book in the other. The sheer size of some women's portmanteaux defies belief, even allowing for the need to carry around a stick of lipstick, a powder compact and those other bits and bobs which loosely fall into the category 'feminine mystique' – and which men would prefer not to have to think about, like tampons.

Marie-Sophie had been especially prone to scattiness

when she was pregnant, but since I had been so in love with her and so proud of the pregnancy, scattiness had registered on my mind as endearing.

One thing I hoped the doorbell did not signify was the arrival of a motorbike courier come to pick up Roger's translation on the Parisian sewage system. If it was I would have to send him back empty-handed. 'Technical difficulties,' I would explain, a euphemism for got up late, then didn't work very hard. Or rather 'found this translation very difficult when also thinking about wife and child'. But it was late on Friday. Surely no one would want it until Monday? My heart sank. A man clad from head to foot in black leather and clutching an oil stained helmet was on my doormat.

'Mr Henry? Would you sign for these please?'

More sewage? There was an unfamiliar look about the envelope being thrust into my hands. For a start it was far thicker than one of my usual bits of work, which rarely exceeded five pages of A4 although the sewage one was part of a special on the whole sector and so much bigger.

In fact, it was a wodge of hate-mail from Rachel Bonham-Lee, including an affidavit sworn by Marie-Sophie. The word affidavit is one of those which you read in a newspaper but never actively use. It is the kind of word that happens to somebody else. Perhaps one's first affidavit is a rite of passage, like one's first cigarette.

The gist of it was that I was a hopeless father, a danger to my child, potentially violent to Marie-Sophie, and suffering from Francophobia bordering on racism, worse than any send 'em back Tory rebel. The document went on to say that Marie-Sophie and Pierre had moved out permanently and weren't coming back. I would be allowed 'reasonable' contact (undefined) with Pierre, but divorce was demanded on the grounds of my 'unreasonable' behaviour. As a parting shot there was the statement that the marriage had broken down irretrievably, with a paragraph devoted to the implication that I was rotten in bed. 'I have not felt able to have sexual intercourse with the Respondent for two years' was how this problem was put. The Respondent? Who he? Me, apparently. 'Me Tarzan, you Jane.' 'Me Respondent, you Petitioner.' Doesn't quite have the same ring.

The bit about our love life, apart from being gratuitous, was untrue. I was a bit hazy about dates, and I wasn't exactly going to instruct my own solicitor to write a letter to hers saying 'Actually, she dared me to rape her the week before.' But, as for two years, well, 'How was it for you, darling?' OK, so there had been a greater easing off than could be explained merely by the normal dip in frequency which follows having a child, but there hadn't been a drought. The fact was that we hadn't dunnit for two or three months and even if that felt like years to her, I couldn't see the necessity of mentioning any of this in a legal document. I read the covering letter:

Our ref: RB-L/M-SDH/53a
Your ref:

Dear Mr Henry,

Re: Your Matrimonial Affairs

We are instructed that by the time you receive this letter our client will have moved to her new flat in Knightsbridge.
Please find by way of service the following documents:

  1. Petition for Divorce.

  2. Section 10 Application under the Children Act for sole residence to our client of the child of the marriage Pierre Yannick Henry, and for reasonable contact for the father.

  3. Affidavit of the Petitioner in support of Application.

4. There will be a hearing at 10.30 a.m. at the Principal
Registry of the Family Division, Somerset House to hear the
matters of Interim Contact and Residence.

A copy of this letter will be served on your legal advisors
and we suggest that you contact them without delay.

Yours sincerely,

Bonham-Lee and Baldinelli

I wondered what 'reasonable' meant. It seemed to me
thoroughly unreasonable that Marie-Sophie had said she
was going off shopping, knowing full well that she had
instructed a lawyer to have all these papers delivered on
me, and that she would not be coming back. Would this
count against her? Presumably Rachel Bonham-Lee would
have thought that one through. Also what about all that
SFLA Code of Conduct reassurance. Sally had been sure
there would be no attempt to remove Pierre while
mediation was ongoing and indeed a previous letter from
Rachel had said as much.

The covering letter was enough on its own to put me in
a daze, but then there was the divorce petition (four pages)
and a whole load of bumf from the Principal Registry of the
Family Division about 'a conciliation scheme for contested
applications for residence, contact and variations thereof'
(three pages). I was going to need Sally the solicitor to tell
me what all this meant. Then there was another document
called the First Affidavit of the Petitioner. I didn't like the
'First' bit. One was enough. It was a chunky document
bound with pink tape, and with a neat little triangle of blue
cardboard in the corner. It was 23 pages long.

To those of us not brought up on the law or Latin the
natural question to ask is, 'What is an affidavit?' My dictionary
tells me that it is the past perfect of the Latin verb *affidare*,
namely affidavit = (s)he has sworn an oath. I swore a different
kind of oath of my own. 'Buggeration, she really has left me

this time.' Actually what I said was a lot worse than that.

In complete contrast to all the horrible documents, the package contained a nice handwritten letter from Marie-Sophie saying words to the effect of 'Don't worry, we're fine, leave it to the courts, they'll decide'. It gave the address of her new flat. It didn't tally at all in the circumstances. You wondered where the lawyer stopped and the human being took over. A more brutalist covering letter from Rachel said words to the effect of 'See you in court next week'. The day booked was Wednesday. No wonder they needed to bike it round.

All thoughts of the Paris sewage system went straight out of the window, or more accurately, down the plughole, as I switched off my word processor, and paced around my study in a futile, impotent way. I was numb. This was happening to someone else, somewhere else – not to me.

First I read the divorce petition on the grounds of my unreasonable behaviour. It stated:

1. On the 23rd day of March 1987 the Petitioner Marie-Sophie Henry was lawfully married to Michael Patrick Henry (hereinafter called the Respondent) at the Register Office in the District of Lambeth in the London Borough of Lambeth.

It continued with various other boring factual details, then paragraph 8 said simply:

8. The marriage has broken down irretrievably.

Paragraph 9 and its subsections then fleshed out a little the irretrievable:

9. (1) The Respondent has on occasions humiliated, frightened and lost his temper with the Petitioner thereby causing her distress.

'Distress?' The poor darling. 'Lost his temper?' Why, certainly, and she with me.

> (2) The Petitioner who is French has frequently been caused distress and humiliation by the Respondent's remarks regarding the French.

More distress. There was a grain of truth in this accusation: I freely admit to having called her a 'frog' on occasion, sometimes in public, and in especially tender moments *mon petit escargot à la crême que je veux manger tout entier*. There were more serious ones:

> (5) On December 6th the Respondent lost his temper in the kitchen and threw plates at the Petitioner and overturned a table thereby frightening her.

Cut-glass salad bowl containing *tricolore* salad actually, and I was the one who cut his finger. It hadn't healed properly and still hurt. And it wasn't in the kitchen, it was the dining-room. Colonel Mustard in the Dining-room, with the Salad Bowl. And did she say I overturned the table? I never touched the table. I was beginning to understand that the demise of that salad bowl could have serious implications for my long-term happiness.

> (6) The Respondent has shown no affection or tenderness towards the Petitioner for approximately two years.

I took exception to this, it was rather the other way around. Me, I was mad about the girl, but every time I touched her she recoiled. Then the whole thing began to get a bit technical:

> The Petitioner therefore prays:
> (1) That the said marriage be dissolved.

(2) That she may be granted a sole residence order in respect of the child of the marriage Pierre Henry.

(3) That the Respondent be ordered to pay the costs of this suit.

(4) That she may be granted the following ancillary relief:

(Ancillary relief? *Qu'est-ce que c'est que ça?*)

(i) an order for maintenance pending suit.
(ii) a periodical payments order.
(iii) a secured periodical payments order.
(iv) a lump sum order.

Etc. etc. . . . I decided I'd translate this one later. Then there was the weighty First Affidavit of the Petitioner. This was a nasty document, and it didn't tally at all with the pleasant 'let's not raise the temperature' reassurances Rachel Bonham-Lee had given me over the phone or in letters and phone calls to Sally. We'd been done, good and proper.

Sally had been reassuring about a snatch when I reported that mediation hadn't gone too well; but, apart from the sheer impossibility of keeping guard over Pierre, I'd been thrown off the scent, and not by Marie-Sophie saying she was going to take Pierre shopping. The two lawyers had gone to considerable trouble, it struck me, to agree a series of mediation sessions. Indeed, the second session hadn't even taken place. I guessed (correctly) that it never would now that a court hearing was booked. But surely a court would take this underhand strategy into account?

I paced round the room some more. It was the element of premeditation that really got me, because the papers just served on me must have been weeks in the preparation. Twenty-three-page affidavits are not spur-of-the-moment affairs. It must already have been half drawn up when we were at the mediators the previous week. Plus there was the small matter of the timing: Friday evening, just as my solicitor was going home for the weekend.

I wondered if Marie-Sophie was sitting in her flat feeling self-satisfied – 'Ha, got him!' Or perhaps she even had a twinge of regret that things had to be done like this – 'Sorry, Michael, there was no other way.' All that time I'd assumed she had been at work over those last few weeks, she'd been in her solicitor's office knocking up this statement.

By the time I'd looked through everything and wailed and gnashed my teeth, I realized I'd better ring Sally. In fact it was the first thing I should have done because all there was at Howles and Easby was an answerphone saying they were closed for the weekend and please leave a message or call again in office hours on Monday morning. I didn't have Sally's home number. I searched the phone directory, then rang up directory enquiries. 'Ex-directory' I was told. Monday and a Tuesday were going to be a rush in which to cobble together a response to some fairly unpleasant accusations.

I took another look at the First Affidavit of the Petitioner:

. . . Sworn in support of my application for a sole residence order of the child of the family Pierre Henry and for the Respondent to have reasonable contact with Pierre, and for an injunction that the Respondent be restrained from taking Pierre out of my care and control and further that he be restrained from using or threatening violence against me and from pestering and harassing me.

Pestering? Harassing? Using or threatening violence? Injunctions? Gasp! We were entering the world of page three of the *Daily Telegraph*. The affidavit went on to give an account of our lives. It was well put together. The early pages contained nothing too vitriolic or hate-filled. It was a blow-by-blow account of our marriage and Marie-Sophie's heroism in holding down the demands of a taxing job at the same time as fulfilling the demands of a taxing child. It gently played her role up and mine down, making me out to be well-meaning but slightly hopeless.

> . . . The Respondent would occasionally bath Pierre, but has a tendency to get Pierre over-excited with the result that often I would need to calm him down when I came back from work.

I'd get him to bed, he'd be nearly asleep, she'd come home, he'd get excited.

It described her plans for him which included a move to a different school, but it was not clear whether she had got him in already, and the school was not named. It was a school near the Petitioner's flat.

From page twenty the document built to a crescendo. It made out that I was as powerful and threatening as Jonah Lomu:

> . . . Although the Respondent has not recently been violent towards me he is fourteen stone and over six feet tall and I am only five feet four inches and he has been physically intimidating and has quite literally forbidden me to leave the house with Pierre.

She had given me an extra stone, and subtracted an inch or two from her own height, errors ascribable to a feeble grasp of Imperial weights and measures if you felt generous which I didn't. The statement went on:

> . . . I have found the strain of sharing a property with the

Respondent intolerable. We have to share a bedroom, although we have not had sexual intercourse this year.

This year? The last two years? Make your mind up, I thought. I wondered why she needed to say that she had to sleep in the same bed as me. She had a sofa-bed in her boudoir and there was one downstairs as well.

. . . Whenever the issue of custody is discussed the Respondent becomes very aggressive and on 6th December the Respondent broke plates in the kitchen although I was not hurt.

The cut glass salad bowl again.

. . . I have decided to take out this application on the advice of my solicitors. First, I have been advised that it is appropriate to obtain an interim residence order for Pierre to live with me. Second, because of the unusual behaviour of the Respondent, I am concerned that he may attend at the flat and try to remove Pierre from my care and I feel that an order of the Court will assist in preventing this. . . . I have also on advice made an application for an injunction restraining the Respondent from using or threatening violence against me or from pestering or harassing me . . . I was reluctant to make an application in these terms since I want to take no action which will strain the already difficult relationship. However, there have been occasions in the past when the Respondent used violence against me and I am concerned that he will be so angry by my leaving the matrimonial home with Pierre that he will take some aggressive action. The first time that the Respondent was violent towards me was about a month after we were married. I told the Respondent that I was unsure about whether we had done the right thing in getting married and he became extremely angry and hit me across the head causing bruising. At this time I was pregnant with Pierre. After the attack I had to attend the doctor the following day.

This was the only occasion when the Respondent has actually used physical violence against me. However, I have found his attitude of late to be more and more threatening as already set out. I am hopeful that the Respondent will feel able to offer suitably undertaking in the terms of my application in order to reduce the friction between us. Of course, I recognize that Pierre needs to have regular contact with his father and will co-operate in any reasonable requests for contact that the Respondent may make. I accordingly respectfully invite this Honourable Court to make an order in the terms of my application.

Sworn by Marie-Sophie Henry

I read and reread all 23 pages of the statements several times especially the bits that really upset me. She said 'The first time the Respondent was violent' then later admitted 'this was the only occasion . . .' You sense a contradiction. If, as she alleged, she was pregnant, then these events had taken place over seven years before. So why mention them? And all this 'Respondent' crap was exhausting, what was wrong with plain old Michael?

For what it is worth, my version of events is as follows. Pierre had already been born. We had a row about, I cannot remember what, in which she lost her temper. It was Miss Peacock in the Living-room with the Contents Of The Mantelpiece. An Airfix Spitfire I had made as a boy made its final flight into a wall. An antique bowl of decorative and sentimental value (but probably not worth much), picked up on travels in China was dashed to the floor. She seemed out of control as she made random-looking sweeps of any *objet* in her path, except that afterwards an inventory of the damage showed that anything belonging to her had miraculously survived.

Then she turned on me, pummelling and scratching. I tucked in my head like a tortoise, not wanting to retaliate. Probably the best thing to have done would have been to run off into the night, but I didn't dare, for fear of what she might do to herself; or, thinking selfishly of myself, of what she might have done to, say, old photo albums of mine. Plus there was a small baby in the house although I never feared she might harm him. I couldn't leave, so I slapped her. I'm not proud of this incident, but I didn't hurt her half as much as she had hurt me, and it did calm her down. Thinking back, we did go to the doctors the next day – Pierre was due to have his measles jab.

I looked at the collection of rather chilling documents yet again. I felt very stupid to have been taken in so thoroughly. Completely fooled. But it was an exceptionally effective sting and it was unclear what I could have done to foresee it. Sally had suggested making Pierre a Ward of Court, but only as a last resort, and Hank had warned me off such a thing. I had chosen to believe that my wife really meant to do things 'amicably'. I'd gone for trust. Big mistake.

<< >> << >>

WITH no Sally at the office, I was a bit stranded. I was somewhat physically stranded too, for, while my wife had abandoned the Former Matrimonial Home to me, she had seemingly taken possession of the Former Matrimonial Car. It too, had not returned from the 'shopping trip'.

I was tempted to ring Roger, but with so many emotions bubbling away inside me, I was scared I might cry if he sympathized, or explode in anger if he made a tasteless joke. Either way, it would not go down in my favour at my place of work. Now was not the time to mess up professional relationships as well as private ones, though quite how I'd be able to concentrate on my work I didn't know. The Parisian sewage system seemed rather trivial all of a sudden.

Even Hank's deli would be closed at this time so I couldn't go down for a pep talk with him. Who did that leave me? My family don't live in London and I didn't want to worry my mother too much. She'd be as devastated as me, especially so if she thought she was going to lose her grandmotherly access to Pierre. It wasn't just me who was going to lose if Marie-Sophie won custody. But we hadn't lost yet. It was time to get tough, solicitors at dawn.

For want of something better to do I did a tour of the house. I had to get my bearings. I felt like I'd been blindfolded and left in a place I didn't know. I paced up and down the hallway for several minutes, went up the stairs and along the landing twice, then back downstairs again. If I wasn't yet walking up walls, I felt pretty close to it. In the kitchen I switched on the kettle and walked around the table until it had boiled (the kettle not the table). In the sink, Marie-Sophie had thoughtfully left me a bowlful of dirty plates from breakfast-time. You had to admire her attention to detail. Excellent departure camouflage.

I looked into her boudoir, almost to see if she was hiding there – I still couldn't believe it – she'd gone? Perhaps this was all just an example of her throwing a very dramatic fit, I thought desperately, a cry for attention, a 'Please, Michael, take me seriously'. I had extreme difficulty in believing that this was not some kind of very cruel April fool. The room was not exactly bare, but was tidy. There were still some files and papers on her desk, carefully stacked, but her lap-top and telephone had gone.

I opened her wardrobe: it was still quite full but there were a lot of empty clothes hangers. Marie-Sophie had heaps of clothes but for the first time I made an effort to distinguish between Next and St Michael on the one hand and Armani and Versace on the other. If there was no

Armani, there was probably no chance that Marie-Sophie was coming back for what was left. I had to acknowledge that in moving everything out from under my nose she had accomplished a major feat. As I hunted desperately for labels beginning with 'V' and 'A' it finally hit me – this was the real thing.

The remaining clothes smelt of her perfume (Diorissimo). I ran my hand over them struggling to rememember which ones had been worn on happier days. I found myself going through her pockets: theatre tickets, the odd tissue, a sweet wrapper. Then I came across a letter from Tiffany. It was dated two years before. It said at one point '. . . I don't blame you for wanting to leave Michael . . . if there is anything I can do to help . . .' Bloody hell. The plot was thickening. I'd got the witches' coven against me – the monstrous regiment of women moving in regimental formation, waving their motto for all to see: *'Omnes homines illegitimi sunt'* (All Men Are Bastards).

I had another delve in Marie-Sophie's underwear drawer. Now that it was empty I had a look under the wallpaper used to line it, not really expecting to find anything. But there it was: a bank statement (not an old one, either) for an account in her name. News to me – we'd always operated a joint account. Even more surprising was the amount: £13,000. In the context of our domestic economy this was a lot and I wondered where it came from, her earnings or a battle fund set up for her by her parents?

Since she had not paid a penny towards our mortgage on grounds of poverty and needing to feed and clothe our family, I felt ripped off. It is a shock to discover that the woman you love has been stashing money away from you. I put the statement on the bed with Tiff's letter whilst I searched on. So many shocks all at once. Too much by half.

After an hour, the only other hostile item I'd uncovered

was a diary she'd written on a filming trip. Some bloke called Jasper had been very understanding of her plight. The name rang a bell – I remembered a Jasper used to ring every so often and leave messages. It's the kind of name that sticks in your mind – I'd felt sorry for him for having it inflicted on him. It was clear from the diary that she had found it a good experience to open her heart to him about her unreceptive husband, but it was unclear whether this was as far as Jasper's uses went. I gathered Tiffany's letter, the diary and the bank statement and left the room.

Pierre's room? I hesitated, took a deep breath and went in there. Most of his things were intact: his latest Lego Technics model, a teddy given by my mother, but not the one given by hers. I lay down on his bed feeling a combination of sadness and anger and tried to think things through.

It goes without saying that sleep was impossible. The worry that I turned over and over in my head was the thought that this might be a prelude to Pierre being moved off to France. Accusing me of violence would make it that much easier for a judge to reach the conclusion that this would be the best thing for the child. I was going to be dismissed as a wife beater.

<< >> << >>

B Y morning I didn't feel much calmer and was knackered from lack of sleep. I made myself a strong cup of coffee and proceeded to make some notes on the offending documents so as to be prepared when I got hold of Sally. I admit to various personality defects, but I couldn't work out from where Marie-Sophie got this version of our lives. All those silly accusations. Why did she feel the need to make them up like that? Why couldn't she just put down the truth:

Of late it has become increasingly intolerable to share the matrimonial bed with the Respondent because he farts in it. That's when he's not snoring or making ghastly sucking noises with his teeth when asleep. Also he is 36 and doesn't have the surging libido he once had. It is well known that men become more and more disgusting as they become older, and as the Respondent is only half-way towards his three-score-and-ten, the thought of staying with him until death us do part revolts me. Further I have heard all his jokes and they no longer amuse. I'm bored with him. Imagine what he will be like when he is 50 or 65. He'll wander around with stains all over his trousers and forget to put his willy away after going to the loo . . . I would ask the Honourable Court to dissolve the marriage forthwith so that I can go off and find myself some nice effete pooftah who at least wears aftershave.

Sigh. I thought I'd been close to the very model of a modern husband, 'New Man' personified. Perhaps I should have stood my ground more, thumped the table and bellowed, 'Where's my dinner?' Perhaps it's the only language some women understand. New Man indeed? New Wimp more like.

I decided that the best thing to do might be to go and intercept Pierre at his new school. I didn't know which school he was going to be in from Monday, although Marie-Sophie's affidavit mentioned two possibilities, a Montessori school in Chelsea and Blenheim Primary School in Knightsbridge, but it wasn't clear if he'd been accepted or had started. Better ask Sally first, but I planned to pop into his classroom and, whatever the teacher said, take him back home, or better still down to granny's until things had calmed down.

I managed to last out until eight on Monday morning before ringing Sally. I left an anguished message on the Howles and Easby answerphone tape. I left another message at a quarter to nine, saying 'It is an emergency' with edited excerpts from the statements. Even so, I probably talked to the machine for ten minutes. It must be horrendous downloading the answering machine in a solicitor's office after the weekend's crop of failed contact.

After a while the machine clicked off. I rang again at five past nine and got it again. Five minutes later I got Mr Howles, who said he was not sure whether Miss Oldcastle would be in that day. She had had a difficult case the previous Friday and it might have run into another day. He wasn't sure. He would give her a message if she phoned in. Unfortunately Mr Howles also had to go to court, and Mr Easby was presenting a paper at a family law conference. Mrs Smith the receptionist and secretary was off on maternity leave, but they had a temp, Miss Middle, who would be manning the fort. Try phoning again at 9.30.

I phoned again at 9.25 and got Miss Middle who hadn't heard that Miss Oldcastle might not be coming in, '. . . Just a moment and I will see if she is in her office.' She was in her office. Phew!

Sally didn't seem unduly worried, but then it wasn't her life. 'Yes, I've just received the papers, too,' she said when I finally got her. She said she had had a very heavy weekend working on another case and so she had come in a bit late. She hadn't had time to look at the papers, so could she ring back at about eleven?

Eleven! I explained the degree of urgency. What other case could be more urgent than mine? Sally said she would deal with it as soon as possible. 'We've got a couple of days,' she continued. 'I think you should come and see me this afternoon. That will give me time to read it all, and think of a few replies. You should write yourself a statement of why you think Pierre would be better off living with you. I think we should consult counsel too.'

'Counsel?'

'A barrister. Anyway, don't worry,' she said, 'There's always an accusation of violence in every petition.'

'What, every one?'

'Pretty much.'

'Do you think there is violence in every marriage?'

'No.'

'Every divorce?'

'No.'

'Do the judges believe these accusations then?'

'It depends. Male judges, particularly the older ones, generally feel sorry for the mother. But I think you've got a good case for custody. Let's hope it is a female judge; you can flirt with her, it will make it easier. Also they don't get taken in when women lie.'

'But you say there is a violence accusation in every divorce?'

'Yes.'

'Why?'

'It makes it easier to get the man out of the house.'

When I went to see her in the afternoon brandishing the statement I had spent all weekend concocting and that morning polishing, I asked, 'What's to stop me going and getting Pierre back?'

'In theory nothing,' she said, 'but it might not look good.'

'But surely it doesn't look good that Marie-Sophie walked off with Pierre, has put him in a new school, and won't let me see him.'

'Well we mustn't raise the temperature.'

'Isn't it sky high?'

'I will have a word with Mr Howles when he gets back from court and then I will consult counsel, but I am not sure if a snatch would be a good idea.'

'A snatch? Hasn't one already occurred?'

'Mr Henry, I think it would be a very risky thing to do.

Leave it to the courts.'

I could sort of see what she meant. I pictured myself arriving at the school. I'd have to get a friend with a red, three-litre Jaguar to wait for me at the school gate. First I'd have to find out which classroom Pierre was in and then I'd have to march into it. The teacher, quite properly, would ask 'Who are you?' Pierre would run into my arms and say, 'This is my daddy. Look Daddy, I've drawn an aeroplane.' He wouldn't be at all upset by his new surroundings because the implications of no longer being with Jake and his other friends would not yet have sunk in.

I'd pick the child up and announce to the teacher that I was taking him home. The teacher would panic, run to the headmistress's (sorry, headteacher's) office and, before I knew it, there would be screaming blue sirens at the school gate and me being dragged by the hair into a police car for fear that I was going to conduct one of those high-profile abductions. The fact that Marie-Sophie had been the one who did the abduction would be neither here nor there. (I remember a picture of the Marquess of Blandford being dragged by the hair during an arrest for non-payment of maintenance. Can you imagine anyone doing that to a woman?)

I, too, might end up on page three of the *Telegraph*:

Police were still combing the countryside last night for estranged tug-of-love father Michael Henry. On television last night wife Marie-Sophie Dufour-Henry made an impassioned plea for the safe return of her child, Pierre. 'Pierre is a sensitive child who needs his mother. Please Michael, wherever you are, give yourself up . . .' she said before breaking down and being helped away by friends.

Ms Dufour's solicitor, Rachel Bonham-Lee, issued a statement last night saying that a judge in the High Court had issued an emergency injunction stopping the father from leaving the country. It was confirmed by the Home Office that

an All Ports Alert had been issued . . . Last night police said
that a red, three-litre Jaguar had been seen speeding away
from the scene and are asking any member of the public who
may have seen it to contact Esther Rantzen . . .'

The article would be illustrated by a school picture of
Pierre, and a blurred, rather sinister one of me taken with
someone's instamatic back in 1973, and a stark press photo
taken with flash of a tear-stained Marie-Sophie in front of a
barrage of microphones. In the background would be
Tiffany looking self-righteous.

I imagined Roger's face as he read it on the way to the
office and wondered if it would distract him enough to
forget to read the *Financial Times* afterwards.

No, altogether not a good idea, I decided. Much as I
would have loved to . . .

<< >> << >>

INSTEAD, on Tuesday morning I phoned Roger and
begged some compassionate leave. He was not
particularly compassionate (I had forgotten to call in the
day before), and seemed to have found his tongue on the
subject of my divorce. 'Don't come complaining to me if
your bonus is down on last year,' he griped, knowing full
well that I didn't get one any way and meaning his.

I went round the corner to Pierre's regular school to
explain his absence to his teacher. She reiterated that he
seemed 'such a well-adjusted child'. I have to admit that I
shed some manly tears at this. Nothing wrong with that.
Gazza does it.

'Look, Pierre's dad is crying,' said Jake.

'He's probably hurt himself,' said James. 'My dad never
cries.'

'No,' said Lisa. 'It's Pierre's mummy. My mummy says

82

she is going away.'

'Perhaps he's killed them,' said Amy.

I was outraged. No doubt the whole neighbourhood knew all about me.

Meanwhile the correct legal redress had to be assessed. Sally consulted with counsel, and counsel, after a lot of umming and aahing, counselled, on balance, against a snatch. When Sally rang back with her Opinion (with a capital O), she explained that both she and Counsel, and indeed Mr Howles, had been in two minds (that made six minds): although there was nothing to stop me doing it under the law, because there was no Order (capital O) in place to stop me, the fact that Marie-Sophie had already put in an Application (capital A) made them worry that a judge might take a Dim View, (D and V), particularly as the actual snatch might physically be quite hard to achieve.

If I was going to pick up Pierre then it must be clean and non-confrontational. No three-litre Jaguars. Just like the one Marie-Sophie had done on me; she'd done everything properly, right down to serving papers on me and handwriting a letter giving me her new address. She had made sure that hers couldn't be called abduction. If my attempt to get Pierre back went wrong, Marie-Sophie would have acquired good ammo for suggesting that I was unstable and desperate. End of custody battle.

I thought what must have precipitated the snatch was a letter Sally had written to Rachel, asking her 'to give your client's undertaking that she will not remove Pierre prior to any decision by a court? If not we will have to consider what steps to take to ensure that he remains in the matrimonial home until matters are fully resolved.' The point was that it might take months 'until matters were fully resolved'. The courts can take three or four to even decide who shall have the child until a hearing proper can take place, if it is not an emergency, because they are so busy. Knowing that there was little way out of giving an undertaking, they had pre-empted it by removing Pierre first.

We were just beginning to draw up our battle plans whilst the enemy were actually carrying out theirs. The temperature was boiling-point as far as I was concerned.

<< >> << >>

I next saw Marie-Sophie on Wednesday at Somerset House where the Principal registry of the Family Division is situated. On page three of the Daily Telegraph, litigants are always 'flanked by their lawyers' or their 'legal team', and, appropriately, I first caught sight of my estranged wife striding into court ahead of us with a person either side of her dressed in black and carrying an expandable briefcase.

I hadn't slept except in snatches since before the weekend and already my heart was thumping. I probably had bloodshot eyes and a crazed look about me. I felt like an England football fan watching his team play West Germany. You know England can win but because they haven't since 1966 you suspect they won't. The feeling is like that but about ten times more intense.

Sally laid a restraining hand on my arm. 'Michael, I want to introduce you to our barrister, Muriel Leach,' she said. Muriel turned out to be a middle-aged, balding, pleasantly plump and down-to-earth lady, whose only immediate shortcoming was that she lit up a Woodbine as soon as she'd said hello. 'Don't worry, we'll sort this out for you, Mr Henry,' she said. I sincerely hoped so.

Once she had asked me a few questions about my daily child-minding routine, we had a bit of time to kill. The hearing booked by the other side was for half an hour,

84

which struck me as plenty for any judge to come up with the decision I anticipated, notwithstanding the fact that the documents filed by the opposition were rather lengthy. Sally and I had not had the time to create a literary epic to counter Marie-Sophie's, but I thought perhaps this was a good thing. To refute each and every accusation about getting Pierre sunburnt or over-excited four years ago would be to see the whole struggle disintegrate into a form of legal mud-wrestling.

It is difficult to describe how tense you feel while you wait in a corridor to go before a complete stranger who will decide the course of the rest of your life. A contested custody hearing has to be the worst kind of stress it is possible to experience, short of being Bosnian. We parked ourselves on one side of a long corridor. Marie-Sophie's party was just along from us. She was sitting very still, looking ahead of her. I had a good look at her barrister. 'James de Vere Crispe,' Sally whispered. I was a bit alarmed by the French sounding name and that he might be some kind of specialist in getting children to France. There was no mention anywhere in any of Marie-Sophie's papers of such an intention, but that didn't make feel any better. One thing at a time, she'd be thinking. Get the child first. Out of the country second. There was something slightly undead about James de Vere Crispe. If the floor had been marble, I was sure his footsteps wouldn't echo.

I couldn't sit still. I also had a rotten headache, partly I suppose from lack of sleep and partly from Woodbine smoke. I looked around for a 'No Smoking' sign, but not seeing one got up and went for a wander around the Principal Registry of the Family Division taking care not to have to walk past Marie-Sophie.

There were lots of corridors, narrow and filled with lawyers and their clients. The clients looked to various

85

degrees tense, ashen in some cases, the lawyers at home. Sally had warned me that it would be a little like this. 'You might hate the other side, but it's our job to get on with them, so don't be surprised if the barristers seem friendly together. They come across each other virtually every day and it helps to reach solutions if they get on well. None of us can afford to get emotionally involved. For you it is the biggest thing in your life so far, but for us it is all in a day's work.' Fair enough, though at this moment I could have done with some emotional support.

I overheard snatches of conversations: 'He will agree to the Saturday night, your client will drop the thing about half-term?' 'Not sure I can get her to agree to that, but I'll see what I can do . . .' How a divorce lawyer can extract any job satisfaction from the hair-splitting that goes on is beyond me. Certainly I observed no one who looked as if they might be doing this 'amicably'.

There were no waiting-room magazines like at the mediation place. They do dish out helpful leaflets – I counted five different ones on different aspects of getting divorced. I wondered why no one thought it worth the trouble to produce anything on how to stay married.

I went back to my seat and asked Sally why all lawyers dress in black. 'We have to dress like this when we go to court, it sort of sets the tone.' Commendable self-deprecating irony. I looked her over. She seemed very calm, but I couldn't avoid the feeling that she was operating in a system against people bigger than she was. She had proved she was all self-confidence when it came to drafting letters to a fellow solicitor, but how would our report stand up before a judge? The way in which she had responded to Pierre's snatch had worried me a little. We couldn't run off to consult all and sundry now.

Then, suddenly, we were on. An usher ushered us into a room – largeish, but not the expected archetypal courtroom:

there weren't banks of oak pews and the judge wasn't sitting on a dais. I was a bit thrown – no *Dieu et Mon Droit* in a vast frieze on the wall, no wigs even. I had the feeling my case was not being taken as seriously as it should.

I was relieved to find that the judge was a her, a rather robust woman. You could almost imagine her riding to hounds but not quite, she looked a bit too Hampstead or Islington. 'In luck,' I thought. Sally had said that, paradoxically, female judges are frequently fairer to men. She sat at the end of the room at a large desk with the odd fat law book on it. There was a long formica table in front of her desk at which we sat, Marie-Sophie and her lot one end, us the other. Muriel Leach and James de Vere Crispe sat nearest 'Madam' – she was only a circuit judge so not 'Your Honour'.

Face-on, Marie-Sophie looked beautiful, almost the girl I had married, but made down, as opposed to up. It must have taken hours to get that understated, slightly drawn vulnerable mother look.

Her paperwork, including letters and various forms, totalled around 40 pages. In addition there was my hastily cobbled together response of ten pages. The judge looked up over her glasses: 'How am I expected to read all this and come to a decision today? There isn't time, the issues are too complicated. This will take more than half an hour.'

'With respect, Madam the issues are very straightforward,' said Muriel Leach. 'The father is at home most and has been the main carer. There is but one child of the marriage, a son, Pierre, who is five . . .'

'Six,' I whispered under my breath.

'Yes, yes, Mrs Leach I can read that myself . . .' said the judge crustily.

'I'm sorry Madam, but the boy goes to a school two minutes walk from the matrimonial home, in which the father still resides. It is a simple matter of ordering that Pierre be returned to the former matrimonial home until such time as matters can be resolved between the parties. The Petitioner's application is for an Interim Residence Order pending a full hearing. It is the Respondent's submission that the boy should stay with him at least until the matter is resolved at a full hearing . . .'

Go for it Muriel, you tell her. I was ready to cheer her on. However, at that moment the Petitioner's barrister popped to his feet. When seated, he had looked as near to a near-death experience as you can get, but once on his feet, he managed to look quite animated (although if he should want to acquire a more healthy complexion he would be well advised to spend a week on the foredeck of an Arctic trawler). He looked like a refugee from one of the flying buttresses on the Royal Courts of Justice (nearly opposite Somerset House).

Like the gargoyles, his face was a little pitted. Evidence of a severe teenage acne problem. I bet he got teased a lot at school, I thought. I shouldn't have been making personal observations of this nature about the man but the truth is that I already hated him even though in supporting Marie-Sophie's efforts to ruin me he was only doing his job. Like the Official Solicitor selling Fred West's papers, I suppose.

'Madam, I cannot agree with my learned friend,' he was saying. 'The issues in this case are not straightforward at all. We have serious concerns about how the respondent might react to the separation, and what he may say to Pierre. The first consideration of the court must be towards Pierre. My client has genuine reasons for worrying about what she considers to be the Respondent's increasingly unusual behaviour, and fears also that the Respondent is not equipped to look after the physical and emotional needs of the child at a time when he is unlikely to be able to resist directing feelings of anger towards the Petitioner. While these feelings may be very understandable, it must be in the best interests of the child for him to be protected from this.'

I suppose he was subtly drawing Madam's attention to the bit in the affidavit about my alleged Francophobia and proneness to violence.

'Pierre has started at his new school, has settled down well, and is enjoying it,' continued Mr de Vere Crispe. 'My client believes that it would be unsettling for him to be apart from his mother while this matter remains unresolved.'

New school! Unsettling?! He had been there for three days at the most. True, Pierre was probably having a great adventure, he didn't understand at all what was happening between his parents. I profoundly hoped this was the case. I felt terribly sorry for him. He was going to be very upset if he thought he wasn't going to be back at school soon with Jake, Harry and Lisa.

The judge repeated that in light of the concerns raised by Mr de Vere Crispe she did not consider that she could come to a decision. She turned to her clerk and asked him to find the earliest possible slot for a hearing: 'Time estimate one day?' She then turned to the barristers, both of whom nodded assent. We could hear the conversation going on between judge and clerk: 'Judge X is on holiday, and Judge Y does not have a free slot until May.' Three months?! To give the judge her due, she wasn't happy with this either. She applied some pressure and a cancellation slot was found two weeks hence but before a different judge.

She also got her clerk to get on the blower to the court welfare department to see if there was an officer available to do a quick report on the situation. It was explained to me and Marie-Sophie that a court welfare officer would make an independent assessment of both our situations by visiting us at our respective homes and seeing us with the child. It emerged that a Mr Wheedle who had been off for several months of sick leave was available because his diary was still nearly empty, so that was arranged.

I didn't know how to translate all these events. It wasn't defeat because we were going to come back to court, but then neither was Pierre going to come home. Sally had explained that the courts are very wedded to the idea of the 'status quo'. The current status quo was Pierre's house and school in Clapham but two weeks from now the status that Marie-Sophie was trying to establish would have become that little bit more quo. Sally didn't need to explain to me that next time they would have more clout in arguing that Pierre preferred his new school, and would find it unsettling to be sent back again to his old one.

Meanwhile, I still had no official access to Pierre. If I couldn't have him back home with me on a permanent basis for two weeks, I was damned if I was leaving the courtroom without permission to see him during that time. Sally had a word with Muriel Leach who spoke to the judge, who spoke to Mr de Vere Crispe. 'I notice that your client proposes that Mr Henry has reasonable access to Pierre. I would guess that she does not object in principle to the Respondent seeing Pierre during the time before the next hearing?'

'Madam, may I take instructions?'

Frantic whispering between Mr Crispe, Rachel Bonham-Lee and Marie-Sophie.

'Madam, in view of the attitude of the Respondent, my client feels that it would be much better if Pierre were not to see the Respondent until this matter has been settled.'

'Mr Crispe, I do not think that it is right that Mr Henry should be kept apart from Pierre for any longer than is necessary. It is the right of the child to contact not the parent. Perhaps you could try a little harder to come up with some sort of arrangement.'

More frantic whispering. Mr Crispe looked apologetic. Miss Bonham-Lee looked understanding. Marie-Sophie looked cross. Mr Crispe leant over for a chat with Muriel. Muriel smiled and I overheard her say 'I'll see what I can do'. She turned and said something to Sally, who was sitting next to me. 'They're suggesting that Mr Henry has Pierre from midday on Saturday until 6 p.m. Mrs Henry is concerned that Mr Henry is not yet ready for the responsibility of having Pierre stay overnight. Do you think he can manage?'

'Manage?' I fumed, not caring in the least who heard me. 'Who do you think has put Pierre to bed nearly every night for the last six years? Why can't he come to me for one of the two weeks? That's equal, that's fair.' I shifted my gaze to the judge, who, to be honest, seemed to view this comment sympathetically.

'Given Mrs Henry's opposition, that's not very realistic Mr Henry,' Sally whispered. It was difficult to discuss tactics when the opposition is three feet from you across the table.

'So, what is realistic?' I whispered back.

'Well perhaps we might be able to ask Mrs Henry to agree that Pierre stays on Saturday night, if you take him back in time for Sunday midday.'

I looked at her in disbelief. I couldn't believe she was so dumbly accepting of just one day's contact and that I was expected to fall in line. To go from seeing your child almost every day of his life to once a fortnight – it was a mad system. But what was I to do? I had put myself in Sally's professional hands and if this was what she advised I ought to agree to it. Feeling rushed and pressurized, I could do nothing else.

The other side agreed that Pierre could come and stay from Saturday lunch-time to Sunday morning on each of the two weekends between the hearings, provided that I gave an Undertaking (capital U) not to harass or molest my wife in any way and to return the child at the appointed time.

'I'm not going to harass or molest her. Why should I agree to that?' I asked Sally.

'Don't worry it won't reflect badly on you, but the other side won't agree to let you see Pierre unless you do. You may as well. Look, the judge has already made clear she hasn't got time to hear the case, you must decide.'

So I agreed to an undertaking not to harass or molest Marie-Sophie and the judge gave her approval, and asked for it to be arranged that a court welfare officer came to pay us both a home visit, during access hours before the next hearing, so that an interim report could be done.

We flocked out of the court. All this might have been enough for one morning except that Sally and Muriel said it would be a good opportunity to sort out the divorce petition. Sally had advised previously that I should consent to a divorce on the grounds of my unreasonable behaviour.

'You haven't committed adultery have you?' she asked.

'No, I haven't, and so far as I am aware she hasn't either, I don't think. Unless she did so over the weekend. Look, this is all too quick, last week I was living with her, this week we're sorting out a decree nisi. Isn't it all a bit quick? Do I have to agree to divorce just yet?'

'Michael, remember if she really wants a divorce, then she will get one. It will be a lot less painful for all parties if we attempt to comply.'

'Why can't we just go for two years' separation?' I asked.

Sally looked weary. 'I've already discussed that with Miss Bonham-Lee but they feel they want to get the whole thing over as quickly as possible. Unreasonable behaviour would be the easiest route. Actually, I do think they have a point.'

'She's the one who wants the divorce, why shouldn't it be on the grounds of her unreasonable behaviour? She's the one who's been behaving unreasonably after all. She kidnapped my child. That wasn't very reasonable was it?'

Sally looked even more weary at this point. 'If you contest the divorce, it will be held in open court, then all the press and public will flock to watch because there are virtually no contested divorces out of 150,000 a year. They are very rare.'

I was running out of steam. 'Why didn't we work all this out before we got to court?'

'I didn't think they'd get to this part today. But as the judge has postponed the hearing I thought . . .'

I suddenly didn't care what she thought. I didn't have the energy to argue with my lawyers as well as Marie-Sophie. I left it to her. 'Except for one thing,' I said. 'I'll agree to the divorce petition on the grounds of my unreasonable behaviour if they agree to let me have Pierre for Friday and Saturday night until a judge's decision is reached, not just Saturday.'

'But Michael, we've just been over all that.'

But Muriel suggested that it might be worth a shot. 'I'll see if I can get them to drop the violence bit out of the petition as well. I think it would be good to get rid of that. It might leave the petition so weak that the judge won't give a decree nisis. I'll see what Mr Crispe thinks.'

So Muriel walked along the corridor for a chat with the undead Mr Crispe. It was strange and frustrating to be in a narrow corridor with my lawyers and my wife's lawyers all within a few yards of each other, yet having to communicate through the proper channels. If Sally wanted to negotiate with Rachel then the form was that she got Muriel to talk to James who talked to Rachel. The overmanning and demarcation in the legal system is as bad as anything at British Leyland back in Red Robbo's day.

You get real professional distance for your money.

Muriel returned saying that James de Vere Crispe thought they could probably get the petition through on this basis, even though the most serious allegation remaining on the divorce petition now was that I had shown the petitioner little or no affection and that she could not thus be expected to continue to live with me. A duty judge would rubber stamp the decree nisi. We could then get this within a few weeks before going for the decree absolute. Six weeks after that we could be divorced if Marie-Sophie wanted. All I had to do was sit back and sign.

I had come to court expecting a quick hearing, with Pierre ordered to be returned home. No such thing had happened. Instead I'd agreed to limited access, undertaken not to harass or molest Marie-Sophie, and agreed to a divorce proceedings on the grounds of my own unreasonable behaviour when I didn't even want to get divorced. If I had ever read Kafka I might have described the turn of events as Kafkaesque.

'What's the address of the school, Marie-Sophie?' I called after her as she started to make her way towards the exit.

<< >> << >>

WHEN I went to pick up Pierre from his new school that Friday afternoon, for my first ever access visit, I got there a little early. I wanted to have a snoop around. I was predisposed to find fault with the place, even though it was in the smartest part of London, and likely to be have lots of children in it from the smart houses round and about – perhaps Lloyds names who had fallen on bad times and decided a private education was out of the question or champagne socialists who move to a certain area because the schools are good.

There were pictures by the children dotted around the walls, and an explanatory note by a teacher ('Class CL worked in different media to produce pictures of trees and animals'). You had to be impressed that she called them 'media' not 'mediums'. I could just hear Pierre coming home and saying excitedly, 'Daddy, today we worked in different media. One medium was crayons and the other water colours!'

My antipathy to the school was fuelled not only by the fact that I had not been consulted in its choice, but also by a letter the Headmistress (oops, Headteacher) had written in support of Marie-Sophie's position, a copy of which I'd just received that morning from Sally. She had also written a cringy letter to the court saying that 'in the difficult circumstances of a separation often school provides the bedrock of stability that a child needs'. This was undoubtedly true, but surely it was an argument for Pierre to stay in his original school, not to move to hers.

I went into the school secretary's office to find out where I would be able to pick up Pierre, and then went in the direction suggested. The first person I encountered was Marie-Sophie walking across the schoolyard. Ahead of her was a motley column of children, following a teacher. I hadn't expected to see her, and I couldn't see what she was up to. It was still a bit early to have been picking up Pierre, and I think she must have been surprised to see me, too. She had probably planned to slip away unnoticed.

'Go away,' she hissed. 'You're not supposed to be here.' She carried on walking. She was carrying a box full of papier mâché animals that the children had obviously been making. She was doing her classroom help bit, integrating Pierre into his new school, responsible parent, etc. Perhaps she was about to become a hands on parent. She'd never shown any interest in what Pierre was up to in class before.

Pierre was in the group of kids ahead of her and

suddenly spotted me: 'Daddy, Daddy!' He reached into the box Marie-Sophie was carrying to show me the animal he'd been working on. I'm afraid I failed to show any enthusiasm for it. We went into the classroom, with my dear ex-beloved all the time trying to shoo me away under her breath. I wasn't going to be shooed.

I met Pierre's new teacher who seemed nice enough. Pierre wanted to show me a picture he'd done earlier. 'Look, I've done a gasometer,' he said, grabbing both me and Marie-Sophie by the hand.

I took Pierre home on the bus, always a treat for him. He was in terrific form. He was very excited to be visiting, even sleeping, at 'Mummy's office' which is how the new flat had been described to him. Given that the court had not yet ruled on his long-term future, this lie was tactful rather than tactical, I acknowledged. He chatted away at random about his Gameboy. I didn't know he had a Gameboy, I'd certainly never bought him one. Marie-Sophie and I had presented a united front on Gameboys: 'Borrow Jake's.'

He told me all about his new school, what he'd done in his lessons. It was a relief to me that he had not yet got wind of what was going on around him. 'I'm going to tell Miss Jardine about my picture,' he'd said. (Miss Jardine being the teacher in his school in Clapham.)

'Where did you get your new Gameboy then, Pierre?' I had visions of a cynical hearts and minds campaign. Under the Children Act the wishes of the child have to be taken into account – what better way than to dish out Gameboys on demand.

'Jasper gave it to me.'

Jasper? The plot thickens. Marie-Sophie's official reason for leaving me was that she needed 'space'. The marriage wasn't working well, she wanted to move out and think things over, she might even change her mind and come back.

'I want a bike with gears for my birthday, Jasper,' Pierre said at one point.

'If you call me that, I'll give you a Barbie doll,' I replied more sharply than I probably should have done, especially as for all I know Jasper was a thoroughly nice bloke.

'Sorry Daddy, I didn't mean to call you Jasper.' Pierre's face was clouded by consternation.

Back home, Pierre went to his toy box and arranged a traffic jam of his favourite cars round the living-room, while I cooked our fish fingers and frozen peas for supper. Marie-Sophie had a Gallic abhorrence of this manifestation of English cuisine, but being like forbidden fruit it was Pierre's and my favourite. I do them in olive oil and a bit of butter, with lots of garlic chopped in, coarse black pepper on mine (not his), herbs from the garden, and maybe a touch of soy sauce. Sounds pretentious, but tastes good.

Then bed and a story, almost the usual routine, except that I couldn't get him to go to sleep. 'Don't go downstairs, Daddy,' he said. Eventually I had to get under the Thomas the Tank Engine Duvet too, until he'd gone to sleep.

On Saturday I hired a car and took him off to see Granny and Grandpa who live in a village in Sussex. My sister Katie was there too with her two girls who are aged a year either side of Pierre. It is a good area for children, with the Downs, large woods for walking in with big piles of scrunchy leaves, and the sea not that far away. Grandpa's garden is half an acre, with a field behind containing sheep and the excitement within a few weeks of lambs. It was big enough for a frisbee, a kite or a model aeroplane, and if there was snow (there wasn't), inclined at a sufficient angle in one corner for a toboggan.

My mother, especially, looked anxious, but didn't say much. 'Is there anything we can do?' she asked. I didn't think there was. Mum's poor boy. Dad carried on more or less as normal, as usual despatching me to chop wood and the like. They had both warned that Marie-Sophie didn't suit me, that I was visibly keener on her than she on me. Now, obviously, they were horrified that a son of theirs was divorcing. But there was no question of either of them saying to me, 'I told you so'.

'Marie-Sophie must be going through a terrible time too,' Mum said, with unexpected generosity, before adding, 'You make sure you make good use of that solicitor.' I felt sorry for my mother, it must be tough for the generation above when the generation below messes up its lives.

One thing I did remember to do was to pay a visit to my old, beaten-up Citroën 2 CV that had been sitting in my parents' outhouse since I'd abandoned it when I was a student. I could never quite bear to get rid of it and had been content for it to become a free-range chicken coop and the like. It looked rather pathetic and sorry for itself but my father said he'd have a go at restoring it for me.

I thought my mother looked quite old when I had to set off back to London at ten on Sunday morning, feeling that there should still have been more of the weekend to go. The only positive thing about leaving then was that it is the only time of the weekend when the A3 isn't clogged with traffic.

I delivered Pierre to Marie-Sophie's new door, pressed one of the ten doorbells and addressed the intercom. 'It's me,' I said. 'Midday, bang on time.' Best not to rock the boat. The building was a 1930s mansion block, not somewhere I'd choose to live even if it was in Knightsbridge. A brass plaque said that there was a translation agency inside. Perhaps I should get some work off them, then I'd be able to infiltrate the building, perhaps sneak along a balcony for a snoop into Marie-Sophie's new flat.

She appeared at the door. She did look tired and stressed out; perhaps she was finding it hard, too, as my mother had indicated. But she also had a more self-confident look about her than when we'd been in court.

I am certain that Pierre still had no inkling about what was going on between us at this stage but equally I am certain that he sensed something. He again grabbed both our hands and put them together. 'Let's go to the park, ' he said. 'All of us.'

'Next time,' we both said simultaneously. I ruffled his hair.

'Bye Pierre.' He didn't ask why I wasn't coming in. I walked away as fast as I could. It was all a bit much for me and I didn't want him to see me upset.

THERE were now less than two weeks to kill before the next hearing. In truth, there wasn't a great deal to do on the legal front. I'd done a hasty affidavit for the first short hearing but there was little to add to it. The other side had written a letter to Sally suggesting that we should agree to the current arrangements, 'access on alternate Friday afternoons to Sunday mornings'. If we were to do so then their client would be in agreement to formalize things on a permanent basis and there would be no need to go to court. I told Sally to remind them that 1) this arrangement was only an interim one, until the hearing, 2) I currently had Pierre each weekend not 'alternate' ones, 3) that I still intended to get a residence order in my favour. Pierre was going to live with me.

I wasn't willing to agree to go from main carer to Disneyland Dad for the rest of Pierre's minority. Saturday afternoon at London Zoo was not my idea of a fair game of soldiers. Solicitors are always seeking instructions, and that is what clients should give them. As far as I was concerned Pierre was coming home.

Meanwhile, recents events were taking their toll. I was

off my food, off my work, off my sleep. When our street had had cable laid we had subscribed to the foreign language channels, including the French one. After viewing it about three times, we decided it was so dire that we were wasting our money, but we hadn't got round to cancelling it. Now it came into its own as a palliative medium. The great merit of cable telly is that you get low-attention-span-junk at all times of night. If you are dog-tired but can't sleep because your mind is racing, it is a brilliant way to slow it down. You get some great films late at night but I'd soon lose the plot thinking about my own thing – 'How dare Marie-Sophie say I only bathed Pierre occasionally . . .?'

My ideal viewing had descended to the level of a compellingly unfunny chat show host called Jay Leno on NBC Superchannel, relayed from America, where he is very popular. Each bit comes in three-minute bursts due to the numerous commercial breaks, so if I did doze off I didn't feel I'd missed anything. Actually, he did crack one good joke once about a dog that survived a nine-floor jump, leaping after its master who was committing suicide – 'remarkable because that's like sixty-three floors to a dog'. He keeps you viewing by promising that some actress you really fancy is coming up 'after these messages' and it always turns out that it is not these messages but the ones after.

As the night wore on the menu would get sparser. There was always an Open University programme – many have presenters courtesy of the Wooden Tops, but there are some good ones. Unfortunately they required more brain capacity than I had available in the state I was in. A low point was when Eurosport went off to be replaced by a sales channel where they concentrate on plugging one product only for up to twenty minutes. I watched all this absorbed by the vulgarity of it, but after a while I found myself actually starting to wonder about all those things you can cook with a hand-beaten wok; or the things you can restore sheen to with the special paint-restoring compound; the things you could cut with the knives which don't need sharpening (as used on the space shuttle); the things you can do with the multi-purpose anti-static magic mops or electrolytic tooth brushes.

The programmes tend to come from America and push American products but are often fronted by a Brit. The Americans have a puzzling attitude to us: we are the only racial grouping that it is safe to cast as the baddy in films these days (the token black actor is always the police chief or the surgeon); and I wondered if this was the principle which made them choose a guy with a Yorkshire accent to put together compelling arguments for the purchase of the three-minutes-a-day exercise machine-cum-bread-baker. It was all I could do to stop myself picking up the phone and ringing the freephone number and committing my credit card to £29.99 (plus p&p). Might as well spend it, then she couldn't have it.

On a Friday night, the German channel dishes up porn. If you miss it, the identical film is repeated on Saturday. Sex was more-or-less the last thing on my mind, but I watched this with the detached fascination of a disapproving sociologist. My gonads were shrivelled with shock not swelling with frustration, besides all the films were blotchy creations shot cheaply in the seventies with Polish refugee actors doing the cunning stunts, dubbed into German. There is another called The Adult Channel, and a third called TV-X, but you have to pay extra, so on my telly they were scrambled. You could hear some intriguing noises, and occasionally make out a left tit, but I doubt that the extra money would have helped me get my mind off my soon to be ex-wife and court case.

Perhaps I would never be interested in sex again. Sigh.

Violins . . . the life of the lonely person. I realized I would have to get a grip. The game plan had to be to get back on to some kind of even emotional keel, fall in love and live happily ever after.

I asked myself, wouldn't I have fewer problems if the brakes on an aged Routemaster bus failed one day when Marie-Sophie was crossing the road? I really did think this, I am ashamed to admit. But I defy any divorcing person to say that they have never entertained similar thoughts. You can bet that Marie-Sophie had pretty advanced fantasies about a spectacular end for me.

It struck me that I was really getting ripped off. If one had to go through all this shit one ought to have done something really wicked to merit it, like deflowering 30 virgins in one night of orgiastic excess. Or even one virgin. Or having a passionate affair with a world-famous supermodel. On second thoughts supermodels are probably a bit overrated – there is an other worldly quality to them which makes me think that if confronted with a naked and beckoning Kate Moss, I probably wouldn't know which bit to touch. Just old-fashioned adultery, done in the missionary position with somebody mundane. Like Jake's divorcee mother – who always used to annoy Marie-Sophie by being too friendly to me in the playground – or in a moment of weakness with a chance encounter on the Costa del Sol. Then perhaps divorce would be my just desserts.

I decided to get a life. Last minute, I accepted an invitation to a party given by that same Michele, to celebrate the fact that she had given up alcohol for two whole months and was now taking it up again. Michele was obviously abreast of my situation, because the invitation had been addressed to me only. I wondered how Jake was coping with the loss of Pierre.

Parties at the beginning of March are a good idea.

Everyone needs reminding that winter is nearly over. Despite being a Monday, it was a wall-to-wall-with-people party, in which you mill around and shout a few pleasantries to half-acquaintances over the hubbub.

I had arrived at the party hoping to avoid the entire topic of divorce, but there must be a homing instinct for divorcees and I seemed to spend the evening talking to complete strangers about how long I'd been separated and answering quite astonishingly personal questions like 'So why do you think your marriage has broken up?' It's amazing how people go into personal counsellor mode and look all caring on your behalf. You sort of wish they'd treat you more robustly, like Roger does.

And then the divorcee homing instinct threw up someone called Marcia. She was a couple of years older than me, with a beautiful but lived-in face. Husband No. 2 had behaved in stereotypicaly bad fashion and left her and three children for his secretary about a year before. We got on well. Afterwards we shared a cab home. Her home. For coffee. She told me that she had just given her new boyfriend the boot. 'He wants to marry me. I don't want to get married again. I've been through all that, I only got rid of my last husband a year ago, I just want to have fun.'

I poured out all my problems. She understood completely, and explained a bit about Marie-Sophie's thought processes. When I got upset and cried, she put her arm round me. It was lovely. And then she gave me a kiss and a hug and said it was time for bed. I wasn't sure whether this was an invitation to stay or what – given her stated desire for 'fun' it might have been appropriate to pounce. Quite what was expected in these situations I didn't know. It had been a long time since I'd played the mating game and I was utterly out of practice when it came to reading the signs. Better to play safe. 'Goodnight,' I said.

'Time to wobble home.'

'We must see each other again . . . soon,' she said.

Back alone in my own bed, I didn't mind missing the opportunity at all, besides which two of the children were young and I didn't relish them bounding in in the morning. But still, nice girl, one way forward possibly. I fell soundly asleep.

<< >> << >>

WHEN I woke I began mulling over Marcia and whether or not I still liked the idea of her now that I was sober. Three children, so been there done that, not some desperate girl in her early thirties with the biological clock thundering. A year or so ahead of me in the divorce market, so probably still quite emotionally unstable and unsure of commitment. As a long-term bet pretty unlikely. But, suitably unsuitable, no question about it.

I hadn't asked her for her telephone number because I wasn't sure if it was the right thing to do. You meet a girl at a party, tell her that you are upset (genuinely), that your wife has just left you, then say, 'Can I have your telephone number?' If I were the woman, I'd run a mile. Filthy male beast with only one thing on his mind. But she had said that she wanted to see me again and soon too. I reasoned that as she was ahead of me in the divorce game, and a second-time-rounder at that, she was well placed to indicate to me the ground rules. Equality of the sexes implies lots of things. I might win custody of Pierre. Marcia might ask me out on a date. But then, what if, when she'd said 'Time for bed' she'd got the impression I didn't like her because I'd gone home immediately. Or she might be thinking he probably needs to be left alone, court case coming up, the last thing he will be thinking of is me.

Being left alone was the last thing I needed, but Marcia wasn't to know that. Well yes she was – she was an old hand at this.

For my part, with all the publicity about men stalking women, and about date rape, since I had last been on the market for a woman, I wasn't sure if I even had a right to ask for her telephone number. I was entering a complicated world as I came out of my seven-year date-free time tunnel, with no idea as to the new rules and etiquette. Dating is the wrong word, I just wanted a bit of female company, strange to say. When a woman was at the root of all my problems it was to women I wanted to turn.

A more or less complete stranger like Marcia was ideal, rather than a more long-standing friend. There are several women I have known for years, and who know parts of me (NB: no *double entendre* intended) better perhaps even than Marie-Sophie, but you can't see a lot of such women without all your other friends finding out and gossiping.

So how to engineer another meeting without making a prat of myself? I wondered about ringing Michele. Risky, I concluded. She might have sent me an invitation and not Marie-Sophie, but I couldn't be sure whose side she was on yet. It wouldn't do for the word to drift back that I was contemplating a fling already, the corpse of my marriage still warm. Even if the Jasper thing was a creation of my more fevered imaginings, I could bet that Rachel Bonham-Lee would manage to turn my transgression into a betrayal and my wife's into a cry for help.

The phone went. Marcia. Dilemma solved. 'I'll make you dinner, sort you out, give you some T.L.C.,' she said. 'You deserve it.' This sounded very promising.

'How did you get my number?' I asked.

'The phone book.' So much for etiquette. 'How about Thursday? I'll have got rid of the kids,' she continued, 'Shane will be on a date, the little ones are off with their dad.'

Great. 'To Thursday then,' I concluded, raising an imaginary wineglass. I wondered what it would be like to kiss her.

<< >> << >>

I figured Roger's compassion, such as it was, was probably exhausted by know. Better get back to the office. However, before heading into work on Wednesday, I visited Hank who, I felt, deserved an up-date after all the help he'd given me, even if some of that had put the fear of god into me. Also, I had a new problem. I wanted to pick his brains on court welfare officers. I'd had a letter from Sally to say that he would be coming round on Friday afternoon to interview me and Pierre. Now I wanted to find out exactly what I was in for.

I told Hank how things were progressing. 'She's got you well snookered,' he said. I'd have this American talking about sticky wickets next.

'Hank, how do I deal with a court welfare officer?'

'Well it depends. Man or woman?'

'A man.'

'It doesn't matter. They are all useless. And dishonest. They lie. For a quiet life he has to find reasons to help the judge award custody to your wife. You realize they know nothing about children, don't you? They come from the probation service. They are trained to look after prisoners most of whom are some variety of behavioural deviant, so their world view is women good, men bad. Let's see, your wife is dark, French, a good-looking girl . . .'

'Sounds like her, how do you know?'

'She used to buy coffee off of me on her way to work sometimes. Presumed you knew. Yep, nice-looking chick, the most dangerous sort. Anyway, the Court welfare officer. They get seconded for five years to the family courts

106

because they are seen as being good at writing reports, then they go back to being probation officers again. They know fuck all about children. Good system isn't it?'

'So how do I handle one?'

'Bug your room. Video the interview. God knows. How's the kid taking it?'

'Fine. A bit clingy. Wouldn't go to sleep without me in the bed, too.'

'You want to be careful about that. An accusation of sexual abuse is an instant win for a woman and a growth industry in family law. They take eighteen months investigating then, when they find no evidence, they still don't trust you with access. Supervised contact in some centre only. There is a whole industry of nut-case psychiatrists and social workers out there poking children's bottoms with probes and giving them male dolls with thumping great erections to insert into female dolls with thumping great holes. If your son is even vaguely good at Meccano, he'll get the hang of it in seconds. The psycho will say "Good boy" and that is the last time you get to give your child a goodnight kiss.'

'Is that what happened to you?'

'No, but I know lots of people to whom it has happened. Believe me, the system is rotten.'

I decided Hank was exaggerating although he was definitely useful for worst-case scenario insights.

'Hey, look. I'm a member of this organization called Families Need Fathers. We meet up sometimes and swap information on judges, call each other and say how cases have gone, etcetera. You want to join us? Might fill you in on the scene a bit. However complicated your problem is, there is someone else who has had it.'

I didn't like the sound of it. I had an image of a horde of disaffected men all revving each other up into greater anger and misogyny. And yet, all things considered, Hank seemed a remarkably balanced sort of person. Yes, he was very angry about his situation and I was only hearing his side of the story. But you couldn't help thinking that a judge must have made some error in preventing him from seeing his child. The more I got to know him the more I believed this to be the case. You just had to see the special, warm, generous, friendly atmosphere he brought to his deli to know that someone, somewhere, somehow had got something wrong.

W ork was a non-starter as I spent most of the day answering questions from kinder-hearted colleagues about my general well-being. That evening I made my very first telephone call to Marcia: 'Sorry, crisis, can't make the date, the court welfare officer is coming, got to scrub the house, visit the Early Learning Centre for some wholemeal violence free toys, etc.' Hank had got me worried and I'd been plagued by his advice all day.

Surprisingly, Marcia was instantly very understanding: 'I'll tell you what, I'll come to your house instead and help you clean it. You can cook me dinner afterwards if you like.' Why the thought of cleaning my house should excite me all of a sudden I didn't know, but it did.

Thus it was that our first date saw her helping me clean my house from top to bottom for the court welfare officer's visit. 'Already looking like a bachelor pad,' commented Marcia, looking at the mess.

When the wife leaves, there are various occupational therapies available to you, such as taking up sport again, throwing yourself into your work or, in an effort not to let personal standards slide and self-pity take over, you can clean your house frantically. I had let things slide. Still, 'bachelor pad' was not completely fair. It had been our matrimonial home for some years and if there were strange accretions behind the cooker and other hidden recesses, not all of them were my fault. A spotless antiseptic kitchen indicates 'Marks and Spencer packet opened and microwaved here' – to my mind an unhealthy attitude to food. We both took eating seriously (with the odd lapse – mine being fish fingers) and proper cooking means mess.

It seemed unfair that the CWO would not have the benefit of seeing Marie-Sophie's housekeeping for what it was. I wished I'd done that photo project of her bomb-zone study. Her newly let flat would no doubt be spotless and, being a gifted television person, she'd have it decked out just right.

Once Marcia got going she made me do things like pull out the cooker and clean in the gap between it and the kitchen units. She pointed out how dirty my light switches were. I'd never paid much attention to my light switches. I was also made aware of a tide-mark of handprints on the doors at a height which corresponded with Pierre's. I was in two minds about touching this. On the one hand the marks were indeed unsightly, on the other they were evidence that this house had a child living in it, surely a plus point. Marcia used vinegar to polish the bathroom taps – now there was a novelty (as was polishing the taps). She also put some aromatic herbs in the loo and a particularly pungent pot-pourri in the bathroom. I realized that subliminal olfactory messages about my domestic competence were not to be overlooked. The thought coincided with my catching a whiff of Marcia's pheromones, but the moment passed.

In fact, the house was beginning to acquire the perfume of an industrial cleaning agent plant, a mingling of bleach and lemon cleaning powder, Shake 'n' Vac and other products which reach the parts that other beers can't.

Marcia promised me that the smells would wear off by the morning and suggested that I put some coffee beans in the oven 30 minutes before the man's arrival to create a welcoming aroma (apparently an old estate agents' trick).

I got on with some heavy work (washing the kitchen floor, cleaning behind the loo) while she moved on to a pile of ironing. 'Leave these out on the ironing board when the bloke comes,' she said. 'Especially Pierre's clothes.' She told me to have a very faintly damp sheet ready to iron shortly before the man came, too; the smell of fresh ironing would also add to the subliminal impression of homeliness.

Having cleaned so hard, we were loath to cook ourselves a meal afterwards and too tired to make the effort to get changed and go out. We settled on take-out pizza and a bottle of good French wine I had in the fridge.

Did Marcia and I kiss on our first date? Certainly not. I will admit to having allowed my body to brush lightly up against hers as we struggled to change a Hoover bag, and it had seemed to me that there was a fleeting response, a hint of promise. But in the end it was only the house that got fresh. Domestos just doesn't have the pheromonal qualities of Chanel No. 5 or the taste of honey.

Should I have really been thinking this way when the corpse of my marriage was not yet cold? Go for it, was my rationale, life was too short for scruples. Besides, my burgeoning friendship with Marcia was better than any therapy going, and even if it all went horribly wrong it still beat Jay Leno on NBC Superchannel.

<< >> << >>

THE barristers had agreed between them that I should pick up Pierre from the new school at noon on the day of the court welfare officer's visit, rather than three, so that he would be settled by the time the CWO came at four o'clock. I arrived at the school in plenty of time but when I visited the office was told that Marie-Sophie had rung in to say that Pierre might be a bit late because of a doctor's appointment. I found myself killing a lot of time in the uninspiring surroundings of Blenheim Primary School, examining the children's progress in 'media'.

The doctor's appointment turned out to be a long one. Marie-Sophie and Pierre arrived just after three, apologizing for having been detained.

'I tried to leave a message, but you weren't there.'

'I was here.'

'I'm sorry, there was a long queue.'

'What's wrong with him?'

'Tummy upset.'

'Can I borrow the car, I'll be late,' I said.

'I'm sorry, I need it,' she said, not looking sorry at all.

Pierre was very excited to see his dad. 'Mummy took me to her office. It's got a bed which folds up which I can sleep on. Can you come and see it Daddy?' I'd have been quite curious but thought it unlikely. I'd have been as welcome in her flat as a Eurostar Express on the Fat Controller's branch line.

Pierre and I got home in a black cab with five minutes to spare. He yabbered happily the whole way back. 'I've been in a taxi lots. Mummy gave me a croissant for breakfast in a taxi.'

Ha! Evidence. So she can't cope with the early morning school run already.

There was no time to prime him, or bribe him properly with some suitable story about the importance of our visitor. A trip to McDonalds would have been fine, but I couldn't say to him 'If you're good, I'll take you for a Happy Meal' because inevitably he'd blow my cover at some stage. 'Daddy says that if I'm good he'll take me for a

Happy Meal.' Discrete bribery of a child takes time and planning.

I'd forgotten to get any coffee beans, so sprinkled some ground coffee on to an oven tray and whacked it into the oven and turned it on full. There was no time to lose in getting that subliminal smell of domesticity as opposed to Domestos wafting through the house. I rushed upstairs and pulled out the heap of Pierre's smalls Marcia had ironed and put them on the ironing board. I'd have to give ironing the faintly damp sheet a pass. I had at least put a basketful of laundry on the washing line for the 'Here's one I finished earlier' impression.

The court welfare officer was a completely unknown quantity. I had asked Sally how I should behave, and she'd just said 'With common sense'. It emerged that she did not really know how CWOs go about their work. If you think about it, all a solicitor ever sees is the report, and the man in court. Even a very experienced solicitor, unless divorced themself, will never have seen a CWO in the process of collecting his material, performing his interviews, and coming to his conclusion. I preferred not to think of the advice Hank had given me. It would be overkill to start installing hidden microphones everywhere.

I think Pierre may have sensed that his father was feeling a touch vulnerable because he started putting a series of unreasonable demands to me of the Can-I-have-some-sweets?/Can-I-go-to-the-park-on-my-bicycle?/Can-I-go-to-Jake's-house? genre. I told him we had a guest, and that he must be a good boy. While I wasn't looking he went to his large box of Lego and upended it on the sitting-room floor.

Mr Wheedle was in his mid-forties. There was the faint whiff of fusty bachelor about him, scurf on the back of his collar, that sort of thing. He was trim, but nonetheless my summation was that he probably still went home to his mother at weekends with a big bag of laundry.

Pierre had been away for a week, and was thus keen to reacquaint himself with those toys that had been left behind. He had now been upstairs to his bedroom and brought down various boxes, the contents of which he was starting to distribute.

'That's a nice little rocket,' said Mr Wheedle pointing to a Thunderbird 2. Pierre rolled his eyes at me knowingly. You just don't call Thunderbird 2 a nice little rocket.

I could tell he had never had children of his own, and there was a certain *je ne sais quoi* about his manner which suggested that he wasn't ever likely to be in the (missionary) position to have any, not with a woman anyway. But I decided it was best not to ask him whether this was indeed so.

We sat at a table while Pierre busied himself with his toys on the floor. I was quizzed about my marriage and why I thought it might have gone wrong. My instincts were to be as nice as possible about Marie-Sophie, and this wasn't too hard, because as angry and hurt as I was, I couldn't deny that I had loved her, nor glibly dismiss that love by making out I held only rancorous thoughts about her. I was still in something of a state of shock about the affidavit, and couldn't believe that the Marie-Sophie I knew had put the nasty bits in all on her own. It didn't make sense. I could imagine Rachel running through a check-list of nasties designed to stir things up:

'Did your husband ever hit you?'

'No.'

'Not even once? During an argument say?'

'Well, yes, there was once,' she would have replied tearfully. Meanwhile, Miss Bonham-Lee set about robbing the situation of its context and making me sound like a habitual wife-beater. It had been one incident, years before which reflected badly on both of us and would have been best left buried in the past. Nonetheless, placed for dramatic purposes at the end of the affidavit it would be bound to colour the impression of me that the reader formed, and Mr Wheedle got to read all the papers in the case.

I couldn't imagine that he would be impressed if I spent the time being rude about Marie-Sophie, besides which Pierre, although seemingly absorbed in distributing more and more toys (the untidiness gene is definitely dominant) would have his radar ears tuned in. I suggested to Pierre that he go off and build a Scalextric circuit, but he was not gone five minutes before he was back.

'Daddy can you help me with this?' I got out one of the plans for a track layout and suggested one for him to go off and do.

'I want to go back to my old school,' said Pierre suddenly and quite out of any context. I don't think he fully understood the significance of the visit of this stranger with all the questions – I'd thought it best not to explain, and I believe his mother had done the same – but he showed that some childish instinct was in operation. He knew something was going on without understanding it.

Mr Wheedle and I exchanged glances, and he wrote it down in his notebook. It seemed to me that the meeting was going well. I decided it was time to offer Mr Wheedle a cup of tea. I opened the kitchen door, to be greeted by billows of smoke. The billows smelt quite pleasant, if a bit acrid. I'd forgotten all about the coffee. I think if it had been beans I might have got away with it, but the ground coffee showed clear signs of ready combustion. I quickly shut the door behind me, threw open the windows and, half choking, started to make the tea. Smoke continued to pour from the oven.

It was not the best moment to discover that Marie-Sophie had nicked the best tea service and that all I had left were some chipped mugs from Esso. Neither was it a good moment to switch on the kettle without first putting water in it. There was a loud pop, a flash of light and the kettle gave up its ghost. What to do? Help. Stay calm. I grabbed a large saucepan and, filling it with water, shoved it on the hob. If Mr Wheedle should come in, I'd have to say it is how the French do things. I gave a quick wipe to the two least chipped mugs, poured in some hot water and cast around for tea bags. There were none. My eye fell on a packet of loose-leaf Darjeeling from Hank's deli. Thank God.

I'd been gone in the kitchen a while and thought Mr Wheedle might be missing me. It was imperative that he did not come for a friendly chat so I put my head round the door and asked him how he liked his tea. 'Strong or weak?'

'Oh, as it comes,' he answered cheerily.

As I put the mugs on a tray, I knocked the packet of Darjeeling over. Only a little came out but some fell on to the electric rings of the hob. Darjeeling combusts nicely. It is right up there with ground coffee but gives off more smoke. I thought of going into the living-room and saying, 'OK, the game is up. Fair cop guv, Marie-Sophie can have custody.' But I am made of sterner stuff. I added a bit more water to the saucepan, then poured the tea into each waiting mug through a sieve.

I joined Mr Wheedle, shutting the kitchen door as quickly as possible behind me. I caught a glimpse of myself in a mirror as I carried the tray to the table, smoke gently rising from my clothing. I called to Pierre to join us at the table.

'Nice tea,' said Mr Wheedle.

I offered him a nice éclair to go with his nice tea. The cream got stuck in his moustache, and the icing on his fingers. I had to re-enter the kitchen to get a napkin. It goes without saying that the best linen had gone with the best tea service, so I got him a couple of sheets of quilted kitchen paper.

Pierre was even less skilful than the CWO at eating his éclair. I had also managed to produce a plate of various biscuits and by the time I came back with the 'napkins', he had helped himself to a handful. He knew it was a capital offence in our household to do so without asking first, but my hands were tied before the CWO.

'Please may I leave the table,' Pierre said eventually, having remembered his manners all of a sudden. With relief, I acquiesced, glad this would signal the end of the crumbs and mess that were beginning to spread everywhere. Impressive good manners, Mr Wheedle, I wanted to say, but it would have been overkill. Besides, he seemed preoccupied with getting bits of paper off his sticky fingers.

We carried on discussing my past, present and future, interrupted every few minutes with requests from Pierre. The problem with Pierre is that he is an only child. Only children require the attention of their parents far more than those with siblings who can amuse each other. If you have two children to look after you have to dust down one of them from time to time when they fight, but it has always struck me that Pierre requires more attention than a child with brothers and sisters. Pierre on his own can be a handful, whereas Pierre with a chum is a delight. You do get respite sometimes because he has reasonable powers of concentration, developed through necessity I suppose, as no parent can or should attend to a child constantly. The trick is to find a project that is easy enough for him to do by himself, but captivating enough to hold his attention. Pierre was now embarked on was one of his favourites: building a house out of the cushions from the sofa and armchairs. He duly demolished the sofa, which was one of those pre-1986 ones made out of stiffish foam of the kind which probably gives out severely toxic fumes in a fire. Its components make brilliant building blocks.

The meeting had by this time gone on for the best part of two hours, and Pierre's reserves of not being the centre of attention were nearing exhaustion. Once he'd been inside his house, and tested the interior with a torch, he got fed up with it. He got up on the arm of the sofa and dived on to his construction shouting 'Geronimo'. It collapsed. Now this was fun.

He then took the cushions and laid them end to end along the wooden floor. Immediately behind the sofa was a window-sill with plants on it and he now got upon this for a longer leap, something he'd done lots of times before. I had to pounce to catch a dislodged mother-in-law's tongue (appropriate in the circumstances), but not in time to stop him leaping over the sofa on to the cushions lined up on the other side. As a game it was a long-time favourite of his and I must admit I had encouraged him in it. I can't stand little cotton wool wrapped children and parents who shout, 'Don't do that, it's dangerous!' If you want children not to have accidents, you have to let them test the limits of their capabilities occasionally. But I could see immediately that it might give the wrong impression. To a rather delicate man with cream in his moustache, with no children of his own, primed by his training to suspect child abuse, neglect or that hyperactivity in children was the result of a dependence on sniffing glue.

Pierre, being quite athletic, managed to land on the second cushion. 'How far did I jump that time Daddy? Fifteen-point-three metres?' He might have jumped four or five feet. I suggested we waited until later and reminded Pierre that I was busy just then. No such luck. Pierre pursued variations of the original stunt such as leaping head first and landing on his tummy or leaping feet first and landing so that one of the cushions slid pleasingly on the stripped and varnished floor for some distance. 'Twenty-three metres, Daddy?'

Mr Wheedle was observing this parent – child interaction with a very serious look indeed, and jotted something down. 'Don't you think this a little bit dangerous, Mr Henry?' he asked. In truth I'd have liked to say that it wasn't dangerous at all. I know. He's my child, I've spent a lot of time and trouble teaching him his limits and, in any case, he has enough natural in-built cowardice to protect him from going to the top of the nearest climbable tree and pretending to be an aeroplane. Against all the odds the overwhelming majority of small boys make it into young adulthood.

<< >> << >>

THE next morning I popped out to the local florists leaving Pierre home alone for ten minutes or so – risky in the circumstances – but I wanted to send flowers to Marcia. I did not think it right that Pierre should witness his father buying flowers for another woman. I definitely wanted to see her again, but even if I hadn't she'd certainly earned a bunch of flowers.

This whole divorce thing was wretched. When he finally worked out what had happened to him he'd be knocked for six. On balance, I thought it was probably best not to explain things to him yet, not until we were through with court and the future was clear. I didn't want to be telling him something in direct contradiction to what his mother had been saying. What is best for the child in this situation? There doesn't appear to be any guidance on offer. Certainly I wouldn't ask Sally the solicitor, nor the court welfare officer – what would either know? The thought that a busy-body type like Mr Wheedle could make a recommendation that might change the rest of all of our lives was too horrible for words.

Pierre wanted to go to the Common. We set off with him on his bike and me running behind him carrying the football, he as happy as ever, me my mind churning. It was good to get out of the house and into the fresh air of which there was lots. It was a cold, blustery day. Marie-Sophie would have had him wearing five layers of clothing and banned him from riding on the pavement. Health and safety, major sources of parental strife. He'd said he didn't want his coat so I let him go as he was and carried it in my other hand in case he changed his mind. It's a little thing, but I was enjoying the freedom to do things my way. It's better if two parents take a united front, but Pierre was used to two cultures, two languages. Looking on the bright side, separate parents might perhaps be just one more thing.

I thought Pierre looked a picture of health and happiness as he raced along on his second-hand bike whilst calling to me over his shoulder to keep up with him. 'Watch where you're going,' I shouted back. We did the ducks, the swings, the see-saw – involving much pushing and bouncing on my part and lots of squealing on Pierre's. We finished up by kicking the football around, which Pierre kicked home while I wheeled his bike.

In the afternoon I sent him round to Jake's house to play, then it was supper and bed at a respectably early and newly-disciplined nine o'clock. I read him Charley the Dragon again. I was on auto-pilot for that as ever while the other half of my brain was on my problems. All the time I reflected how the very ordinary things I was doing, like feeding my son and putting him to bed, could be taken away from me and there was a constant knot in my stomach like the one I used to get before exams.

Every so often I still have a nightmare in which I relive my university finals. With two weeks to go I'd done almost no revision. I was studying French and fortunately a friend had a set of excellent 50-page cribs from France on Baudelaire's *Poèmes en Prose* and the other set texts I was supposed to know inside-out but didn't. I scraped through with a 2:2, avoiding the ignominious third. Waiting for Mr Wheedle's report and the following examination in court felt exactly the same (but worse).

'Kiss goodnight,' I said finally.

'Yuk,' said my loving son. 'Daddy, where are you sleeping?'

'In my bed with the door open so I can keep an eye on you.'

'Will I see Mummy tomorrow?'

'Yes, at lunch-time.'

'Don't you and Mummy love each other any more?'

'Yes, I do love your mother.' Should I let him have it and say 'but she doesn't love me so she's left me'? Of course not. 'Mummy's very busy with work so she would like you to help her by staying at her office and going to the other school for a while.'

'Can Jake come to my new school?'

'Possibly. Go to sleep and we'll talk about it in the morning.'

What does one say to a six-year-old? The dreaded moment when Pierre put two and two together was on its way. Had I been a coward or done the best thing by falling in line with the story about Marie-Sophie's work? My godfather got divorced when I was seven. I only started to realize because the Christmas presents sent by his wife stopped coming. The separation and Pierre's new circumstances were something he deserved to have explained to him, but how? There is no guidance on this outside of dense, unreadable psychological treatises.

If I was thinking of the child's rights and best interests and not my own, should I, for example, be the heroicly selfless father and simply slip away? For the sake of protecting the child from his squabbling parents, hard though it may be, should I write a letter of farewell for him to open when he is older, saying 'If you feel like it, look me up when you are eighteen, feel no pressure, but I will always be there for you'; and then limit my involvement to a generous amount of maintenance for him and the sending of birthday and Christmas presents? I was pretty certain that must be wrong although I also thought it was what Marie-Sophie would have liked.

There could be nothing worse for Pierre than to be kept permanently guessing. But I could make it worse by saying the wrong thing. I had little idea of what Marie-Sophie had been telling him. It occured to me that if she hadn't snatched him, we could have sat him down and explained it to him together. It would have been the fairest thing to do. I'm not sure that I could have done it, though. If I'd taken on board earlier that Marie-Sophie really was going to take him away, I would have put up a fight. We had both been selfish in putting our own needs ahead of his.

They say that children often blame themselves for their parents' divorce. I'd have to make sure that Pierre never thought this and, above all, I must make him understand that I was not living apart from him through choice.

<< >> << >>

I took Pierre home the next morning. He didn't continue his line of questioning so I let it lie also. Marie-Sophie came to the door of her mansion block for the hand-over. She was polite but distant – I was the same.

'Bye-bye Pierre,' I said, 'be a good boy.' He tugged at my sweater so I picked him to give him a kiss. He clung to me really hard. 'Come on Pierre, down you get, I've got to go now,' I said, but he wouldn't let go. His little hands had taken a handful of my sweater and were holding it very tightly.

'I don't want to go to Mummy's work,' he said in a quiet voice, 'I want to go home.'

I didn't know what to do. I could see that Marie-Sophie was getting cross, and also there was the small matter of an interim court order. I'd be in contempt if he didn't stay here. I found myself prising his hands gently off me when I was dying just to head off with him. Finally I got him into her arms. I was touched by his loyalty and found the whole thing too awful for words, particularly as I reckoned he was for the high jump when she got him indoors.

<< >> << >>

WHEN I got home I found Michele at my front door in the process of writing me a note. 'Just popped round to cadge a cup of coffee and check things aren't going too badly.'

'How badly can they go?'

'I'm sorry. Look forget the coffee but if you're feeling low would you like to come round for some supper tonight? Nothing fancy, just me and the kids.'

I wasn't sure I really felt like it but then thought it was probably a better option than moping at home alone. Besides I've never been good at thinking up quick excuses so I said yes.

'Seven OK?'

Supper took place in Michele's kitchen – big with an Aga in it – with Jake and his sister, Charlotte, who is a few years older than him. The food was good, plain, wholesome, nothing out of a packet. I made a mental note to start cooking properly again.

The early part of the evening passed without incident and I even started to unwind a little. Over the pudding however the homing mechanism whereby divorcees end up discussing divorce with each other clicked into gear. I forget how, but Michele touched a raw nerve which caused me to have a little sob into my apple pie. This was an annoying lack of self-control, especially in front of her kids. She then put her arm round me which annoyed me more even though it was well meant. I didn't want people to start feeling sorry for me. I wanted to wallow privately in my grief.

After the children went to bed I told her about the incident handing over Pierre. She told me that she'd had a similar thing with Charlotte when her father came round to take her away for a weekend. Charlotte is mad about her dad, but she'd taken to saying she didn't want to see him. On one occasion she'd locked herself in the loo. As a means of getting attention from both parents at the same time it had worked a treat. Dad was distraught because his daughter said she didn't want to see him. Mum was embarrassed because it looked as though she'd set Charlotte up to it. 'There are plenty of mums who would do that, but I wouldn't,' said Michele. 'Anyway that phase is passed. Charlotte's fine about going away now. Pierre will get used to it, too.'

I didn't want to pick a fight with Michele, but 'get used to it'? That presumed a lot. She went to the fridge and got a bottle of champagne out. 'May as well,' she said. I'd always liked Michele for her innate generosity of spirit and kindness. Despite the house she didn't have much cash, but would still take pleasure in treating friends.

She knew Marie-Sophie too, and in rallying round me she wasn't taking sides, it was just that I was still local. There was a lonely side to her too: despite her many friends and active social life, she had two quite difficult children and she had admitted that they played up if she got close to a new man. Invariably the man would be scared off. But she'd always put her children first and could never get involved with someone they really didn't like.

I'm sure she was enjoying having me around to look after. This was the second invitation in a short time and I got a slight impression that she had tried to make it seem low-key. I studied her a bit closer. She was dressed in jeans but had put on a touch of lipstick, which I thought was something she didn't normally do, and nail varnish. Strange as it may seem for a man who misses most things about a woman's apparel, I am up to speed on nail-varnishing habits. It's something I always make a point of noticing – states of fingers are an immensely useful index for assessing a woman's personality. Long, perfectly manicured ones have always been a turn off for me because they are useless and fragile and get in the way. They can't hold a tennis racket, go in a washing up bowl, weed a flower bed, play the piano and I've never understood why any man should want them raking down his back. Marcia had short practical ones; Michele had fingernails bitten to the quick, and this evening they were covered in nail varnish.

<< >> << >>

THE next morning a motorbike courier came to my door with a package of papers for which I had to sign. It was another affidavit, but this time sworn in the name of Marie-Sophie's friend, Tiffany. I needn't have been surprised. After all, the letter I had uncovered did say 'I don't blame you for wanting to leave Michael. If there is anything I can do to help . . .' It might be two years old, but still.

The package contained more gratuitous unpleasantness, more fees for Rachel Bonham-Lee. The affidavit alleged that my family had been mean to Marie-Sophie, saying she had encountered hostility from my father and mother. This observation was, perforce, at second hand, because Tiff had never met them. Paragraph 17 read:

> Pierre is a very well bought up and charming boy, which I am sure is down to the way in which the Petitioner has guided and cared for him. She is a kind, considerate and polite person. On the other hand, I must say that I have often found the Respondent off hand and rude. Certainly the Respondent was unpopular with some of the Petitioner's friends.

You could just imagine them: 'Oh, oh, here comes the Respondent, dive for cover girls . . .' Paragraph 23 was about what an uncaring father I was:

> Once when I was babysitting, Michael came back early, and woke Pierre up to give him some medicine because he was suffering from a cold. In all the time that I have known the Henry family this is the only time that I witnessed Michael acting as a father.

Paragraph 25 had a little anecdote about my giving Pierre a ride on the back of my bicycle, Pierre falling off, and having to go to casualty at St Thomas'. This was true, but Tiffany hadn't even been there. She had been rung 'in great distress by the Petitioner'. If the incident had been that serious, you would think that the Petitioner herself would have remembered to put it in her own 23-page affidavit. Paragraph 29 expanded further on my alleged proneness to expose Pierre to life threatening situations:

> On another occasion Marie-Sophie was cooking for a number of friends, of whom I was one. Myself and the other women guests helped while Michael sat watching TV in the lounge

with the men. Marie-Sophie was concerned that Pierre, who was a toddler at the time and into everything, would have an accident if he kept coming into the kitchen, and urged Michael to look after him, but Michael just carried on watching television. I think it may have been a soccer match. It was therefore left to those in the kitchen to pick Pierre up and take him out of the kitchen. This happened several times. My sister and I were surprised and appalled at Michael's lack of responsibility and I recall that in the end my sister's boyfriend Trev (whom I would not normally consider to be interested in children) entertained Pierre to keep him out of harm's way.

Her sister's boyfriend Trev? How do you counter stuff like this? It was pathetic. I couldn't even remember Tiff's sister, let alone Tiff's sister's boyfriend Trev. And so the affidavit wended its pointless way. At least I thought it was pointless. It did paint a picture, though. 'The only time I witnessed Michael acting as a father'. How dare she, the unmarried, childless, feminist bigot, devoid of any experience of the business end of a baby, how dare she say that?

With this latest batch of paperwork, including exhibits of significant correspondence between the two solicitors, the evidence had passed the 100-page mark. Pity the poor judge who eventually had to read it all the way through. I remarked on this to Sally when I rang up to ask whether we needed to do anything about Tiffany's affidavit.

'Oh, don't worry,' she said. 'Judges are paid enough.'

That was not the point I had been trying to make.

<< >> << >>

THE day before the hearing Sally rang me to remind me, as if I could forget, to be on the steps of Somerset House at 10.15 the next morning. She had just heard that we would be before a Judge called Stern, but when I asked her if he lived up to his name, she didn't really have an opinion, never having brought a case before him. Mr Wheedle had not yet filed his report and things hinged on that to quite a large extent. It was a rush he'd said but a report would be ready for the trial.

I was supposed to be ploughing on with another translation at home but I persuaded myself that I should nip down to the deli to get the gen on Judge Stern from Hank. Having been to court around 80 times over the eight years of battles over access to his son, he might even have been before him Even if he hadn't he'd have heard of his reputation through Families Need Fathers who, he'd said, were putting together a 'Good Judge Guide'.

'Fix Michael a cappucino,' he shouted to one of his assistants.

I braced myself for a dose of worst-case scenario. Mental health-wise, it might have been better to stay home, and not go and see gloom-monger Hank, but I reasoned that if I heard the worst, and everything did indeed go horribly wrong the next day, I would be able to handle the disappointment better.

Hank's pep talk was as confidence building as I had feared. The essence of it was that I was stuffed. He had been through it all himself so many times that he found it a mystery why judges bothered to turn up, so rarely did they go against the opinion of the all-seeing, all-understanding court welfare officer. CWOs themselves almost never find in favour of fathers. If they did, it would be regarded as so peculiar that they would never be taken seriously again. Pay and prospects would suffer accordingly.

To recommend in favour of the father: (a) the CWO would have to do an unhealthily severe hatchet-job on the mother which would make everyone feel sorry for her; and (b) the judge and opposing barrister would then give him such a hard time that, for the sake of a quiet life, it was not really worth the trouble. For professional approbation, take the line of least resistance and do the severe hatchet-job on the father, it's expected.

'If you say you changed lots of nappies they won't believe you. And they'll blame you for not breast-feeding the child. Stern, quite well known as a mother's judge.' He made it sound like a hanging judge. 'I managed to get something out of him though because he's a jazz freak.'

'Jazz?'

'Yeah. He saw in my affidavit that I like jazz, and that my son likes it too. I once had to apply to court to take Christopher to a jazz concert. I won but the other side had legal aid to stop me, so those tickets cost the taxpayer about a thousand pounds.

'When the other side went out for something he asked me if I had a particular jazz album he really liked, a 1920s New Orleans recording, which is very rare. And I did have it. We had a discussion about whether the tracks on the earlier one were better than the tracks on the later one and I said I thought they were. I think he'd have liked to borrow it. Anyway, I think that is why I got my staying access restored. He knew the child would be listening to good jazz. The case had been going very badly up to that point. Unfortunately my ex soon started stopping Christopher coming. That's why I'm still going to court the whole time. I was lucky with Judge Stern. Normally you're stuffed. He thinks that women should stay at home and look after children.

'There is an unlikely alliance of out-of-touch sixty-year-old public school boys and man-hating feminists. Stern thinks that women don't work, not proper jobs anyway, they look after children. If you point out she works more than you do then he concludes that she has to skilfully juggle mothering and work, and it's all your fault she has to because you are such a hopeless provider.

'The feminists think they should have the child and the money. Male involvement limited to supply of sperm in glass phial. Sperm bank and cash dispenser then fuck off. That's what the judge thinks too.'

Hank was firmly on his soap box, no dislodging him. 'OK, so she abandoned you, uprooted your son, put him in a new school away from his friends? But the child must go where the bond is strongest.' He put on his finest mock British judge voice, '". . . and so I order that the child must live with the mother, this mother breast-fed her son for months. He needs her." How old is Pierre? Six? You could argue that he's done with the breast for now and needs a male role model. Actually he needs both. But not one more than the other, but that's not the way they see it. It's winner takes all.'

I left Hank's feeling profoundly depressed as usual. I couldn't decide if forewarned is forearmed or whether I was developing masochistic tendencies. I wondered if Hank was a member of the 'Men's Movement', something I had always doubted the existence of. It is an imaginary enemy created by the women's movement – of a group of men intent on keeping the sisters as undereducated, underachieving baby machines, a cook in the kitchen, a maid in the drawing-room, a whore in the bedroom. Sounds good to me. (I know that's not funny. Only joking, girls.)

<< >> << >>

AND SO to court, for the second time. This time for the Big One, a day of legal argument which would probably settle the pattern of the rest of our lives.

Kick off in the courts is not until 10.30 a.m., which gives the judges time to get in from Godalming, but obviates the need to rub shoulders with ordinary commuters. As agreed, I met Sally and Muriel on the pavement outside Somerset House at 10.15. They seemed relaxed enough. Before leaving home I'd failed even to get a bit of coffee and dry toast down and I hadn't slept.

Somerset House is a beautiful building, not gothic and forbidding like the Royal Courts of Justice on the other side of the Strand. Until you get inside, that is, when it becomes dark and grey and institutional. I seem to remember a debate some years back about changing its use from a place for the record of births, deaths and marriages, and making it into an art gallery. Now, of course, it is used for the deaths of marriages, with a couple of floors devoted to this purpose upstairs. The Principal Registry of the Family Division is something of a misnomer. The day-to-day work of the place is not about registering families so much as dismembering them. Of course the dismemberment is registered afterwards.

There was no sign of Mr Wheedle or his report. Shortly after we arrived Marie-Sophie, Rachel, and the sinister James de Vere Crispe appeared in the corridor outside the courts. Marie-Sophie was again made down as opposed to up, dressed in motherly Marks and Spencer, rather than vampish Versace, a long way from her usual knock-'em-dead glamour. We steadfastly avoided each other's gaze.

Again, pre-match nerves were a severe problem for me. Being congenitally incapable of waiting patiently for something to happen in a claustrophobic corridor, I went in search of the loo. I think I ended up going about three times. As you walk along the corridor you notice the names of the judge assigned to each court: Angel, Aglionby, Conn, Artro-Morris. It was busier than last time, crowded with other litigants, some with their children lolling around.

It is a surreal place: the couples collected here are all in nearly the same position as yourself, perhaps a dozen couples who used to love each other even perhaps to distraction and who know every intimate detail of the other's personality and physical habits, who know what deviation from the missionary position excites the other the most, who once enjoyed sufficient intimacy to produce a child but who are now at each other's legal throats. Bizarre.

Maybe because of the extra people, the building was horribly stuffy and over-heated. There was a poster up saying 'Energy Conservation Week, October 23rd to 30th'. This seemed a good idea even in March so, for want of anything better to do, I started to turn off some of the radiators. There was a lot of my taxes going up in hot air in this building, which could be why the Inland Revenue is in another wing of it.

As we continued to wait for Mr Wheedle we passed the time we had in a silly game of lawyer's names. Muriel told me that in addition to Messrs Angel et al., there was a Butler-Sloss, a Cazelet, a Sir Roualeyn Cumming-Bruce, a Mr Setright, a Mr Valentine le Grice and a Mr Spon-Smith. You could never imagine a barrister with a name like John Jones.

A new addition to the enemy team was Marie-Sophie's key witness Tiffany. I looked forward to watching Muriel giving her a suitably humiliating hammering in the witness box. I couldn't believe that Judge Stern would be massively impressed by the leggings she'd turned up in either, although black was definitely this year's colour in the courts, just as it had been since 1723. There was the odd statement against black – James de Vere Crispe had on a foppish bow-tie in bright red which matched his more than usually red lips. You really could imagine him coming out of the mist in the woods of Transylvania.

At five to eleven Mr Wheedle finally arrived and thrust a copy of his report into Sally's hands. He looked pleased with himself. 'Hot off the press,' he said chirpily, with the air of a man who has just finished a job well done. He handed another copy to the opposition.

On the front of such reports it says: 'This report has been prepared for the court and should be treated as confidential. It must not be shown nor its contents revealed to any person other than a party or a legal adviser to such a party.' So if I reveal its contents, I shall find myself in contempt of court.

It was eleven o'clock and the combatants in the previous case came out and we were on. The main problem with the report was getting to look at it at all; we only had one copy between us and had had it for only five minutes. Muriel and Sally had grabbed it and were poring over it together, while James and Rachel read theirs. I tried to look over my lawyers' shoulders, but without much success. They had started reading it from the back, always the logical place with which to start any report. 'What does it say? What does it say?' I whispered anxiously, but realized that both were concentrating, and it wasn't the moment to interrupt.

Muriel broke the news to me: 'I am afraid it recommends that Marie-Sophie has residence,' she said. 'But, look on the bright side, it recommends generous access.'

What to think? What to do? I couldn't take it in. 'I want an adjournment,' I said to Muriel. 'I haven't even had a chance to read this report. Why does he recommend that? He's got it wrong. He didn't listen to what I said. We've got to have time to find out where he went wrong.'

'If we ask for an adjournment we will end up waiting. We were lucky to find a slot in two weeks. Next time it could be two months. Best to get it all over with now. Now ssshh, I've got to read the rest of this,' she said.

'But what did he say?'

'Ssshh,' she repeated.

After a minute or two Muriel got up and went for a little

conference with James de Vere Crispe. She came back and said they wanted to go on now, too. He was offering to settle in line with the report. Pierre lives with her, alternate weekends to me, with one night to stay on alternate weeks.

How could I agree? I couldn't, it seemed so unfair after we'd spent our married life sharing the child rearing. I couldn't accept that the recommendation was the right one. I wanted to know why he'd come up with it but there was no time to read the report. OK, so I'd burnt the coffee and filled the house with smoke, Pierre had broken his personal long-jump record, and the CWO had got a humiliating amount of cream stuck in his moustache. If ever there was one, now was the moment when my expensive barrister must strut her stuff. I hadn't asked how expensive or been told either, somehow it hadn't seemed appropriate to ask. Two hundred quid, a thousand quid? I didn't know.

We went in, except for Tiff, who as a witness had to wait in the corridor until she was called. I wished upon her much lonely wrestling with her conscience in the bleak corridor. The courtroom was a small one again, putting you at a disadvantage if you haven't slept the night before and are thus a twitching wreck. Probably, Marie-Sophie hadn't slept either but as in the previous hearing she had achieved a look that seemed to denote 'careworn but coping despite my horrible ex-husband-to-be'.

The judge said that he had read the papers but not Mr Wheedle's report. Where was it? My hopes lifted. Surely we would have another adjournment. How could he make a judgment if he had not read the facts?

'Your Honour, we have only just received it, but I believe you should have received a copy . . .' said Crispe. The judge looked across at Mr Wheedle, who said that he had given a copy to the judge's clerk. The judge looked at the judge's clerk who handed him the report.

The judge read it, which took another five minutes,

while the rest of us sat in silence. 'Mr Crispe . . .' he started. And that was it, battle enjoined. First up in the witness box, because he had other things to attend to, was Mr Wheedle. I suppose this is the moment CWOs live for. Imagine being an expert court witness, and having a judge who, despite his authority, status, years of learning and wisdom, would bow to your special insights . . . 'Your Honour it is out of the question that the defendant could have used bi-pheno amino hydrazine which is completely harmless except in enormous quantities. The traces found under the victim's fingernails are most likely to be the result of . . . blah, blah, blah.' What fun.

There was an insouciant casualness, a sort of 'look no hands' panache with which Mr Wheedle took the Bible and promised us all that everything he said would be the truth the whole truth and nothing but the truth. Although these are not complicated words, when it came to my turn I knew that the sense of occasion would get to me, like saying one's wedding vows, and I'd need to read them.

'First of all,' said Judge Stern. 'May I express all our thanks to you Mr Wheedle, for pulling out all the stops and producing a report at such short notice. We know that you are a very busy man. Mr and Mrs Henry, Mr Wheedle is a one of our most experienced court welfare officers, and we are all very lucky to have at our disposal his report.'

I thought this was overdoing it a bit. In what way was it lucky for me? I had neither had a chance to read it or come off well in it.

A sort of cabaret double act seemed to develop between Judge Stern and Mr Wheedle. The judge constantly referred to Mr Wheedle's experience. Each mention of his experience would cause Mr Wheedle's chest to inch out a touch. Mr Wheedle's interpretation of events seemed to be that I was obsessed with my marriage, obsessed with Marie-Sophie and that I was unable to accept that it was now all over.

I'd gone to special pains not to say anything too derogatory about Marie-Sophie. There were a million mean things I could have said about her but his diagnosis was that I was obsessed.

In due course, he said, he hoped I would come to terms with the end of the marriage but, meanwhile, the hurt I was feeling had so incapacitated me, that I couldn't think clearly and it would therefore be better if the child stayed with the mother, where he was settled and clearly thriving. She had been planning her move for a good time before she left and had been very sensitive to Pierre's needs, doing everything she could to protect him from the conflict between his parents. He didn't think I was as capable a parent as she and frankly he had been alarmed by some of Pierre's antics when in my charge. He said I had seemed to lack control, whereas Marie-Sophie had managed Pierre at all times with calm and poise.

If Muriel hadn't been sitting between us, I think I would have throttled the man. I suppose that is one reason for employing a barrister – as a sort of buffer. Questions and observations were popping into my mind the whole time. Go on, Muriel, I silently urged, ask him if he has any children of his own. I bet you anything he hasn't. I know it's not relevant to my case, but what does he know? He's a bloody probation officer.

When Muriel was on her feet the only means of communication with her was via pieces of sticky yellow paper. Muriel had certainly got the picture with Mr Wheedle, but she seemed curiously reluctant to question him assertively. She had one line of questioning which started to sound promising:

'If all things were equal, and there were nothing to chose between the parents . . .' she started.

'All things aren't equal,' Mr Wheedle interrupted.

'But if all things were equal, there were nothing to chose between the two parents, both had contributed equally to the child's upbringing, both were equally competent . . .'

'The premise is faulty,' replied Mr Wheedle. 'Of greater importance is who lives where. The child should live with the more competent parent.'

The judge smiled. You could see that the CWO was enjoying his joust with the barrister.

'No, but imagine for a moment if you will, Mr Wheedle . . .'

Judge Stern interrupted. 'Miss Leach, I fail to see where this line of questioning is taking us.' To me it was obvious: we both cared for the child, best not to uproot him if there was no material difference in the two homes. If the judge 'fails to see' that this is so then Muriel's job is to tell him in a suitably euphemistic barristerial way that he is thick − 'Perhaps I can explain it differently Your Honour . . .'

Muriel wouldn't. 'Your Honour, it should be obvious that the child should have stability, he should stay put in his familiar environment . . .'

'But Miss Leach, it is clear that the child is already out of his familiar environment. I am bound to say that my preliminary opinion does not make me feel that this line of questioning is going to take us anywhere useful. We must remember that Mr Wheedle is a very experienced and respected court welfare officer and he has come to the conclusion, and I am sure he has not done so lightly, that this child would be better off with his mother. I think we need to examine the reasons for that.'

Muriel was swimming in treacle. She tried a different line of questioning. 'Mr Wheedle, your report mentions challenging behaviour . . .'

'Yes, Pierre was jumping off the furniture and the father was unable to stop him.'

'But this is the normal behaviour of a child who is understandably excited because he hasn't seen his father, to whom he is very close, for quite a time. He was not in any danger was he?....'

We were on the defensive, and she had asked him a question which he could answer any way he liked. He wasn't about to say, 'Oh, silly me, you're quite right, I think I over-reacted to Pierre leaping about the place. It wasn't dangerous at all.' I passed her a piece of yellow sticky paper with a message on it about Marie-Sophie delivering Pierre to school late on purpose, which was a key to understanding why Pierre had misbehaved. She'd had time to bribe him into model behaviour, I'd had none.

' . . . He was unsettled, inevitably over-excited at seeing his father again, at finding himself back in his home with all that was familiar in it,' Muriel continued before Mr Wheedle could reply. Perhaps she sensed her mistake. She looked at my note but she didn't seem to grasp the importance of my hastily scribbled message.

'In my opinion, the child could have hurt himself.'

'But he didn't did he, Mr Wheedle? This is the kind of robust behaviour which is normal in a boy of six is it not?'

'Not that I have regularly observed. He could have hurt himself and I was worried. It was more than robust behaviour.'

What a wimp! It had been obvious to me from the start that Mr Wheedle had little experience of children. Definitely a man who folds his pyjamas, I thought.

I was next in the box. Muriel asked me some friendly questions, so that was fine as a warm up; it gave me the chance to emphasize what a hands-on father I was, how it was me who did more. Warming to my subject, I was still in the box when we came to lunch time. I said, 'Can I look at that report?'

'I'm afraid you can't,' Muriel said.

'Why on earth not?' I asked.

'Because you are in the middle of being examined. It's just that, an examination. You're not allowed to go back and look at what is in the report to refresh your memory, and we can't give you any legal advice either.'

Coaching in the middle of examination would be Contempt of Court. Rules is rules, I suppose. But it seemed unfair. Since I wasn't allowed to talk to my lawyers I went off to lunch on my own. I certainly wasn't hungry so I went for a stroll along the Embankment. While I was there, some out of season German tourists asked me directions to Big Ben, clearly visible along the Thames. I'm afraid I told them to 'fuck off'. Talk about visiting your misfortunes on others. I've felt remorse about this ever since.

Back after the recess I don't think I was caught out especially by James de Vere Crispe, except on a couple of points. He had me in tears on the subject of the last time I'd handed Pierre back after access when he'd clung to me and said, 'I don't want to go to Mummy's work, I want to go home.' I was being accused of having primed him by instilling fear into him with the words 'Mummy is going to take you away'. I had never said anything like that. I might have said 'You've got to go with Mummy now', I can't quite remember, but nothing so loaded.

The judge asked his clerk to get me a glass of water. He looked a little impatient. Later I found myself facing a Crispe crescendo led from the chin. It unnerved me, because I couldn't see why he needed to become quite so oratorical. Family cases are held in private, there is no gallery, no jury to impress, only a judge, who has surely seen it all before. 'Do you mean to tell the court that you expect your wife to pay you maintenance?'

I was perplexed by this question, because the answer was so obvious. In this age of equality of the sexes, if I had custody of Pierre and Marie-Sophie earned more than me, and she was the one who had walked out, and I had to cut down on work a little to look after him, then obviously I thought, it would be normal that she pay me maintenance for the child. That's what the Child Support Agency is set up to organize surely? But there was something about his tone, and the serious look on Judge Stern's face that stopped me saying it. I looked at my lawyers for guidance, but I was in the witness box, they couldn't help. I didn't know what the party line should be on such issues.

He repeated the question. 'Well, what's wrong with that?' I finally asked. He paused theatrically, saying nothing. I sensed that I was not doing well.

Crispe also asked me who had been in the habit of making the child-care arrangements. I saw no harm in answering that honestly. 'My wife choreographed things,' I said. 'You see, she was the one with the irregular timetable, and since you could more or less tell where I would be from day to day, it was easier for her to decide things. She had no idea from one day to the next where she would be filming. I just did what I was told.'

I have to admit that Marie-Sophie was devastating as a witness, managing an enticing combination of domesticity and femininity, as well as appearing like a flower waiting to bloom but kept in the dark by an unsympathetic husband. Judge Stern would have had great difficulty imagining the sharper, professional side of her job. He clearly found her delightful. At times, she sipped nervously at a glass of water, apparently close to tears. She may have been, it was an emotional time. When her voice wobbled at one point during Muriel's cross-examination, the judge was visibly moved. Mainly she told the truth, but where she scored was in damaging little assertions, of themselves harmless, but put together, a deadly picture of a mother struggling massively against the odds.

Anything I had done for Pierre was neatly turned

against me. I had brought him back from skiing terrified and sunburnt (read 'elated and tanned'); the Scalectrix I had bought at a car-boot sale was dangerous, he could have got electrocuted (at this point I passed a piece of yellow sticky paper to Muriel: 'Only 12 volts' it said. But Muriel put it to one side, and didn't point out the obvious. With hindsight I've thought that perhaps she didn't know that 12 volts can't kill either. Can't even tingle.)

'But your husband did a lot of the cooking, did he not?' she said.

'Cooking? Yes, if you call fishfingers and baked beans cooking. Or getting a hamburger from McDonalds, cooking,' my wife replied with wonderful Gallic haughter.

How dare she say that? I wanted to cry again. What about my *sauté de veau maregno* cooked for her bloody friends? It wasn't my fault that half of our guests turned out to be vegetarian, and all disapproved of veal (the eating of which is a French habit anyway).

I knew little about cross-examination but I thought some of Muriel's questions were suicidal from my client's point of view. 'Have you any other criticisms of Mr Henry as a father?' What a daft question! Just give Marie-Sophie *carte blanche* to be beastly about her husband.

She embarked on a vexing tale of my parental imcompetence: 'Recently after access, I couldn't find Pierre's jacket, and I asked my husband where it was, and he said he left it somewhere in the park. I asked him to please go and look for it but Michael refused to do it. He did not do that, therefore I have had to buy another one for Pierre which I cannot afford, having only just moved and bought his new uniform. Michael knows this.' (True I had left his jacket behind. He'd got hot on his bike and I'd left it near the swings. As he had a thick jumper on and didn't feel cold, neither of us realized what I'd done until he was due to go back to Marie-Sophie. Even if it had still been there, which was unlikely, I was damned if I was walking all the way back there when she had the car.)

When she was examined by her own barrister photos of her new flat were passed around. It looked like a real *Home & Garden* home, with profusions of cascading plants, all freshly bought from some top florist no doubt (certainly they were in wonderful nick compared to the houseplants in the Former Matrimonial Home, which got a lot of attention, but only from inexpert me. I don't talk to them enough probably).

There was a photo of Pierre in the bath playing with a complicated plumbing toy from the Early Learning Centre. He looked as delighted as any small child would who has just been given an amazing new toy. A photo of his new bedroom showed him on the floor in the middle of a vast network of wooden railway. Again, he looked delighted. There were ABC posters round the walls and piles of new or borrowed teddy bears (I hadn't seen any of them before) and wholesome books like *Alice Aux Pays des Merveilles* and *Les Aventures du Roi Babar des Elephants* and what looked like a complete set of Tintin books. I was impressed. Perhaps I should withdraw my case; she deserved custody if she was about to become a reformed hands-on mother who would go to this sort of effort. But I couldn't see it lasting, somehow.

When it came to the amount of access she thought suitable for me, she said that she had found Pierre difficult upon return, but that she would accept the court welfare officer's recommendation – namely, alternate weekends, Friday through Monday morning, and mid-week staying access on alternate Thursdays; holidays school and otherwise, to be agreed between the parties.

By the time Marie-Sophie had finished her evidence time was getting on and Judge Stern made it plain that he had heard enough. It was agreed that Tiffany would not be called, a disappointment in a sense, because I would have liked to see her grilled about her sister's boyfriend Trev.

Depositions were over. Mr Wheedle came back in, timing his re-entry perfectly, obviously having finished whatever other business he had to attend to. Strictly speaking his involvement was over, but I could see that it would be dull for him to miss the denouement.

Sally whispered to me that we were about to get the judgment. It is lucky she did so, because I was unclear as to what was going on. Certainly as Judge Stern started speaking he didn't say '. . . and the winner is . . .' The suspense was unbearable. First he summed up the backgrounds of the two parties: 'The couple met in Paris and it is clear from the evidence that both families were aghast . . .' and continued with a brief history of the marriage, the birth of Pierre and where, as he saw it, the union had gone wrong. 'At first the husband was slow to see that the marriage was in trouble, however it must have become completely clear to him that the marriage was near an end when his wife announced that she intended to move out, and even clearer, when on a day in February she did indeed do so . . .'

Get on with it, man, what have you decided. Spit it out.

He droned on. It was like a striptease as he gradually revealed his thinking – but you'd only get to see it all at the end. Hank says all judges do this. First they have a story to tell. I knew my story. I just wanted to know the end.

'. . . I accept what Miss Leach says when she describes the father as a loving father, and further, I accept what she says when she argues, very persuasively, I may say, that this father has been closely involved with the child's upbringing . . .' My hopes began to rise. 'But I am also very indebted to Mr Wheedle. Mr Crispe, Mr Wheedle, you will both agree with me that things are not always accomplished so quickly in the Family Division. I found this a very helpful report,' he smiled at Mr Wheedle, 'I am satisfied that Mr Wheedle got it right when he identified Mrs Henry as the main carer. As the father admits, she "choreographs" arrangements. This was a very elegant way of putting it . . .' he smiled at me, as if to share with me his joy at my command of language. 'I must say also that there were areas where the evidence of Mrs Henry on the one hand, and Mr Henry on the other were not in accord. Having listened very carefully to all of the evidence I have to say that where it conflicts, I prefer the evidence of the mother . . .'

I stopped listening. My world had fallen apart. We filed out of court and in the corridor I sat down in silence. Marie-Sophie came out shortly afterwards. Tiffany looked at her inquiringly, but the smiles on her face said it all. She threw herself into Tiffany's arms for a hug of relief. Sally and Muriel told me that I had done extremely well. It was not quite the image of success I'd had in mind when Sally had advised me that I had a good case.

So there we are. I was trounced. Pierre would come to stay every other weekend, Friday through Monday morning and every other Thursday night, exactly as recommended by the court welfare officer. Why bother with a judge?

<< >> << >>

A FEW days elapsed during which I took unpaid leave from work and went to stay with my parents. I was not in good shape, and not the best company to say the least but by the following Wednesday I had managed to pull myself together. I went into work. Roger took me to the pub to commiserate. 'I'll give you some advice, Michael, what you need now is a good casual bonk. I'll see what I can fix up for you.'

'I'm not going near any prostitutes,' I said, the puritan within me rising in alarm, even after three pints.

'Don't be stupid. You're a single man in his thirties. It's a buyer's market. Loads of girls in their thirties, desperate, gagging for it. Out there is demand waiting to be supplied. Supply it. Go for it.'

Roger was misjudging my mood, but he was probably right. In retrospect, perhaps a bit of shock therapy would have done me good – a bit of 'Snap out of it, at least you're not Bosnian.'

Back home that evening, I realized that navel contemplation was self-indulgent and a less satisfactory way of passing time than revenge contemplation. Legal avenues were closed to me for now, Muriel had said. She didn't think an appeal was on. The judge had covered his tracks too well. I didn't really understand why, but it was something to do with his having said that he had listened carefully to all the evidence, weighing it all up; and some of it conflicted so he had had to exercise judgment. To win an appeal the judge had to be 'plainly wrong'. I thought he was plainly wrong, but it wouldn't be plain enough to an appeal court panel who don't rehear all the evidence.

I revisited Marie-Sophie's room. A further inspection of the wardrobe revealed drawers and pull-out compartments that I had not really noticed before. It was not nearly as bereft of belongings as I'd thought, she had actually left quite a lot of stuff.

Mr Wheedle's report was supposed to have been about children but had strayed on to money. She'd told him that that she earned £2,000 per month. This had been pure news to me but, apart from the initial shock at the deception (similar to finding out about her secret bank account), as the battleground shifted from child to money, it was good news. She could look after herself financially.

I began a manic unloading of the outfits one by one on to the bed, jotting an inventory down on a piece of paper. First of all I counted out 98 empty coat-hangers. Even given that wire coat-hangers tend to breed when left alone in the dark this was a lot of coat-hangers. Comme des Garcons suit, two-piece. Five other suits, designer unknown to me. Cashmere sweaters, six (yes six). It continued. I logged and photographed the lot, all the time thinking, 'My God, if this is what she left behind, imagine the First XI she took.'

Then I rang Marie-Sophie and said, 'Take your bloody clothes. I don't see why I should be a warehouse service for you. Besides which I want to let the room.' It was the first I had thought of letting the room, but I was angry and improvising.

'I haven't got anywhere to put them,' she said.

'That's not my fault, you left, not me, you should have thought of that. I think it is only fair that if you decide you want me to live without you, then you should co-operate by removing all remaining traces of yourself. If you don't come and get them within twenty-four hours I will dispose of them as I see fit, in fact I might dump them on the pavement outside your house.' I hung up pompously.

Within the hour a motorbike courier delivered me a letter from Rachel asking me not to dispose of the clothes. Half an hour after that Sally also rang through anxiously urging me to agree to this in order not to 'raise the temperature'. I authorized Sally to write a letter promising on my behalf not to dump the clothes on the pavement, then went to the Frock Exchange in the Fulham Road and sold the lot.

Now was the time to hit her where it hurt her most, in the pocket. And the sleeve, the trouser-leg, the belt. Vandalism is not my way. These clothes were of themselves innocent and should at least go to charity. In marriage, what's yours is mine and mine is yours. The charity should be me.

The next morning I received a letter from Fletcher Clare & Co: 'Certificated Bailiffs and Agents to the legal profession'. That put the wind up me. When I opened it I realized that it was about not sending a cheque for our council tax. Amidst all the other legal excitement going on in my life, council tax had taken a low priority. Conviction *chez* the magistrates followed and these bailiffs had been detailed to get the money off me. No matter, I was cash in hand now. Marie-Sophie was just about to pay her first bill.

<< >> << >>

I agonized about giving Marcia a call. I'd not returned any of her messages and I felt bad about it. I should at least have rung her to tell her what had happened re. Pierre. I had just got too wrapped up in being miserable, to the point where I was even beginning to like being miserable. I decided it was too late. I'd blown that one.

Michele, meanwhile, was being kindness itself. She seemed to take it for granted that I'd be eating at hers every night and, no matter how hard I protested that I wasn't up to going out or wasn't hungry, she wouldn't give in. The result was that I was becoming a bit of an *habitué chez* Michele. She was so considerate and I must admit she did get me out of myself and back into company. Her nature was such that she was constantly throwing impromptu parties for 25 of her closest friends. Impressively, they tended to be a different 25 each time, the common denominator at each of course being me and her. I couldn't fault her but I did end up feeling slightly under seige.

My acceptance of her invitations made it difficult to turn her away if, for example, she popped round for a cup of coffee on her way back from dropping her children off at school. She seemed to develop an unerring instinct for when I was working at home, but no understanding of the fact that I was busy – but I could scarcely refuse her a coffee if I had been for supper in her kitchen the evening before. I was conscious that I was building up an unhealthy entertainment deficit, but what the hell, I wasn't angling for invitations.

My first access to Pierre after the court's decision was a full three weeks after the hearing. After the judgment there had been a debate as to when contact proper should start, and the judge had accepted the other side's argument that Pierre needed to be settled before it started even though I'd already had him to stay on the two weekends before.

It was the weekend of Jake's birthday party, to which Pierre was naturally invited, and I had been press-ganged into helping by Michele. It was going to be an effort to keep that friendship going when I had Pierre so infrequently and with trips to his grandparents, uncles and aunts and their children to fit in.

At the party, I stuck around with the mothers. This was partly because Michele had assigned me various jobs, like operating the music during the musical chairs (I wondered which had been the angry ones in her relationship counselling scenario). Another reason was that Marcia was there in her capacity as mother to two of the guests. There was nothing for it but to be honest I felt, so as soon as there was an appropriate lull – when neither of us was needed for judging or mopping up fizzy drink and losers' tears – I made an effort to explain myself. I said I was sorry I hadn't called her. At first I hadn't felt like calling, but after a while I'd begun to feel that too much time had elapsed. In short I'd been a bit shy about the whole thing.

'I understand,' she said. 'I didn't call you either. I guessed things hadn't gone well for you. They always give custody to mothers.'

'That's fine for them, but very unfair to me.'

'I agree. I'm sorry for you, and Pierre, which one is he?' I pointed him out. 'Nice-looking boy,' she said.

I was chuffed. If only Marie-Sophie could be like Marcia, I thought. She let her Tom see the children whenever he wanted to. She said she had even let him have a key to her house.

Michele interrupted. She needed someone to operate the music for the pass the parcel. The children weren't too clear as to what to do – too many parties paid for by professional parents in gymnasiums or with hired magicians at Thank God Its Friday or McDonalds. They liked the prizes though, so I had to introduce an element of forfeit as well as profit, otherwise they ended up greedily hanging on to the parcel, waiting for my hand to twitch on the switch. Every so often I got one of the children to eat a pot of jelly while standing on his or her head. If it was a boy, sometimes the forfeit was 'Give Michele a kiss'.

'Oooh yuk, give Michele a kiss.'

This meant that the parcel zipped round at a good pace. I had to fix it so that all the children got a prize, and to stop Jake, host and Birthday Boy, from scooping up everything.

When my duty was over I went back to Marcia who smiled at me but looked a little concerned. 'Michael, why does Pierre screw his eyes up like that?'

I'd noticed he'd been doing it all day, but I'd taken him swimming and put it down to an irritation from the chlorine. Now, he was doing a sort of peculiar double blink, screwing his eyes up in what looked like concentration as he played the latest game. It didn't look nice at all. I'd have to buy him some goggles before we went next time.

'That's a nervous tic,' said Marcia with some certainty in her voice.

I was quite shocked at the suggestion and I didn't think it could be but I promised I'd keep an eye on it. I also promised to give her a call.

By the morning the 'tic' seemed to have vanished – definitely the chlorine. I'd decided to take Pierre to see his grandparents again. As usual they were overjoyed to see him and made a huge fuss of him. The lambs were now out and about so Pierre spent most of the day outside with my father.

My mother gave me a bit of a lecture. 'They're not all bad you know, you'll find a nice one, it may take a while but you'll probabaly even get married again.' She was a bit worried that a misogynist streak was developing in me. I didn't even necessarily disagree with the idea that I might remarry. I certainly wanted more children. I didn't blame the institution of marriage particularly, it was more a problem of the participants in our particular one.

No, I think Roger's advice was probably the best. A bit of misbehaviour was what was required, but not with Michele. Too close to home, by half. Pierre's best friend's mother. No way. In the absence of other candidates my target was looking more and more like Marcia. I'd see. I certainly wouldn't tell my mother though.

All in all though, it was a good weekend.

<< >> << >>

COMPLETE insomnia was something I had been suffering from off and on (but mainly on) for a couple of months now. It must have meant I was in a bad way because my usual difficulty is staying awake. It was getting to be a problem at work (the only place where I had no difficulty sleeping) where I would collapse on to my word processor with fatigue, the words I was translating swimming before my eyes.

Others take sleeping pills and tranquilizers, but I've always been one who uses medicine as a last resort. I am whatever the complete opposite of a hypochondriac is, and will probably die of a monstrous tumour that I was too lazy to show to the doctor soon enough.

The trouble with a major life event like losing custody of your child is that you can't stop thinking about it, turning over 'What if . . .?' scenarios in your head the whole bloody time. It is permanent, you cannot get rid of it, it takes over your every moment. One night I got all the way to the end of the Jay Leno show, all the time thinking I really must find something more interesting to do like ring up the credit-line subscription to the grunts and groans of TV-X. I finally managed to drift off in the middle of US Market Wrap, in which they were talking earnestly about a corporation I'd never heard of in Idaho taking over a corporation I'd never heard of in Iowa.

After I'd fallen asleep I had a completely revolting experience which woke me up again. I was sopping wet in the kind of muck sweat that you associate with malaria victims. The bed was completely soaked, my pyjamas were dripping to the point where you could ring them out over the bath, my hair was matted, the pillow heavy, everything had the consistency of a thousand squash shirts. Nothing like this had ever happened to me before. I'd grown accustomed to a constant knot in the bottom of my stomach, and to a mind racing over every detail of the court welfare officer's report, every inflection and nuance of the court hearing: all that was to be expected, but a physical reaction of this kind was very peculiar. I was tired but I wasn't ill and yet I was dripping wet with perspiration.

I wonder if this happens to everyone who goes through a divorce, or if it was happening to Marie-Sophie. You never know, she might even be suffering from divorce remorse, a new phenomenon identified in America (where all social trends start) amongst women especially. A bit too early in the process for that though.

My tiredness wasn't helped by my social life. Concerned friends – not just Michele or Roger – were rallying round; some I hadn't had much to do with for years because Marie-Sophie hadn't liked them. She had a particular dislike of those friends who knew me better than she did, old university friends and the like.

My wet dream (the wrong sort) was a strong signal that

it was time to attempt a return to the real world, and escape the surreal one of judges and affidavits. A sort of bush telegraph was operating in my hour of need: 'Get him out, keep him busy, get him drunk (and if you can, get him laid).' Whilst I could see the therapeutic value of this last, I have to say that getting laid was still not really on my personal agenda. Less libidinous I had never felt in my life.

Having not been able to get myself out of the house, I now entered a phase in which I couldn't bear to be in it. I didn't want to be alone. Once out of the house, I think I may even have been quite good company, not navel-gazing at all.

'Divorcing? You look in quite good shape on it,' somebody said at one party. I thought this couldn't be true, but then lack of sleep puts you on a high all of its own. You get drunk, for example, after only half a pint of beer.

'What I really need is a liaison with somebody completely unsuitable, you know, a tart with a heart.'

'What you really need is a bonk.'

I didn't explain. He was right, but the real point about somebody completely 'unsuitable' was that that is what she would have to be to have anything to do with me in my state. I was beginning to get quite a lot of duty as the spare man at dinner parties so I began to live in hope, then there was always Marcia who I was pursuing with insufficent vigour even though she was sufficiently unsuitable.

One Saturday morning I decided it was time to drop in on Hank. I could do with his advice again. I hadn't seen him since the trial which I felt as bad about as not having phoned Marcia.

He was good enough not to say 'I told you so'. I was also relieved that he didn't say to me, 'What you need is a good bonk'. He had just started Rock 'n' Roll classes he said, why I didn't I come along some time. He said that there was always a shortage of men and a surfeit of women, I'd be spoilt for choice. I quite like Rock 'n' Roll, but the last time I did dance classes was a series of Salsa lessons in which I attempted to swirl someone round in one of those moves where you turn her arm over her head – I'd dislocated her shoulder. Fortunately it had not been Marie-Sophie's.

'I think this could be my chance to go for someone beautiful and twenty-two,' I told him.

'I disagree, I always go for older women,' Hank replied. 'They're far nicer. Women in their late forties they're just the best. Ian Fleming said "Older women are best because they always make love as if it might be the last time" you know. He's right, it might be. And they do. You should come along to Rock 'n' Roll, plenty of great girls in their forties. They'll be all over you.'

'I'm not that desperate,' I said. 'In fact I think I've retired.'

'Rubbish man. Don't believe you. You'll change your mind.'

<< >> << >>

THE next morning an envelope flopped on to my doormat and when I saw it wasn't from Rachel Bonham-Lee I was relieved. Any letter not from Bonham-Lee was a relief. I'd even got to look forward to my Visa bills.

In it were a couple of photocopied pages from a book written in 1864 called *The Life and Times of Benjamin Franklin* by one J. Parton. It was a letter written by Franklin to a friend. Included was a card from W.H. Smith saying 'In Deepest Sympathy, Thinking of You at the Time of Your Bereavement'. It was from Hank. Inside he had written 'They're not all bad (most, but not all). PS: Older women are best'.

According to Benjamin Franklin I'd got to get married again. Meanwhile if I couldn't face that, then the proper solace was women, older ones.

PHILADELPHIA, Penn 1726 1757,
Benjamin Franklin

Oder Mistress Apologue

My Dear Friend,

I know of no Medicine fit to diminish the violent natural Inclinations you mention; and if I did, I think I should not communicate it to you. Marriage is the proper Remedy. It is the most natural State of Man, and therefore the state in which you are most likely to find solid Happiness. Your reasons against entering into it at present, appear to me not well founded. The circumstantial Advantages you have in View by postponing it are not only uncertain, but they are small in comparison with that of the Thing itself, the being married and settled. It is the Man and Woman united that make the compleat human Being. Separate, she wants his Force of Body and Strength of Reason; he, her Softness, Sensibility and acute Discernment. Together they are more likely to succeed in the World. A single Man has not nearly the Value he would have in that State of Union. He is an incomplete Animal. He resembles the odd Half of a pair of Scissars. If you get a prudent healthy Wife, your Industry in your Profession with her good Economy, will be a Fortune sufficient.

But if you will not take this counsel, and persist in thinking a Commerce with the Sex inevitable, then I repeat my former Advice, that in all your Amours you should prefer older Women to young ones. You call this a Paradox, and demand my Reasons. They are these:

1. Because they have more knowledge of the World and their minds are better stor'd with Observations, their Conversation is more improving and more lastingly agreeable.

2. Because when Women cease to be handsome, they study to be good. To maintain their Influence over Men, they supply the Dimunition of Beauty by an Augmentation of Utility. They learn to do a 1000 Services small and great, and

153

are the most tender and useful of all Friends when you are sick. Thus they continue amiable. And hence there is hardly such a thing to be found as an older Woman who is not a good Woman.

3. Because there is no hazard of Children, which irregularly produc'd may be attended with much Inconvenience.

4. Because thro' more Experience, they are more prudent and discreet in conducting an Intrigue to prevent Suspicion. The Commerce with them is therefore safer with regard to your Reputation. And with regard to theirs, if the Affair should happen to be known, considerate people might rather be inclined to excuse an older Woman who would kindly take care of a younger Man, form his Manners by her good Counsel, and prevent his ruining his Health and Fortune among mercenary Prostitutes.

5. Because every Animal that walks upright, the Deficiency of the Fluids that fill the Muscles appears first in the highest part. The Face first grows lank and wrinkled: then the Neck, then the Breast and Arms; the lower Parts continuing to the last as plump as ever; So that covering all above with a basket, and regarding only what is below the Girdle, it is impossible of two Women to know an older from a younger one. As in the dark all Cats are grey, the Pleasures of corporal Enjoyment with an older Woman is at least equal, and frequently superior, every Knack being by Practice capable of improvement.

6. Because Sin is less. The debauching of a Virgin may be her Ruin and make her for Life unhappy.

7. Because the Compunction is less. The having made a young Girl miserable may give you frequent bitter Reflections; none of which can attend the making an older Woman happy.

8. And lastly, they are so grateful!

Thus so much for my Paradox. But still I advise you to marry directly; being sincerely your affectionate Friend.

Ben Franklin

Married and settled. Sigh. Not an immediate possibility for me. An older girlfriend? Marcia was nearly forty but only a bit older than me. She hardly qualified. I decided I didn't go for this idea. My natural tendency was towards women I found good-looking and I was pretty certain that if the field was one of fifty pluses, I would find it hard to play. I was quite happy to have one who studied to be good as long as they were unstudiedly handome while they did it. The *Guardian*'s Women's page runs regular features on how unfair 'lookism' is, how lookist men don't go for fat, ugly women with nice personalities, but prefer beautiful bimbos. I read in the *Economist* about research showing that ugly women have worse job prospects, too, and marry less well off men. That's terribly unfair. But we men are victims of this propaganda, too. We've been driven by the media and Hollywood into lusting after visions of feminine perfection like Sharon Stone or the one I'd like to meet (French women again), Isabelle Adjani. As a result of this media-imposed drive we overlook far nicer women who may have a floppy bust-line and a hint of cellulite.

Additionally you have to have some sympathy with thirtysomething women when you look at what is available on the market. It is either out and out rotters like Roger or unwanted goods like me.

One of the problems of getting involved with any woman, as I saw it, was the difficulty of making it a victim-free crime. Someone was bound to get hurt and not me – I was still smarting from Marie-Sophie withdrawal symptoms and no one else was likely to capture my deeper affections for quite a while.

<< >> << >>

I decided to hold a dinner party. This would be my coming out party where I emerged from the depths of despair and took a grip on life.

I rang up Marcia and invited her. There was something

about her that intrigued me. My still limited acquaintance with her suggested to me that her needs might be similar to mine. Separation-wise she was nearly a year ahead of me in the cycle whereas Michele was three years ahead. Marcia would be looking at most for a fling, not yet to replace her lost love. If not much older than me, I could relax in that she was a mature woman. With her I would be safe from divesting any romantic girls of dreams of white dresses – I should be so lucky. Actually, I invited Michele, too. It was a good opportunity to reduce the entertainment deficit and Marcia was her friend.

The party went very smoothly. Whatever Marie-Sophie might allege, I am a good if improvisational cook. There was a motley collection of friends present; we all ate and drank far too much and a good time was had by all. Marcia and I agreed that we would go and see a film together so that was one goal accomplished.

My guests departed one by one, including Marcia who had to get back to relieve her babysitter. Michele, however, appeared to be lingering. 'Can I get your coat Michele?' No, she didn't want her coat, she didn't have to rush, her babysitter was staying the night. But she did want to help with the only part of the arrangements that could be improved – many great artist's studios are very messy and my kitchen reassembled a bomb zone.

'I'll help with the washing-up,' she said.

'No really, Michele, don't worry, it can wait till morning.'

As usual, she would have none of it. And, just as there is no such thing as a free lunch, there is no such thing as a free rack of clean dishes with no strings attached. 'Thank you for doing the washing up, Michele, a nightcap?'

Anyway, to cut a long story short (shorter than I care to admit – but allowance should be made; I was both out of practice and drunk), I awoke at about five in the morning to find the other side of the bed empty and Michele dressing to go home.

At the key moment she had asked, 'Have you got your goloshes?'

'Goloshes? No.' I didn't know what she was on about.

'Don't worry, I've got some,' she said, and reached for her handbag strategically placed by the bed and found me a condom. Welcome to the nineties.

When she had gone I clutched my head, aching not just with hangover, but with remorse. What a piece of work is a man. How noble in reason, how infinite in faculty, and what a stupid git. Pierre's best friend, Jake's mum. How to extricate myself from this one? You could argue that I needn't have feelings of guilt because after all it takes two to tango, and I could be the emotionally fragile one who was being used. The trouble was that this was not the victim-free crime I'd been hoping for. In Michele's mind this was not, I feared, a one-night stand.

Still, I couldn't help this triumphant little voice in my head saying, 'Not bad going . . . pretty good actually'– I'd scored. It had been a little like losing my virginity all over again, if slightly less pathetically fumbling this time round. In the heat of the moment I had enjoyed myself, and so I believe, had she. 'Thanks Michael, that was great,' she'd said. Post-coital small talk never having been one of my strong points, I'd replied, 'Was it?'

First new notch on the bedpost for, was it really nearly eight years? Back to earth with a bang, so to speak.

<< >> << >>

MEANWHILE relations with the ex-wife-to-be had showed no signs of improvement. There had been no more word from her on our divorce so I wasn't quite sure how 'ex' she was. However, one thing I was to discover is that rows with the wife don't end with separation.

On the second or third occasion that Pierre was due to come and stay, I arrived at the school to pick him up, only to find him gone. I was very disappointed. I was already growing to hate the gap between Friday morning when I dropped him off at school, after mid-week staying contact, and the next Friday afternoon when I picked him up again for my alternate weekend access. For me it was too long. The teacher explained that Marie-Sophie had arrived and picked him up earlier than usual. Naturally I was furious. I had been looking forward to seeing Pierre but I couldn't vent my fury on the teacher, it wasn't her fault.

When I got home a message on the answerphone from Marie-Sophie informed me that Pierre had an appointment with the dentist. She really ought to have warned me in advance, indeed chosen another day. My time with Pierre was precious, not to say sacrosanct. My immediate suspicion was that she'd done it on purpose, part of an attempt to start whittling access. She could easily have phoned me the night before, or if afraid to talk to me direct, sent a message via Rachel and Sally. I thought she'd probably carefully chosen a time when she knew I'd be out to talk to the answer machine.

I nearly rang her up to say something fierce but decided to ring up Sally the solicitor first. I had undertaken not to harass and molest my wife after all. 'Is she allowed to do this?' I asked. 'She knows perfectly well it is my contact day, and she books a dental appointment. Can't we go back to court. It's obvious she wants to cut him out of my life. I should have custody, I wouldn't do this to her.'

'Technically she is in breach of the order, but I don't think it would be wise to do anything yet,' she replied. 'We must be careful not to raise the temperature.'

Don't raise the temperature. I was sick of not raising the

temperature. What this expression appeared to mean was you are stuffed anyway so roll over on to your back and allow your tummy to be tickled.

I ignored her advice and rang Marie-Sophie anyway. We were separated, why should I put up with the power she had over me for the rest of my life. She said that the dental appointment had been booked since before the court hearing and it would have been too difficult to change. This seemed unlikely but could just about have been true.

'Call yourself a parent,' she said, 'You don't even know when his dental appointments are.'

'I could just have easily taken him as you. You only had to tell me.'

I decided that this was the moment to pick a fight about her having delivered Pierre late on purpose for the court welfare officer's first visit. As with most domestic rows, I remember little about it, except that it really ignited when I said 'I bet that lawyer of yours with the fat legs told you to bring him late' and then moved on to a discussion about whether or not the court welfare officer had children. 'No way,' she said, laughing. 'It's obvious.' The irony was that he was the kind of low-life she herself despised and yet she'd spun him around her little finger.

When I accused her of inventing the doctor excuse etc. it provoked a tirade about how difficult it was to juggle her work and look after the child. I said this difficulty was optional: 'I can look after him just as well as you can.' The row went nuclear shortly afterwards. One of Marie-Sophie's shortcomings is talking about her problems. It was one of mine, she had always said, that I wouldn't discuss them with her. 'Men can't communicate', it's a mantra of the age.

I slammed the phone down on her but she rang straight back. Once she's in full flow you can put the phone gently down, go off and make a cup of tea, agonize over hobnobs or digestives, discover the milk is off and open a new packet, then pick up the phone again to check on progress. Yep, still ranting.

The important thing though was that it was all taking place on her phone bill.

<< >> << >>

I finally got Pierre on Saturday afternoon, picking up him up from my wife's front door and walking him off into the car without a word. My old 2 CV was finally MOTed and on the road again. Pierre liked it, especially with the roof off, or when you opened the ventilators and could see outside through the wire mesh that stopped flies hitting you in the face.

'How were the teeth?' I asked him. He screwed his face up, but didn't answer me. Odd, I thought. Still he'd never liked the dentist. I noticed that his face was still twitching, if anything worse than last time.

Since the night of drunken passion with Michele I'd taken the coward's route and avoided her. I was still ruing my lapse of discipline. I hadn't meant to be so weak. My only excuse was that at least it showed that I was on the path to recovery, with normal mechanisms in full working order. As luck would have it, the most direct way home is past Michele's house and we passed by just as Jake was getting out of her car. Moreover, with a grinding inevitability, we were forced to a halt by an oncoming lady driver. There was easily room for both cars to pass but she seemed to think she was driving a three-metre-wide Sherman tank instead of a Mini. My sexist prejudices were definitely reinforced.

I groaned. If I was lucky, Michele wouldn't notice me in the strange car. But if she did she would think that I had stopped on purpose. Unfortunately for me, Pierre had now worked out how the 2CV's side windows flipped up and was yelling at Jake. A couple of instants later Michele was opening the passenger door. The two boys hared off inside the house. To cap it all, the lady with the mini had vacated a parking slot. I was well and truly trapped.

'Tea?' asked Michele.

It was a very embarrassing cup of tea this time, during the consumption of which neither of us could quite look the other in the eye. My coward's role saw me act as if nothing had happened, hoping the problem would go away – our night of lust had been an aberration, we'd both been drunk. I am a coward but didn't I have enough on my plate without having to exhibit concern for the feelings of another woman? Hadn't she been as precipitate as I in leaping into bed with me when she knew I was damaged goods, vulnerable? Who took advantage of whom? I had a vision of two emotional cripples propping each other up and I didn't like it.

Charlotte came into the room and, as usual, wanted my attention. However, while I was prepared for a rendition of who did what to whom at her school that week, I was thrown when she announced in a voice far more knowing than I normally associate with ten-year-olds, 'Mum went to your house on Wednesday and didn't come back until 6 a.m.'

I knew then for certain what I had been pretty sure about all along. Got to extricate myself from this one. I'd have to talk to Michele but not in front of the children. For now I'd leave it.

<< >> << >>

I took Pierre for my Sunday shop at the Brixton Tesco, a struggle for any parent, even though Tesco claim to lead the market with 'Sweet-free checkout counters'.

One purchase I surreptitiously made was a packet of condoms, placed in the basket beneath the streaky bacon and the digestives. If I was going to be having more dinner parties, I would be prepared in all areas. It seemed realistic to buy a packet of three, with its neat slot-'em-in-your-wallet-just-in-case packaging, rather than a dozen, which in terms of unit price would have worked out cheaper. They should really sell them by the score – it is the obvious collective noun for these objects.

The trouble was that a bulk-buy might well survive their 'Best before' date. This was June 16 in the year of the chiliad. I use this word a little self-consciously (probably wrongly, too), but I want to be the first to give it currency before it becomes hackneyed, as it is bound to do. At a time when every newspaper carries at least three articles a week, and politicians scream 'forward to the millennium', no one is saying 'Forward to the Chiliad', which according to my dictionary means exactly the same thing. If you are a 'chiliast' you believe in the doctrine of the millennium. For some this is the notion that the world will end the moment the clocks strike midnight on December 31 1999 (or is it 2000?); for me, the notion that I wouldn't score again this century.

Michele had provided grounds for more confidence, however, so I arrogantly took the use-by date as a mark of the supreme quality of the product rather than of the manufacturer's natural pessimism about the chances of a customer with the market profile 'sad bastard who dreams'. I wonder how many unused condoms there are sitting in wallets around the country. Scores, I expect.

I managed to slip my packet of three into the basket without exciting Pierre's curiosity, but if he'd asked I'd have told him that it was very strong headache medicine for grown-ups. He must leave well alone. I'd have got away with that. As far as Pierre was concerned babies came out of tummy buttons and his mother was still 21. My own father never told me the facts of life, I had to find them out for myself. He had discovered with my brother that teaching them was unnecessary. Looking up from his *Daily Telegraph* as my brother passed one day he'd said, 'Son, do you know the facts of life?'

'Of course, Dad,' which was probably bluff, but never mind.

'Thank goodness for that,' said my father and dived hastily back into his paper.

When I got to the checkout counter with the condoms I had the traditional embarrassment associated with such purchases. The girl didn't say anything, but I could tell what she was thinking – What, only three?

<< >> << >>

THE Monday morning school run was a bit of a culture shock for me having been used to walking three minutes round the corner to school. There was no straightforward route by public transport from Clapham to Knightsbridge so I'd drive, dump Pierre, then head for a residential road in Stockwell to leave the car before getting the Northern Line to work. This may be no worse than many people's school run except that most other people manage to share theirs whilst mine was too irregular for that.

At least Marie-Sophie had not upped and offed to Newcastle, a problem faced by plenty of fathers. They have to face not only the travel time, but also the expense. I read somewhere that nearly 50 per cent of fathers fall out of contact with their children after separation, and you can see how. I was determined not to become one of them.

One of my biggest worries was still that she might

disappear to France or apply to emigrate with Pierre. On form the courts would let her go which seems incredibly unfair to me. Surely if the 'best interests of the child' really are to be served then the courts should use what pressure they can to keep a family in the same geographical district. If Marie-Sophie were told that a decision to live in France would result in a reversal of custody, she'd stay in London, simple as that. It could be argued that I was someone who was at home in France but why should I uproot myself in order to follow an ex-wife around? Besides, if I did, I'd end up being accused of dogging her footsteps. To keep up my access would be difficult, expensive and exhausting.

The upside of such school runs was that the journey gave me a chance for a chat with Pierre. I stuck to safe topics like Michael Schumacher being better at driving than Damon Hill or men being better at driving than women. I still hadn't worked out how to go about telling him that his mother and I were getting divorced. I'd tried to speak to Marie-Sophie about it but she'd cut me short and told me I should raise the matter with Rachel. I was damned if Rachel Bonham-Lee was going to dictate to me what I could and could not say to my own child.

A child's thought process stays on track with as little readiness as Damon Hill, so suddenly you have to handle the unexpected.

'I've got a new friend coming tonight, Dad,' he said.

Dad? He was growing up, I thought. 'That's nice, who's that?' Pierre was beginning to develop a little life of his own. He'd soon start to move apart from his friend Jake.

'He's called Jasper.'

Jasper? 'Is he in your class?'

'No silly, he's a grown up, he gave me my Gameboy.'

Aaargh! So that Jasper. There was nothing other than some very circumstantial evidence to suggest that he was

Marie-Sophie's new lover. It was just that his name kept cropping up. Perhaps Pierre didn't fully comprehend Jasper's presence either and was indirectly seeking my approval. I'd had what I hoped was a flingette with Michele but nonetheless the name Jasper made me feel jealous.

'Dad,' Pierre interrupted my thoughts.

'Yes Pierre.'

'When can I go back to my old school? I don't like my new school, I don't like my teacher. I want to go back to my old one.'

Music to my ears in a *schadenfreude*ish sort of way. I, too, thought his teacher was a bit sub-standard. She'd put up a picture by Pierre Dufour-Henry, which annoyed me (his name is not double-barrelled), and then labelled it 'Horse and Carridge', so she couldn't spell either.

He had almost said the same thing in front of Mr Wheedle, but Mr Wheedle hadn't thought it worth mentioning in his report.

'Hasn't Mummy told you?' I ducked.

'She doesn't tell me anything.'

'Well you can ask me anything you like.' My instincts told me that parental *glasnost* must be the thing. There was no possibility of synchronizing stories with Marie-Sophie so better just tell him. The truth is neutral and you can't be criticized for telling it.

'When can Mummy and me come home?'

Mummy and I. Tricky. Who do I blame? His mother for removing him in the first place? I think she is to blame, but I can't say that to him. I could blame it on the abstract forces of law and order, Judge Stern and Mr Wheedle. But at age six he had no idea what a judge was or what Mr Wheedle had been doing. I decided to explain.

'Your Mummy and I decided not to live together any more. We both love you . . . we both love you . . .'

'I know that. Mummies and daddies have to love their

children.'

'. . . and we both wanted to live with you . . .'

'So why don't you live together? Don't you like Mummy?'

'Of course I like Mummy but . . .'

'Mummy likes you. She said so.'

'I'm sure she does, Pierre, but we can't live together anymore because if we do we just argue, and that's not very nice. We both wanted you to live with us, but we couldn't agree, so there's a man called a judge and we had to ask him.'

I described the process in the simplest terms possible making Mr Wheedle the judge for the sake of narrative simplicity (he was effectively).

'Can I go back to my old school if I ask the judge man?'

The answer in my embittered mind was a complicated one. The courts are supposed to take into account the wishes of a child but where these are inconvenient they can be overruled by his 'best interests'. The courts think mum is best willy nilly, they're biased. But how do you transmit that idea without shattering a small child's idealistic trust in the world of adults? The answer is you can't and shouldn't. It's the same as teaching children the facts of life too early. They'll find out soon enough.

'Did you see Damon Hill spinning off into the sand trap, Pierre?'

'I think Mr Wheedle is stupid,' said Pierre. *That's ma boy*.

Nonetheless I thought this conversation had gone far enough and I moved on to the intricacies of Formula One and the vicissitudes of the various racing drivers. This occupied us until I got him to school, but I knew we had unfinished business.

<< >> << >>

THAT night was supposed to be my cinema date with Marcia. For the umpteenth time I wondered if I shouldn't put it off with some excuse about a work crisis to cover the real reason. 'I'm sorry Marcia, but I slept with your friend Michele last Wednesday, in fact the same night as I asked you out on a date.'

When she rang into the office at four o'clock and said 'Still on for tonight . . . ?' all my well rehearsed excuses deserted me and I meekly said, 'Yes, see you at the Peckham multiplex. Seven? Yup, that's fine . . .'

'Got some bird then?' asked Roger.

'No, solicitor's office.'

'What, seven o'clock at the Peckham multiplex? Can't you take her somewhere decent?'

I ignored him.

Just before I left home for the Peckham multiplex I fielded a call from Michele. 'Haven't heard from you for a while. I've got some Irish stew on, it will stretch to four.' Stretch to four. She'd probably bought sirloin in my honour knowing Michele. So big-hearted and generous.

The fact that I was freshening up for my first formal set-piece date with Marcia made me feel very guilty indeed as I fobbed her off with a 'You're too good to me'. I'd already slipped a condom into the dark recess of my wallet.

I didn't think Marcia would be the type to object to the premeditation, indeed I had got the feeling that she came from a *milieu* in which that sort of thing was expected. The worst aspect of condoms is mentioning them. 'Condom' – could there be a more unromantic sounding word? 'French letter'? A bit dated even for me (first recorded 1864 apparently). The French say *capote anglaise* – might as well blame each other for the invention of the hateful things. I doubt most English women would have any more clue what this means than I had with Michele's 'goloshes', which is a bit twee and a bit too squelchy sounding.

'Prophylactic' sounds too like 'laxative'. 'Durex' sounds like a cure for headaches. 'Mates' sounds a bit bestial, they might as well have been called 'Shags', except that that would have had connotations of sheep. 'Barrier method' has the wrong ring to it. 'Dunky' is one quite good term I heard, but really we are stuck with ugly sounding 'condom'.

Once in the cinema, Marcia and I shared a carton of popcorn. We managed a tentative brushing together of hands. It was not too difficult to overcome the hand on leg problem. I am very tall and have to sit at an awkward angle whatever the circumstances, which means that I can press my legs up against the girl next to me without it seeming too sexually threatening. I developed this technique as a teenager, and it's like riding a bicycle, you don't forget these things.

She pressed back. This is easy, I thought. We were still in the adverts, and the date was going splendidly. What we needed now was for the projector to break, so that we'd have an excuse to head off home and rip each other's clothes off. We were soon holding hands.

They were doing a repeat of the Meg Ryan film *Sleepless in Seattle*. I'd missed it first time round and we could have got a video but Marcia said it just wouldn't be the same. In it, a dad (Tom Hanks) with a small son has lost his wife. The son gets on Christmas radio and tells the whole of America of dad's plight, after which dad is bombarded with letters from women who want to help. Meg Ryan is one of these women but the relationship is geographically challenged by the fact that he lives in Seattle and she in New York. However, they overcome fabulous odds and it is implied they live happily ever after.

If I had known a bit of the plot beforehand, I would have been even more apprehensive about the date than I had been. The Tom Hanks lonely-man-with-child character was obviously based on me. The only difference was that his wife was dead.

I could imagine the thinking behind it: 'A divorced man hero? Pairing off with a thirtysomething woman? OK, so we got millions of those out there in that situation. Our public will identify. The problem is that no one will sympathize with the character. It's messy. They will assume that he left his wife. OK so divorce, everyone's doing it, I've done it, but it still has stigma. So how are we going to stop the abandoned wife getting all the sympathy? And how do we get the cute child pushing Tom Hanks into the arms of Meg Ryan? Real life children try to push their parents back together again.

'If the mother didn't have custody, either she has something wrong with her, or she is a huge victim, because mothers always win custody. A victim mother would be a distraction; that makes her too big a character, she'd take over the script. Everyone loves a hard done by mother. If we make her nasty, that will piss off all the women with romantic fantasies. She will get in the way of Tom Hanks getting off with Meg Ryan. We'd be seen to be promoting separation and infidelity. Not box office. This is a feel-good movie with a happy ending.'

Pause for thought. 'We kill the mother off. Open movie with scene of vast vulgar Chevrolet hearse pulling away from grave, beautiful view of Seattle in sunlight – could be a challenge, it always rains. Tom Hanks and precocious male child actor hug each other in desolation. That way sympathy for Tom Hanks character introduced immediately. Meg Ryan becomes substitute mother figure instead of wicked stepmother/temptress. And we only have to pay one actress, plus get a coffin (cheap) as a prop.'

Worse, Meg Ryan, having decided that Tom Hanks is the one, gets rid of her blameless but asthmatic fiancé who loves her. You had to give the film-makers credit for finding a disability to make fun of in the politically correct world of Hollywood, but still the film's message to women rings loud and clear. If you are a bit bored with your mate, and he has some irritating shortcomings, bin him and get another. It is part of the culture whereby 70 per cent of marriages end with the woman either leaving the husband or booting him out. Even though I am in love with Meg Ryan, *Sleepless in Seattle* began to get on my nerves. My date with Marcia was going rather wrong, although in the darkness of the cinema she hadn't yet realized.

There was one positive message in the film for me: it promoted the Man and Child as a bit of a role model. It's a pity Raphael didn't do an iconographic picture of it. The thought that some women might actually find me attractive because of, rather than in spite of, having a child was an extraordinary but encouraging one.

Marcia had obviously found the film tremendously uplifting, and bubbled amorously in the car all the way to her house. As for me, I gloomily declined her offer of a coffee, and went home. 'Men!' she must have thought, 'What do you have to do to please them?' Still, Marcia was very intelligent and it wouldn't take her long to realize that what she should do for our next date was hire the video of *Basic Instinct*.

<< >> << >>

B Y the next morning, I felt ashamed of myself. My feelings towards the film were unchanged but I very much regretted my sulky behaviour and hoped I hadn't blown it with Marcia as I assuredly deserved to have done. I rang her.

She had a slightly busy week or so coming up, but how about doing something on Saturday week when her children were off with Tom?

As it happened it was a Pierre weekend and also I had been inveigled into playing rugby for a company team scraped together by Roger to play a bunch of clients. Roger himself was too paunchy to play but for some reason I agreed. I hadn't played since before I married. I'd never been the world's greatest player, too slenderly built, but I'd always enjoyed it. Unfortunately the first casualty of a serious relationship with a woman is often a man's sport. Even if it doesn't impinge on their time, wives don't like the idea of their man going off for a day with the lads.

I was once having a few sets of tennis with a friend in a beautiful setting – grass courts with plenty of space around for children to play safely. The man's wife appeared with pram and toddler just as we had finished a set. 'Fancy another one?' I asked. It was obvious he did. 'Yes, but I'd better go and make sure it's OK with Julia first.' I watched a slightly tense conversation going on and overheard her saying, 'But I've hardly seen you today, Richard.' I saw Richard's shoulders drop slightly as he came back to me and said apologetically, 'Sorry Michael, I'd think I'd better go.' Outrageous – the wife appears in a place where the child could be let off the leash and proceeds to bollocks up a game of tennis just because she can't play.

So it had been with my rugby. But, now, being separated, virtually divorced, I could look forward to taking up a few abandoned interests. Dilemma. 'Marcia, do you like rugby by any chance?' I warned her that there would be a knifing wind and that she might have to witness loads of boorish men misbehaving in the bar afterwards. She said she didn't like rugby but she'd come and watch anyway. 'I've a lot of experience of boorish men,' she said. Dilemma solved. Added bonus – she could also watch over Pierre for me, while I was playing.

Saturday of the game came. Michele called. She needed to take Charlotte to casualty for a cut finger. Could I possibly have Jake for her until she got back from the hospital? I could hardly say no, in fact it saved me ringing up Michele under pressure from Pierre, and saved me from guilt at the thought that she might think I was avoiding her (I was). I got Jake without strings which was good because two children are so much easier to look after than one.

The four of us set off for the game, an hour's drive outside London. The wind wasn't knifing at all, it was a warm spring-going-on-summer's day and we were all in fine spirits. Pierre and Jake were trying to outdo each other with crude verses about poo picked up in their respective playgrounds. Charlotte had passed down quite a few to Jake so he had the advantage.

I had given Marcia strict instructions for no lovey-dovey hand holding stuff. 'Not in front of Pierre,' I had explained. She could see the logic of this; she understood that it was too early for Pierre to see his dad holding hands with a strange woman. I didn't want Jake seeing me holding hands with Marcia either, he'd tell his mum too. I just had to hope that Jake wouldn't say anything to Marcia (or Pierre come to that) about Michele staying out until the early hours of the morning on a certain Wednesday a few weeks ago.

My age isn't too towering for rugby, but charging around on a Saturday afternoon when not fully fit and without the necessary musculature was probably a bit silly. The game went quite well, and I didn't get injured – if it ever looked like I might have to do a tackle I did a despairing dive and just missed. It even had therapeutic value. I could pretend that the ball was Rachel Bonham-Lee's head, for example. Over an hour of energetic play all sorts of tensions were released and on the touchline, lying in the grass, Marcia seemed to be getting on very well with the kids. I am not sure how it happened, but there came a point where I found myself with some forward momentum and Rachel's head in my hand, and before me James de

Vere Crispe and Mr Wheedle blocking my passage to the try-line. Eschewing my normal policy of passing immediately to somebody more willing to be tackled, I smashed both players to the ground and went over for five points and back-slapping congratulations from the team. Afterwards I trotted casually back, before tossing the ball nonchalantly to the kicker and risking a glance at my fan club which I imagined would be jumping up and down ecstatically on my behalf. Marcia was sitting on the grass reading a book to the boys. None of them were looking. So much for my moment of glory.

Well-knackered, well-satisfied, uninjured. It was a shame it was so near the end of the season, I could get back into this.

By the time we got in the car to go back it was clear that Marcia had won Pierre and Jake over well enough. The two boys chatted happily in the back describing various incidents on the touchline involving a football and some other child's bicycle. Then their conversation slipped back into the competitive vein of the morning, in which they were attempting to talk dirty by interspersing their utterances with words like 'pooh' and 'wee'.

'That's enough of that, mind your language,' I said.

'Dad's not really cross, are you Dad?' said Pierre.

'Yes I am,' I said and tried to sound it.

Then Jake hit on a scheme for teasing the grown ups: 'Marcia, is Michael your boyfriend.'

'Well, he's a friend and he's a boy, so you could say he is a friend who is a boy, or a man really,' she answered.

'You love Michael, don't you?' he persisted.

'I think he is very nice,' she said.

'So do I,' said Jake. 'But you love him. I saw you kissing him.'

Did he? Just a discreet little peck, nothing much.

Jake switched his attentions to me: 'My mummy says

173

you are getting divorced. Does that mean you are going to get married to Marcia?'

What could I say? 'No comment'? 'We are just good friends'? 'Haven't even had it off yet, certainly not thinking of marriage, Jake'?

'What does divorced mean, Dad?' asked Pierre, before I had a chance to reply to Jake. It was clear he was still not up to speed on this but it wasn't the moment to explain further, but fortunately we came up behind an enormous mobile crane with police outriders so we had a big discussion about that instead.

We dropped Jake off at Michele's. It might have been more tactful to keep Marcia in the background but Michele wouldn't be fooled, and it might discourage her.

'How's Charlotte's finger?'

'Oh fine. I've told her time and again not to play with penknives. I don't know how she gets hold of them. Let me make you all supper, I've got plenty of pork chops.' It was generous of her because I think she'd got the picture about me and Marcia. We stayed for supper while Pierre and Jake played, which was fine except that Jake started to tease him about his funny face.

We finally got back to my house at about ten in the evening. I got Marcia a drink then I put Pierre to bed. There was a fax sitting on my machine that I hadn't noticed. Being a weekend it wasn't going to be from Rachel. It turned out to be a direct message from Marie-Sophie instead. It said that Pierre had the beginnings of a cold and I should be careful to wrap him up when I took him outside, in fact probably better not to. I was glad I hadn't seen it before going off to play rugby.

When I came down from putting Pierre to bed Marcia was looking through my CDs. They are mainly classical and she chose one of Mozart's flute concertos. 'Used to play this when I was at school,' she said.

'What on your gramophone?'

'No, the flute.' I was impressed. Marcia could play the flute? You should never judge a record by its cover.

We had a few drinks, a few too many drinks, probably, as we edged closer and closer together on the sofa. It felt very adolescent. We were soon behind the bike sheds, so to speak.

'Would you like access to me?' she asked, demonstrating a facility with repartee which would probably get her a job as a scriptwriter on *Blind Date*.

'I think I am getting enough access,' I replied. It is probably best not to talk on occasions like this. Body language is the thing although mine was beginning to ache all over from the rugby, feeling sinuous rather than sensuous. Besides, small-talk will always end up being small. We had fumbled our way to a partial state of *deshabille* and I was getting a first look at her bottom.

She had a nice bottom, but it was tattooed with a butterfly. Being middle class, at least a B2, if a long way from being an A1, I'd never before touched a bottom with a butterfly tattooed to it. But, as my old woodwork teacher once remarked to me with regard to a dovetail joint, 'If you can't hide it, emphasize it.' So rather than skirting delicately around the subject I asked her to explain it.

'Bloody hell, what's this butterfly? Why did you do it?' She said that she had had it done, conscious that it was permanent, when she was nineteen. 'It was a *folie de jeunesse*, but I like it. Whatever happens to me, whoever I fall in with, I know that with a tattoo on my bottom, I will never be square. Your place or your place?' she asked. 'Come on let's go to bed.'

For sure, the occasion called for more than was immediately sensible behind the bike sheds, but I had to say no. For one Pierre was sleeping in my bed and I was worried that he might come downstairs unexpectedly and discover me with Dad's new friend naked on the sofa, bebutterflied bum and all. It would be too much.

'We'd better not, Marcia. I'm worried that Pierre might wake up and find me with a strange woman.'

'I am not a strange woman.'

I hadn't meant to say the wrong thing. I don't see how I could have said the 'right' thing. I mean I did say the right thing.

'I'm sorry,' I said.

'Never mind.'

She left shortly afterwards, and I retreated to check on my obliviously sleeping son, conscious of *my* squareness and reflecting that I didn't understand women and afraid that I never would. That was two dates in a row I'd blown.

Quite aside from the rectitude or otherwise of Pierre finding a strange lady in his dad's bed, my mind was still on other things – my custody battle, for instance. It was something that I was living, eating, sleeping and now, apparently, hoping to fuck. I couldn't get this divorce thing out of my mind for more than five minutes.

Still, this time I had definitely blown it with Marcia.

A few days later I got the backwash from my rugby weekend, not from Roger taking the piss out of me at work for having the girlfriend with the lived-in face (although he did), or indeed from Marcia herself.

It was on the Thursday afterwards as I was just spreading a piece of breakfast toast with peanut butter and mum's homemade jam. The early morning light filtering through trees was making me think the world was not such a bad place after all. Then I heard the flutter of paper on doormat and what for a normal person would be a moment of anticipation (*pace* the Visa bill) was for me one of instant apprehension. I was scared stiff of what the mail would bring.

Item number one was obviously junk mail, and addressed to Marie-Sophie. Bin. Item number two was addressed to me in lettering applied by hand with real ink, so I opened that one next. In it was what could only be described as an out-of-season Valentine, a languidly erotic, but unsigned poem. As poetry goes it wasn't too bad; it didn't show signs of having been written by a budding Emily Dickinson but it was worthy of the back of a popular music album.

> The two stoned sphinx
> are staring at each other.
> Out of their lips is running
> blue water.
> We took off our clothes.
> We shut out of the door
> the houses, the dogs,
> the gardens, the statues,
> My hands remember you
> deeper than my remembrance
> Bodies deny words,
> naked and silent
> communicate.
> death.
> Do you know that?

This was either a hoax from Roger or something enigmatic from Michele. I didn't think this was Marcia's style. It certainly couldn't be from Marie-Sophie. Still, hers and Michele's were the only hands that had recent memory of my naked body. If it was Michele then she had obviously gone to bed with me in good faith and not for a drunken pretend-it-never-happened-the-next-day bonk.

The next letter I had left till last because I knew it would be unpleasant.

Dear Miss Oldcastle,

Re: The Matrimonial Affairs of Mr and Mrs Henry

Our client is concerned that a cheque for £1,000 may have been paid in error into your client's Visa account. She requests that these monies be returned to her without delay.

Yours sincerely,

Bonham-Lee Baldinelli

Bank error in my favour! There's a thousand quid you let slip through your fingers, darling, and you won't be getting that back.

I read Sally's covering note, which I expected to be suitably triumphalist.

Dear Mr Henry,

It might be better to pay this money back for the sake of keeping the temperature down. Could you give me a call to discuss this and the other letter enclosed . . .

What a wimpette was Sally. No question of my repaying the money. The use of the word of 'repay' is wrong anyway. It had been a joint card, with joint debts on it. But we were no longer married. What isn't mine isn't yours. I didn't owe a thing.

I delved in the envelope to find the other letter, a three-pager from Rachel.

Dear Miss Oldcastle,

Re. Pierre Henry

Our client is becoming increasingly concerned about Pierre's welfare and his health. Over the past few weeks Pierre has shown clear signs of disturbance which unfortunately appear to be more severe immediately after contact with your client. In particular, he has developed a nervous tic and on several occasions he has wet his bed. Pierre is also becoming increasingly quiet and morose and prone to illness. Such signs of disturbance in Pierre, we are sure you will agree, are extremely worrying particularly as he has always been a lively and outgoing and gregarious little boy. Part of the change in Pierre is likely to be a direct result of the separation of his parents, however it would appear from various matters that have come to our client's attention and in particular from conversations she has had with Pierre that his unhappiness and the related physical manifestations have been exacerbated by the following:

Our client has been informed by Pierre that when he stays with your client on contact Thursday nights he has sometimes been taken by your client to other people's houses for late dinner parties. This has meant that Pierre has been put to bed in somebody else's bed and has then been woken and taken home late that evening. Although Pierre appears to enjoy such visits sleeping in other people's beds is very unsettling and disturbing for Pierre particularly at the present time.

By way of example, our client instructs us that Pierre told her that on a recent weekend access with your client he was taken to the house of a friend called Jake. This was despite the fact that our client had told the father that Pierre was not well. It appears that your client told our client that he put Pierre to bed at this house at 9 p.m. returning Pierre to the former matrimonial home at around 1 a.m. The following day Pierre's health had not improved, and he had a temperature. Your client however did not keep Pierre in bed but took him to watch a rugby match in the cold. Although this might have been enjoyable for Pierre the day was very cold and as a result Pierre became ill and my client had to keep him off school which resulted in her having to take time off work.

Pierre has also been disturbed by comments that have been made by your client to him. In particular:

179

1. Daddy asked me if I could ring him in the week.
2. Daddy says that he wants me to stay with him more
3. Daddy said that Mummy argues with him
4. Pierre has frequently referred to the Court Welfare Officer, Mr Wheedle whom he has told our client that your client described as 'horrible' and 'stupid'.

Pierre has clearly been upset by these comments and in particular in relation to 4 above. Such comments make Pierre feel confused and upset.

Our client is very concerned that disturbed sleep patterns in different environments, late evenings and the comments made by your client on contact visits have all contributed to Pierre's present unhappiness. We have therefore advised her that if such continues we shall consider the possibility of making an application to the Court to vary the existing order for contact.

Meanwhile we should be grateful however if you would urge your client to ensure that Pierre is put to bed in his own bed at a reasonably early hour, particularly when he has school the next day and to refrain from making any comments to Pierre which may upset him particularly when they concern our client's relationship, her impending divorce, and your client's unhappiness with the present order for access. We are sure that you will agree that it is important that both our clients should reassure Pierre of the love they both undoubtedly give him and of their support and protection that they will both continue to give him. If this can be done, we are certain that Pierre's present unhappy situation will pass and that he will once more be a lively, well adjusted and happy little boy,

Yours sincerely

Rachel Bonham-Lee

This letter probably reads to an outsider as the heartfelt concerns of a mother for her child as transmitted in the formal language of the solicitor, but it put me in a complete panic. I could see an agenda taking shape here, one in which my contact with Pierre was gradually whittled down prior to an application to take him to live in France. They'd be able to argue that I hardly saw him anyway, so may as well let him go.

It wasn't an accurate letter either. The dates were confused. And if Pierre had been genuinely ill neither Marcia nor Michele nor I had seen any evidence of it. It was true that his nervous tic had got worse and I'd noticed that sometimes it was not just a double blinking of the eyes but a twisting of the whole of the left side of the face, like a child with mild cerebral palsy. I hadn't really wanted to acknowledge it and thought it best to avoid making Pierre self-conscious about something which might disappear in time.

On the other hand, he had never wet his bed when staying with me. Most nights he had insisted on sleeping in my bed so I would definitely have known if he had. Surely if he wet the bed at Marie-Sophie's house, that meant he was unhappy at *her* house. If the tic was worse when he got back from access, then that could as likely have meant disappointment at returning to her as a measure of anything I had done or said.

Pierre was generally fine with me: happy, energetic, funny. Surely the cure was not less access but more?

<< >> << >>

No court welfare officer or judge seemed to want to believe my version of events, so how to change that? I entertained fantasies about sending Pierre back to his mother with a bug buried in his teddy bear. Roger's flat was not that far from Marie-Sophie's. It occurred to me that a communications interception base could be set up there. I took him out for a beer the next day, a Czech or Slovak Budweiser – even the rate of divorce amongst countries is rising these days – and explained my plan.

'Don't be ridiculous, Michael,' he said, 'but if you are really serious, and I hope you are not, I do have a friend who has a friend who is a private detective, why not try her?'

I had a mental image of my detective rummaging through Marie-Sophie's rubbish for evidence. Evidence of what I was as yet unclear but, nonetheless, there would be Evidence (with a capital E).

I needed something to release the control Marie-Sophie would apparently exert over me through Pierre until he was eighteen. At least with prison, say, you can roughly calculate your release date with time off for good behaviour, but with Marie-Sophie as arbiter of that my stretch was open ended.

What about this Jasper then, who was he? Did he pick Pierre up from school? Was he bonking my wife while naïve and trusting little Pierre played with his new toys next door? My detective would tail Marie-Sophie on the school run and see that she was lying about how convenient the school was and that often Pierre missed register due to Marie-Sophie's inability to get up in the morning. If Jasper was staying over, I'd have even more fun with this bit. We'd go triumphantly back to court, and then she'd be sorry, and be put in prison (plus all that stuff about frozen peas and fish fingers – how dare she lie about my cooking – that too would be struck from the court record). Ha!

WHEN I spoke to the detective the first shock was that she couldn't bug the telephone for me. This is apparently illegal, which isn't to say that it absolutely can't be done, but that it would involve breaking and entering and be very expensive.

Additionally, she said that her experience of the divorce courts was that they would not be all that overwhelmed by evidence that the trip to school takes 30 minutes as opposed to 15. Now, if it could be established that my ex was holding regular orgies, that would be a different matter. 'But, Mr Henry, you don't suspect her of that, do you?' Well no, I didn't.

And as for Jasper, she is entitled to sleep with him, because, 'She is separated from you, Mr Henry. A judge would not be terribly impressed if she does take a lover to bed, but then he is not impressed with divorced people full stop. He wouldn't do anything about it. Have you been sleeping with anyone since your separation, Mr Henry? And have you introduced your new girlfriend to Pierre? Was that wise? Might you not be the pot calling the kettle black?'

My kind detective was telling me in the gentlest way possible to forget it. 'I get a lot of calls like this,' she said. 'If you really need me, then you have my number. I charge thirty pounds an hour, double after eight p.m. So, to find out if this Jasper was sleeping with Marie-Sophie might have cost me around £600. And that was if I caught him on the first night. I was not sure if I needed to know that badly.

<< >> << >>

INCREASINGLY I was finding that Hank's unsettling take on matters was the most reliable one so I went to see him.

'Panic Hank, they're trying to stop me from seeing Pierre, what shall I do?' I waved Rachel's letter at him.

'Let's take a look.'

He offered me a coffee which I took but couldn't drink; I was jittery enough as it was. He began to read.

'Don't worry,' was his first comment a couple of

paragraphs in. 'I've seen hundreds of letters like this. They have different letters for different occasions ready written on their word processor. Change names and dates, add a little local colour, then make out it took three hours to write, and charge accordingly.'

He read on.

I sat there nervously drumming my fingers on the table top.

'Stop drumming your bloody fingers,' said Hank. 'Well, I can see that you are an appalling father, it stands out a mile. I think you should get a one way ticket to Clifton Suspension Bridge. Let's just go through the list of your shortcomings. Pierre has a tic. That's your fault. He wets his bed at her house, that's your fault. You stayed at somebody else's house, Jake, that's Michele's kid, right?'

'Right. No, I mean well I didn't stay, but we had dinner and stayed quite late while he played with Jake. We were just having a talk.'

'Well, that's your fault. What else? You made him ill. You took him to a park when he had a temperature?'

'Well, a rugby match except that I was never told he had one. He never complained and I didn't notice he was any hotter than usual. He was racing around with Jake and sure, he got sweaty.'

'You should have. That's your fault too. Let's carry on. Oh dear, you asked him to ring you. You didn't ask Rachel first? That's bad. Real bad. That's harassment. You referred to the court welfare officer as "horrible" and "stupid". Is that true?'

'Well, he is horrible and stupid. I don't think I said that. I was trying to explain to Pierre why he didn't favour me. I think we agreed between us that he is horrible and stupid.'

'Well you know if this ever goes to court again, he'll get to read that you called him that. It's quite a clever letter as well as being complete bollocks obviously. You're still using that solicitor right.'

'Yes.'

'Drop her and do it yourself.'

'It's fine for you, you're American and you're black, everyone expects you not to conform, but I won't get taken seriously if I represent myself.'

Hank shrugged. 'Get your solicitor to write back then but give her a bit of backbone, don't let yourself get pushed about. Maybe if Marie-Sophie's going to start whittling you should be applying for more contact, maybe even residence. You won't get it but it might make them think twice about messing you about in future.'

He-Man Hank. I didn't know. The whole thing scared the pants off me.

<< >> << >>

THERE was the odd bit of light on the horizon. In a brief preliminary crossing of swords over financial matters I had won effective custody of the Former Matrimonial Holiday Booking. It had been made in my name, but in a brief flurry of letters and faxes Rachel Bonham-Lee tried to persuade us that I should cash in the deposit and share it out. I could not see how they would force me to do this. Except that they might hold a gun to my head and say I wouldn't be able to take Pierre off to the villa on the island of Elba we'd booked. This had its ironies because one of the reasons for choosing Elba had been Marie-Sophie's desire to catch up with her Corsican forebear Napoleon.

In the original pre-break-up plan Roger was going to come with whatever girl he had on the go at that moment, as was Marie-Sophie's mate Tiff. Obviously the latter two were now out of the picture and Roger said he would recruit some other girls.

185

After a couple of letters each way the correspondence lapsed, presumably because the opposition realized that this was something over which they could make no headway short of going to court, which would have involved expenses greater than the value of the holiday. The judge would get cross with the party that brought the action (them), and that might undermine credibility in future actions over financial matters such as maintenance. So they backed down with a letter saying something feeble like, 'We strongly urge your client repay to our client her share of the deposit . . .' Get lost, doll.

Anyway, in the end, fate intervened. Marie-Sophie drew the short straw at work and got the rota at her news station for that period and couldn't get a nanny. I had got Pierre by default. Ha! Her child-care systems breaking down already.

<< >> << >>

I was getting the uneasy feeling that divorce and solicitors and my ex-wife were going to be 'till death do us part'. Divorce in haste, repent at leisure as Oscar Wilde might have said. I thought Sally had been doing her best but that her best wasn't particularly startling. She'd lost what I'd been promised was a strong case. It had all seemed stacked against me in a way I found unfair. The opposition seemed to have a battle-plan with all this correspondence about nervous tics (serious) and holiday bookings (trivial). There had to be an overall strategy for escaping from the control Marie-Sophie was exerting over me.

Because I kept protesting, Sally suggested a conference one afternoon with Muriel in her chambers to decide what should be done next. Before I went there I decided I wanted a second opinion from someone really top notch – Princess Di's lawyer or equivalent – so an hour before my meeting with Muriel and Sally I booked an appointment nearby with the solicitor Michele had used and now recommended to me.

This was Camilla Wilson of Milliner & Co., solicitors to several members of the Royal family. They have their offices in Lincoln's Inn Fields, a pretty square built, I would guess, during the early part of the reign of Queen Victoria or a bit before. It is a stark take on social justice that the fat-cat lawyers' offices occupying the houses look out across a square which is stuffed full of the canvas and cardboard abodes of tramps. Must spoil the view completely. They are an interesting testimony to the ability of the best legal brains in the country to get them removed.

Milliner & Co. are situated in an imposing Georgian-looking townhouse, of the kind which would make an upper-class client feel that he was dealing with gentlemen, and a *nouveau riche* client feel that he was dealing with a lawyer who dealt with the upper classes. It would make the shady wheeler dealer with his Rolls-Royce and ten-bedroom Barratt home with indoor pool and Jacuzzi think that the three marriages were worthwhile. He had finally got to employ Milliner & Co.

Which all begs the question, what was I doing there? I wanted to see if they would have done things differently, whether they would be able to add several hundred pounds an hour worth of value to the quest of improving my future life.

You go past the brass plate outside into a large reception area which in former days would have been an imposing hall and staircase. Architecturally, it has been spoilt by building regulations which require the imposition of fire-doors in places of work. But the stucco ceilings remain impressive, as do large oil paintings of the likes of Josiah Milliner 1773 – 1832 and various other Milliners, as well as HRH a Prominent Member of the Royal Family, their client.

The waiting-room, a former drawing-room, was rather more agreeably appointed than the marriage councellor's. There was that hush you get in smart clinics in Harley Street (I imagine – never having been to one). The magazines on offer were the same though: *Country Life* and *The Lady* for redistributing property and hiring domestics.

Shortly afterwards I was ushered into an impressive boardroom kind of place and introduced to the frighteningly together and professional-looking woman in her early forties that was Camilla Wilson. She was accompanied by a younger man, late twenties probably, whom I took to be her assistant. She wore a Tory woman's business suit of the kind favoured by Cherie Blair, above which was well-topiarized blonde hair, the kind of blonde which cannot be obtained without a touch of help from one of the bi-products of a large chemical cracker in Ellesmere Port.

We shook hands and sat down at opposite sides of the boardroom-style table with a leather top. Repro not antique, but nice stuff.

'May I introduce to you my assistant, Mr Davies, who has also read your papers. Now what can we do for you?'

Or do you for, I thought uneasily. I was beginning to feel out of my depth. This place was for big-league divorces: Bill Wyman v Mandy Smith, Bob Geldoff v Paula Yates, or Prince Andrew v the Duchess of York, but not Michael Henry v Marie-Sophie Dufour.

She looked like a Mrs Wilson rather than a Miss or Ms Wilson. I checked the rings on her fingers, the fourth one on the left hand had a socking great cluster of diamonds on it and a wedding band. As with Sally's lack of one, I didn't know if such was encouraging –happily married, thus emotionally distanced from my problems?

I explained what I saw as the grave injustice done to me.

The young Mr Davies spoke. 'We know Miss Bonham-Lee. We don't rate her terribly highly. We've looked through the documents, but we couldn't find any copy of the judgment. Where is the judgment Mr Henry?'

'What judgment?'

'The judgment the judge made, we need a copy of that.'

'It's in there,' I said fishing out a piece of paper from the pile.

'No, that's not the judgment, that's the order,' said Mrs Wilson. I felt like a silly little boy. She started reading: 'That the Respondent do pick up the child Pierre Henry' We can't advise you unless we see what the judge actually said, what reasons he gave for making the order he did. Do you see? You can get a transcript through the court.'

'How do I do that?'

'Well we could get it for you, but first we would have to be on the record as your solicitors. We would order a transcript and, depending on how long the judge spoke for, it might cost anything from twenty to several hundred pounds, but it is unlikely to be under a hundred. Could I just ask you how much you earn and the value of estate in this dispute?'

I told her. Roughly £25,000 a year as a translator, house worth £120,000, mainly represented by mortgage.

'Have you been warned how horribly expensive we are?' She said this with a certain proprietorial pride, not devoid of charm. 'My charge is two hundred and twenty pounds an hour. Mr Davies is somewhat less. We charge one hundred and forty pounds an hour for his services, and we don't do legal aid work. I think perhaps that we may not be the right solicitors for you.'

Were they suggesting that a cheaper solicitor would do just as well for me? Don't you get what you pay for in this world? Ah, but of course: the law is universal and has nothing to do with being rich. They can't make much money charging those prices then …

Despite a business-like style, Mrs Wilson did have a certain softness too, and I could see she would be capable of switching skilfully between being as hard as nails and exerting gentle feminine persuasiveness. Any but the toughest of opposition would be routed. If you had the money, you might get value for it, but provided the estate you were squabbling over was worth well in excess of a million.

It didn't take Einstein to come to the sudden realization that the egg-timer in this particular meeting was dropping sand at the rate of £220 + £140 = £360 an hour. Six pounds a minute and they were telling me that they couldn't give me any advice because they didn't have a copy of the judgment. When I had rung her she had asked for the papers. Now it was put to me like this I could see that the judgment might be important, so why didn't she tell me it was needed?

I said I would think things over and get back to them. I went for a sandwich and a pint of beer in a cheap looking pub before heading for Muriel's chambers. I was despondent. It seemed to me I'd just wasted £300 on being told that unless I came armed with the judgment they could give me no advice at all.

<< >> << >>

MURIEL'S room is in one of the Inns of Court, down some steps the other side of the Strand from Lincoln's Inn Fields, in a setting more Nottingham University than Oxford. I met Sally outside and together we made our way through a maze of corridors painted in prep-school grey.

Muriel had a small room, dark at slightly below ground level. She made us some tea and offered a Rich Tea biscuit.

I thought she might at least have splashed out on Boasters for her clients, especially as I was not a cut-price legal aid one. We then chatted about this and that.

'How are you Michael?'

'Fine, thank you.'

'Managed to get away on holiday yet?'

'No, schools don't usually break up till July. We had a bit of a tussle about that didn't we Sally?'

'But we won it,' she said.

'Oh, well something to look forward to then ...' said Muriel.

She seemed to want the occasion to develop into a very pleasant tea party. Bonhomie, smiles all round. We were discussing everything except the matter in hand.

'Could we perhaps discuss ...?' I said. I was already a few hundred quid down on the day's business and no clearer where I was going, and although Sally is cheap, Muriel is not. Well I didn't think so, although Sally said she was good value. (A day in court with Muriel costs £600.)

We had to decide what should be done next. We eventually decided it would be best to see how things went over the summer and then if I felt I was still getting a raw deal and Marie-Sophie was continuing to whittle away at contact then it might be right to apply for a directions hearing to define contact, perhaps even reverse the residence situation.

'What's a directions hearing?' I asked.

'One where you go before a judge and he decides what paperwork and reports, like another welfare report, need to be done before the final one, and sets a date.'

'Can you get rid of Mr Wheedle for me?'

'He's terrible isn't he? The last case I did when he was involved the judge gave him a dressing down at the end. Mr Wheedle is well known. Our hearts sink when he is on one of our cases, and then you had bad luck with Judge Stern who is not well known as a father's judge.'

So Hank had been right. Well, I would have liked to have been party to this kind of knowledge from my legal team first time round. Then perhaps I would have been better prepared mentally for handling the double act. How come she didn't manage to get him dressed down when he was on my case?

'We'll give getting rid of him our best shot,' said Muriel.

I'd believe it when I saw it. I didn't have much confidence left in either of them. I liked Sally and Muriel, we'd had a jolly tea party, they were both very pleasant people but I couldn't help feeling we had made little progress. As I went home I mulled the possibility of going it alone. Maybe Hank was right; perhaps divorce lawyers were a waste of space. In the corridor or in her chambers Muriel would talk tough, but in court she would come over all deferential. I suppose they go before a Judge Stern every other week so can't afford to get on the wrong side of the guy, whereas I only got one shot.

Given what you got for your money – not a lot, for a lot – there might be something to be said for representing myself like Hank suggested. Those letters for example: Sally would get one from Rachel, she'd then ring me to ask what to say, I'd instruct her as to what I wanted said, she'd write the letter. Why not just write it myself?

Sally and Muriel wouldn't mind being fired, wouldn't notice probably. They had plenty of other clients. The problem I had with them was that they were just too nice, whereas Bonham-Lee was not nice at all.

<< >> << >>

MARCIA finally phoned me for a chat and I told her where I was at on the legal front. 'Do you know, I said to Tom when we separated, look, you get a solicitor if you want, I'm not going to OK. He thought you had to get a lawyer when you divorce, but you don't, it's all part of their propaganda. You see he bought the *Which? Guide to Divorce* which says you have to get a solicitor. That's the Consumer Association view. OK it was different for me, I was in a strong position. Anyway, he didn't get a lawyer and things have worked out fine. For him, too, I think. More importantly, why don't you come round for some supper. I was looking for an excuse to pack the kids off to their dad ...' Send the kids off to their dad. If Marie-Sophie was like that I'd drop all thought of further legal action.

Quite why I should inflict upon Marcia my sea of troubles and expect her to listen sympathetically while cooking me supper I didn't know, but no matter – it was her suggestion. I checked the dark corner of my wallet. I noticed the oval outline was now firmly sculptured in the leather of the zip-up bit. Pathetic. Tonight I would throw caution to the wind, suppress my moods, this would be it.

The whole process was remarkably straightforward and angst free. I went round to her place for supper and sympathy, got plastered and, before I knew it, was being shown her etchings (viz. one tattooed butterfly on bum) upstairs in her bedroom. She leant her arms against my chest as I went for the buttons down the front of her shirt. Consumed by a frenzy of passion, before we knew it we were lying on the bed naked.

I shouldn't make it sound quite so easy. In the filthy bits of films they always cut to the naked actor and actress in bed, or rather on bed. Clothing seems to slip diaphanously to the floor. Bras unclasp without a hitch and Michael Douglas never gets stuck with his socks on. In real life socks are a problem: if you are in a frenzied clinch, you can't stand on one leg and bend down to remove your socks for fear of losing not just your balance but worse that intangible atmosphere of soon-to-be-fulfilled desire. Intangible? Wrong word. There is nothing intangible about a good bit of tit and Marcia's were lifted and separated in a bra the discoupling of which was beyond me.

'It's a front loader,' she said.

I fumbled further. 'Give me another clue.'

'Haven't you ever done one of these before?'

'Thousands of times,' I murmured, deciding that giving an impression of past promiscuity was better than giving one of past underperformance. I pulled the straps off the arms and took the thing down over her waist.

'Darling, shall we become romantically linked,' I said as our bodies entwined on the bed. Around us the waves crashed, the wind roared, the lightning flashed, as, dear reader, why don't you mind your own business.

Afterwards, Marcia said, 'That was great. Did you know that some women don't enjoy penetrative sex?' She said this with a tone of proprietorial pride that reminded me of Camilla Wilson of Milliner & Co. telling me how expensive she was. I rather wished she hadn't said anything. All this 'You were great darling' stuff doesn't do anything for me. Also, I like my women mysterious, and I get queasy if they get too gynaecological on me. Regular bulletins about how their periods are going, for example, I find off-putting. I am sure I speak for all men on this, including New ones. Exchange of any information of a vaguely technical nature should be done on a 'need to know' basis, which is just how the military keep their secrets. Still, I was pleased to have been of service.

Notch number two on the bedpost. Not bad going, given that surveys indicate the average human only manages six partners in the course of his entire life. To have been in this position so soon after my marriage had ended made me into something of an over-achiever. It was good for morale, if not for morality, and is to be recommended to anyone fortunate enough to have access to such therapy. A good bonk is worth a thousand sleepless nights, or several thousand pounds spent with a Harley Street bereavement counsellor.

Next morning saw Marcia alone in bed, not because I am the wham-bam-thank-you-ma'am type who flees the moment he has had his wicked way. Far from it. Both Real Man and New Man, I was downstairs with a towel around my waist, continuing to help fulfil certain mutually held needs – not just sex, but heart to hearts and hugs and in this case a cup of coffee.

I turned the gas on under the percolator. I'm a coffee snob and I was glad to find that Marcia was, too. The doorbell rang. I could hear a child. Panic. It must be Tom bringing the kids back early. Then I heard a key in the lock. Bloody Hell! I remembered about Marcia's acrimony-free divorce and how she trusted Tom enough to give him a key.

The kitchen was off the hall, so I could remain undiscovered for a short while. I had about 30 seconds in which to make myself scarce. It is a small Victorian terraced house, and if I had had my wits about me I might have made it out of the kitchen, into the hall and up the stairs, where I could have cowered under Marcia's bed as I'd done all those years ago at Marie-Sophie's parents' flat.

'Hang on, I'm coming ...' yelled Marcia from upstairs. I could hear her casting around for some clothes. With just the towel round my waist I felt as naked and exposed as I had ever done. So where to hide?

It is bad enough cooking in somebody else's kitchen (you can never find the salt) but hiding in one. This one was small, a bit more than a galley kitchen but by no means big enough to host an Aga saga. The first cupboard I opened was fully occupied by the hot water tank. Why wasn't the bloody thing upstairs like normal boilers? The second turned out to be a cleverly disguised freezer. The third was packed with large pans, colanders, graters, a steamer three storeys tall, a wok, all things which stash neither neatly nor naturally. The top pan lurched at me threateningly. I grabbed at it to stop it and its colleagues from making a mass break out from their dark prison. I found myself lodged holding this top pan, which hissed sibilantly at me while the pile as a whole shifted to the crazy list of a ro-ro ferry which has recently lost its bow door in heavy seas, as I crouched for cover below the breakfast bar, out of sight of the hall.

'Mummy, Mummy, we're home,' a child was shouting excitedly. As I held the Tower of Pisa of culinary objects I heard the front door swing open, and felt the blast of cool morning air. Considering it was once his house too, I expected Tom to march confidently in and put the kettle on or raid the fridge – usually my first port of call. I froze. Perhaps I should brazen it out. 'Hi Tom, nice morning, er, nice to meet you at long last, heard lots about you, none of it complimentary. That Marcia of yours, see why you liked her . . .' or perhaps an excuse: 'My water's been turned off and I had to make an early start so Marcia said I could borrow her shower . . .'

There was a scramble of little legs up the stairs. 'Mummy, mummy . . .' a child was shouting excitedly. I was fond of Marcia but had no mandate for her children who I had only met once before, briefly at Jake's party. No matter that she'd told me Pierre was good looking, the overwhelming impression I'd got of hers had been of encrustations of snot.

I popped my head up to look at the garden, examining it for hiding places. Marcia's elderly neighbour was out hoeing his vegetable patch. I took it that he was not used to seeing stray men running into his neighbour's garden in various states of undress, but it would brighten up his life. I reached one hand towards the bolt while keeping the other against the cupboard door. Bolt drawn I prepared to bolt . . . Locked. Shit! Where was the key?

My other arm was getting cramp. I took a risk and slowly lowered the pots to the floor. With a heartstopping wobble they obeyed silently – I decided against opening other cupboards. Through the window, I eyed the children's climbing frame which had a tent construction on top. It was one of those June days where the cricket is as likely to be snowed off as rained off and I didn't fancy spending time in there while Marcia sweet-talked her husband out of the house again. Besides, the man with the hoe would be bound to take fright and call the police.

I spotted an intimidatingly large and clanky looking bunch of about fifteen keys in a fruitbowl. No chance of getting the right one. Maybe the window would be easier? But the route to this was over the previous night's washing-up, of which there was quite a lot, and then there were the double glazing and triple locks to deal with.

A child could be heard coming down the stairs now and I dived to the floor again. Where was bloody Marcia? If she could cause a diversion for a few minutes, I could be in the back garden in no time.

A small, grubby body made its way into the kitchen and towards the cookie jar on the opposite units. Maybe if I had leapt out and said 'Boo!' it might have collapsed dead from shock. It was Marcia's three-year-old, Jason. I held my breath There was a chance he might recognize me as the Pass-the-Parcel Man. I remained crouching, my heart thumping and calves tingling from the effort of keeping still in my cramped enclosure. Meanwhile Jason rounded on the jar and, after a second or so of deliberation, stuffed three chocolate fingers into his mouth and attempted to put the lid back. Somehow he got the whole lot off balance and I could see him wrestling with a decision about whether to drop his biscuits or save the jar from toppling.

He turned. We eyed each other, both looking like someone caught in the act. With his mouth crammed full, Jason could articulate very little so the onus was on me. I made the decision for him and grabbed the jar and put it straight. I don't know why but I found myself mouthing the words, 'Hello, I'm the plumber.' Whatever, the child's stiff frame relaxed. He gave me one of those disinterested looks which belong to very young children who have not yet worked out that it is not normal to encounter strange men clad in a towel crouching behind the breakfast bar in their mother's kitchen.

I thought I'd got away with it when he finished a biscuit and ran into the hall. 'Daddy,' he started, 'there's a man …'

I was ready to meet my doom but, just at that moment, Marcia bounded down the stairs. 'Tom, I'm sorry. I've had a terrible night, I must have overslept.' (Thanks Marcia, *quelle ingrate*. I could picture her giving a flick to her dishevelled hair).

'Mummy, mummy, there's a man …'

'Tom,' she interrupted, 'you couldn't take them to see the ducks and come back in half an hour could you? Just give time to have a quick soak …'

Suddenly I was forgotten. 'Ducks, feed ducks. Ducks,' chorused Jason.

However, his sibling, who until now had presented no danger, complained. It wanted to watch telly and, more worryingly, it wanted a glass of milk.

'Shoo,' said Marcia. 'Daddy will buy you a drink on the way.'

There was the sound of quick kisses. Then of the front door opening and shutting again. Poor, poor Tom, he must have been very confused.

The voices receded. I came out of my hiding place into the corridor. Suddenly, there was a huge metallic crashing sound from the kitchen.

'There you are,' Marcia said, walking through the open door and giving the scattered pans a puzzled look. 'Time for a quickie?'

'You must be joking.'

'Oh, come on. Once they get on the swings, there's no getting them off.'

She had on a very sexy négligé. I wondered what Tom had made of that – his ex-wife so alluring, he dispatched to the park.

'All right then, but we'll have to be quick.'

'That shouldn't be a problem for you ...'

'Up yours.'

'I hope so.'

Dear me. How vulgar can you get? Quite takes the romance out of it.

<< >> << >>

I received a polite reminder in the post to pay Sally's fees. I'd had a bill earlier which had somehow never made it out of my 'in' tray. If it wasn't Marie-Sophie's solicitor it was mine. Was I never to get out of Chancery?

I'd decided to treat it like those bills you deliberately leave until the third red reminder. In advertising speak the purchase of this service is what is known as a 'distress purchase', something that nobody enjoys purchasing like loo paper or petrol.

Dear Mr Henry,

We do not seem to be able to trace any record of having received payment for the fees invoiced to you of £4,916.58.

We would appreciate payment as soon as possible, and would remind you of the terms of business letter sent to you when you first instructed us.

I am sure you will understand that in a time of recession

that it is important for any business to ensure that it is paid on
a timely basis.
   We look forward to receiving you remittance without further
delay.

Yours sincerely,

Esmee Smith
(Accounts partner)

The pathos of it. Solicitors, surely, benefit from recession.
Financial pressure equals reluctance to pay, equals
litigation. At the personal level financial pressure is at least
one thing that tips people into divorce.

I had to reflect too that Bonham-Lee and Baldinelli
were a smart West End divorce boutique of which Rachel
was the senior partner. So if my bill was around five grand,
given Marie-Sophie's love of the phone, hers was going to
be ten and the rest, meaning that the former family unit was
up to the fifteen grand mark, and that was before we'd done
more than skirmish over the financial settlement.

I could well imagine that for some a solicitor becomes a
confidante – a dangerous relationship as the meter doesn't
stop running while you pour your heart out. Michele told
me that she had had a lot of problems with solicitors,
sacking two before settling down with Milliner & Co. The
first one had been kind, reasonably efficient about his work
and they'd developed a good relationship. Then one
evening, sharing a taxi to their respective homes, he'd put
his arm around her and attempted to snog her.

The second solicitor was younger, equally good
professionally, but no less danger. He bit the dust because
Michele found herself at a dinner party at which two of the
other guests, complete strangers, suddenly said 'Oh, we've
heard all about you'. It emerged that Michele and her
divorce had been his chief dinner-party conversation
material.

She's looked into complaining about both men to the Solicitor's Family Law Association, except that she discovered the SFLA doesn't entertain complaints until a case is completed, which of course takes ages. Once her case had come to an end, she found she no longer had the energy or the will to engage in disputes with her two former solicitors.

Looking at Sally's bill I could see that a lot of it represented just ringing up for a chat. It wasn't her fault, but what ever did I talk to her about?

Marcia was a better emotional prop anyway. I still thought it best to keep Marcia under wraps. Like Michele, she was proving to have a heart of gold, but I doubted that my mother, for example, would approve of her. It was not a question of being insufficiently grown up to go out with a girl without my mother's approval (I had done so once, big time, let's not forget) simply that my divorce had put my parents through the mill. No need to make them even more anxious about their boy's welfare. For a start the fling (or affair, or deep long-term relationship – too early to say which) was indecently hasty, and although I needn't mention the tattoo, other biographical details – her age, the fact that she'd already had two marriages – would set warning lights flashing unnecessarily. My parents should be spared that, I felt.

I liked Marcia better all the time. But I didn't think that I was falling in love with her. I had a feeling of guilt every time I kissed her, which is strange because I really didn't owe any loyalty to Marie-Sophie.

<< >> << >>

HANK finally prevailed upon me to go to a Families Need Fathers meeting. He said he was chairing the meeting that week.

'You're like a lead guitar in a second rate band who wants me to come and watch his gig, is that it?' I asked.

'Something like that. Look, if you are ever going to take my advice, dump your solicitor and represent yourself, you need to meet lots of others who've done it and understand why they did.'

Depressed Dads Anonymous, I thought. But Hank had been good to me, and he deserved a little bit of my support in return. Besides, I was beginning to think he had a point, especially after Sally's invoice.

The venue was the upstairs room of a pub called The Churchill, near the Mount Pleasant sorting office just off Gray's Inn Road, not so far from the most densely packed area of lawyers in Britain. 8 p.m. every Tuesday if you're interested. All are welcome.

The first thing that struck me was the sheer range of participants. Unlike Alcoholics Anonymous, Families Need Fathers is not big enough to sustain a posh chapter or a celebrity chapter so the meeting was all races, all classes, probably all political persuasions. Dotted around were a stockbroker type, a man in a turban, another with dreadlocks, construction worker type with tattooed arms, men in suits and men in jeans, perhaps fifty in all. There were some women too, which surprised me. Celebrity was represented by a well-known comedy actor from the telly, quietly nursing a pint in the corner. The one thing most had in common was sad tired eyes. Is that what I looked like?

As I listened I realized that my problems were mild compared to some and that Hank had not been exaggerating when he talked about his. Those who sought advice were invited one by one to tell their tale. Hank would allow about ten minutes to each. He knew the answers to many of the problems but often turned to others in the group many of whom were clearly old hands. There was also a queuing system for a barrister who was giving free advice downstairs.

I quickly discovered that my problems were at the lower end of the tragedy scale, in fact I was doing very well seeing my son every other weekend and mid-week on Thursdays. Some of these guys hadn't seen their children for months, in a couple of cases for years.

There was more than one person who had been the victim of a false accusation of sexual abuse. A big investigation had been conducted and no evidence found but the man was still not being allowed to see his daughters. He had not seen them for two years. The psychiatrist had gone further and said he thought the evidence had been made up. But, just in case, the judge had decided to deny access because the obvious conflict between the parents would be bad for the children. In other words, she makes the allegation, creates the conflict and he doesn't get to see the kids.

Until I heard this account, I had always presumed that Hank was laying it on a bit thick on the topic of child abuse, Woody Allen and all that, but these were every-day people with every-day lives. The advice the guy was given was to keep plugging away, but the feeling you got was that he did not have much chance of seeing his children before they came to search him out as adults. Then the children would be so appalled once they learnt the truth that they'd turn against the mother, quite virulently probably, in itself a disaster.

'Anyone else got a problem?' asked Hank. Three more hands went up. He managed the meeting in the same way as he managed his deli, with charm and authority, but every so often there would be an over-excitable guy who he couldn't get to shut up. One kept spouting off about 'Jungian this' and 'matriarchal that', a guy who was obviously heavily into social-anthropological theory. You could feel the room getting restless. You couldn't help thinking that whatever his wife had had against him, she'd had a point.

Overall, though, the occasion left me scared shitless about the power Marie-Sophie had over me. Suppose she accused me of sexual abuse? Pierre liked to sleep in my bed on visits. Should I stop him? He'd developed a nervous tic which I'd been blamed for. Suppose the fact that he often slept in my bed was misconstrued? Better ban him from my bed.

As if Hank could read my mind, he suddenly said, 'To stop you all rushing off to Beachy Head immediately, we will now have a session for good news.' Various hands went up.

'Went to the court of appeal, representing myself, Trevor here was my McKenzie friend, got me parental responsibilities.'

'A Parental Responsibility Order,' explained Hank portentously, 'gives an unmarried father standing in law. Without it, even your name on the birth certificate gives you no status as father, except if the Child Support Agency wants to come after you for money. Unmarried fathers here will be sad to hear that our members often find themselves refused a PRO in the lower courts; they will be glad to hear they always win the appeal, and I mean always, but what an expensive waste of time. If half the judges knew the law that wouldn't happen. Why did you represent yourself?'

'Refused legal aid.'

'What grounds?'

'Solicitor said he couldn't get it but my wife had it.'

'Sack the solicitor,' went up a chorus.

'I did.'

Another man spoke. 'Not exactly good news, but some encouragement.' He said that he had been through two years of hard fought legal stupidity before he and his ex-wife had come to their senses, more-or-less simultaneously. This moment coincided exactly with the resolution of their financial affairs and the disappearance of the solicitors back into the background.

'My former wife and I are not exactly friends, you'd have to describe our relationship now as cordial. There was a time when we couldn't even agree about the weather. A couple of weeks ago we even had a joint birthday party for our child, instead of two. It took us four years to get there, but we've done it.'

'Lawyers, dontcha hate 'em,' said Hank from the chair and then he was off on the the spiel I now knew by heart: 'In my experience about seventy-five per cent are a complete waste of space. Worse than a waste of space because they stir things up, often deliberately, and do actual damage. We do keep a list of ones who are OK, but by and large, represent yourself ...'

The whole experience was a real eye-opener for me. For a start I wasn't alone. Here was a group of people who were experiencing problems similar to mine – from what I had gleaned from this meeting, actually worse. Even the few who were whingeing about nothing in particular seemed to benefit from being told in Hank's firm but gentle way that they were whingeing about nothing in particular.

I found I was left with mixed emotions. From what I could surmise, I was getting 'good' contact, but it could be improved so that mid-week contact happened every week, not every alternate week. Almost everyone else there was suffering from some form of contact whittling and uncertainty like me. The thought that I might spend ten years being uncertain about when I'd next see Pierre was too fatiguing for words. It isn't much wonder that so many dads quietly give up.

On the other hand it was brought home to me how vulnerable Pierre's relationship with me was. I was particularly alarmed by one guy whose ex-wife had announced she wanted to leave London and live in Blackpool, and there was another where the mother had got an order allowing her to emigrate to Australia with her new husband. What price access at that range, even by telephone?

The overall feeling was that no matter what it took, a father musn't give up. If there were rows, tears, legal fees, these wouldn't effect the child nearly so badly as would their father walking out on them for good – even if this was to protect the child from the conflict with an implacably hostile mother.

I mulled over what I had learnt on the way back with Hank.

'There is certainly a great deal of hostility in that room,' I said.

'Yep, but it passes. We keep going. We get through it. We have to use that hostility constructively. We have a right to see our children and they have a right to see us. So we fight for that in the best ways we can.'

<< >> << >>

PIERRE'S sports day was not on my access day, but Hank said that school was a neutral place and I had every bit as much right to go to it as she did. So, I went. God I hated this inner-city school near Harrods. Every time I looked at the displays of the children's work it was the lowest common denominator all the way, by which I don't mean stupid children, but so little ambition amongst the teachers for the kids.

'Every term our teachers have inset days [aka another day off] in which their skills are enhanced in training programmes. This term they went on a course to enhance their skills in teaching art using various media. Here are some prints created by the teachers.' Pierre could coat a dead fish with paint and splodge it on to a piece of paper more artistically than the best of them. I'd prefer them to have taught him to read.

The school was not good about keeping me abreast of things like sports day. I certainly wouldn't have heard about it from Marie-Sophie. Originally I had missed occasions such as new parents' evening, because I was never informed of them. It wasn't until I'd looked at a notice board that I realized what was happening. The school had needed a certain amount of training in the form of a stiff letter to understand that Pierre had two parents. Again, par for the course to have to do this, said Hank.

Marie-Sophie flounced into the playground looking like a million dollars as the children were filing out into the playground, lining up by class. She didn't see me at first, but when she did she was all smiles. I soon learnt that the smiles were strictly for effect. 'What exactly are you doing here? It's not your day. You haven't requested permission to see Pierre.'

I launched into an explanation of my rights according to Hank. Also my responsibilities: I should be there. Either way, Pierre was excited to see us both. 'Mum, Dad,' he shouted when he saw us together.

There was no sack race, no egg-and-spoon race, no parents' race. Just a series of non-competitive physical jerks, like passing the ball round a circle of children, not even against the clock. The children all had big smiles (it beats learning to read) but it can't be a surprise that most of the nation's children are becoming video cabbages.

As somebody who used to do a lot of sport at school, these non-competitive games worried me. It is a tragedy for the children. There will always be some children who will hate football whatever, so there should be a let-out for them to go off and play chess, do embroidery or learn an instrument, but no football at all is a kind of cruelty.

If I despise the anti-competition ethos, it is not a political statement. Missing out on competition is missing out on a lot of fun. Victory and defeat: '… if you can treat those two impostors just the same …' you are a boring old twerp.

At the end, Pierre bounced up to us, grabbing us both by the hand and pulled us close together. I sort of shied away from Marie-Sophie as she did from me. 'Let's all go somewhere together, three of us,' said Pierre. I was half on for it, it might help clear the air between us, but the time wasn't right.

'Another time Pierre, I've got to get back to work, I'll see you at the weekend,' I said. As I went home I mulled over something I had sometimes thought of when Pierre was back in his original school in Clapham, namely to institute some kind of football club for boys (and girls if they wanted) of Pierre's age. I could manage one afternoon a week. I'd been thinking about it for a while, but had done nothing.

What I witnessed at Blenheim Primary School was a spur. I was getting my act together on various fronts. Women, work, legal affairs, so why not Pierre's sport? It was a bit late this term to get something organized but would make a project and a channel for energies once the autumn term started.

<< >> << >>

I had to ask Pierre's teacher for a copy of his end-of-year school report. 'Oh, I already gave it to your wife, you should get a copy from her,' she informed me.

Oh no you don't I thought. You treat me the same as you treat her.

Hank told me that uncooperative schools are a common

complaint for fathers and the way to deal with them is to threaten to take the school and education authority to court for sex discrimination. Sex discrimination policy stops at the important issue of whether or not to say headteacher or headmistress. Fortunately schools have no budget for legal stuff, so they cave in immediately.

I went into the headmistress's office and said politely but firmly that the law gave me a right to expect my own copy of the school report and all future reports. I hoped that whilst actually being polite, I looked sufficiently crazed for her to worry about future action if they failed to comply. The next day she rang me up, apologized, and said a photocopy of the report was ready for me whenever I needed it. Who needs a solicitor?

The report was fine, unfortunately. I had been slightly hoping that my son was doing appallingly badly, was a total nervous wreck, twitched beyond belief with grief when not seeing his dad, and thus needed to go back to his old school. But instead it said that he had settled in well, that his reading was all that could be expected of a child of his age and that he was a lively and enthusiastic member of the class.

Nonetheless, I found myself spending an idle morning at the office typing up a letter which I'd send direct to Rachel Bonham-Lee, cc Sally Oldcastle. I thought I'd have a bash at representing myself for a while. I'd stay on an umbilical cord with Sally, copy her into correspondence, but handle everything except major crises myself rather than get her to write letters I could perfectly well write myself.

Dear Miss Bonham-Lee,

I have just noticed that on Pierre's school report, his name is given as Pierre Dufour-Henry. His name is Pierre Henry. I have no objection to 'Dufour' being used as a second given name, if my wife so wishes.

After Pierre's name was registered at birth, Marie-Sophie said that she wished we had also had 'Dufour' slotted in as well, but we never got round to the paper work. If she would like to do so now, then I will create no difficulties, although I would be entitled to.

I do not however, agree to his surname being changed, or to his being caused to be known in the community as having any surname other than 'Henry'.

I liked that last bit. It echoed the paragraph in the copy of the Children Act 1989, which I now had sitting in the loo for light relief. You are not allowed to have a child 'caused to be known in the community' by anything other than his real name.

The letter I got back affected not to understand what I was on about. Me, I thought it was perfectly clear. So I got out the big Oxford Dictionary and copied out the definition of 'given name' to her.

Dear Miss Bonham-Lee,

I am puzzled as to why you are puzzled at my letter about Pierre's name.

'surname': n. & v.t. 1. Additional name of descriptive or allusive kind attached to a person & occas. becoming hereditary; the name common to all members of a family. (cf. CHRISTIAN NAME or GIVEN NAME) or 2. v.t. Give to; give (person); (p.p.) called by way of additional surname, having as family name.

'given name' = one given to the child by his parents (unless the child is a foundling or other variety of waif). Some refer to this as a 'Christian name'.

My son's mother is a lapsed Catholic, and so in order to avoid giving offence I used the more modern term 'given name', rather than Christian name, which is regarded as out-moded in some quarters.

My son's SURNAME is 'Henry'.
My son's GIVEN name is 'Pierre'.
My objection is to his surname being known as 'Dufour-Henry'.

I have no objection to his acquiring a new given name, such that his full name becomes, Pierre Dufour Henry, or P.D. Henry, which will give him handy initials if he decides to become a detective novelist, but am opposed to his becoming Pierre Dufour-Henry, in other words P. Dufour-Henry. This is partly because it is the law, and partly because I think that double-barrelled names are silly and pretentious, and would never wittingly visit silliness or pretentiousness on any child of mine.

I am sorry if my last letter confused you. Perhaps I could draw your attention to the series of very helpful reference books published by The Oxford University Press, constantly updated, which give guidance on the usage of troublesome items of vocabulary. I believe they are now available on CD ROM should your practice be in the possession of a computer. The thirteen volume version of this work is more than most require, but could I recommend The Shorter Oxford Dictionary in just two volumes. I am sure that the Legal Aid Board would be grateful for some of the savings in letter writing that the acquisition of this would allow. It can be obtained quite inexpensively (compared to law books) from all good book shops.

This letter failed to elicit an answer, but it made me feel better.

THE summer holiday and our trip to Elba was approaching and I for one needed a break from this permanent feeling of being Mr Angry about everything. I'd received a couple more petulant letters from

Rachel Bonham-Lee accusing me of handing Pierre back exhausted and undernourished. 'We would be grateful if your client would take great care to ensure that Pierre eats his Weetabix and goes to bed on time ...' or words to that effect. I had become a divorce trainspotter if you can imagine such a thing. 'Did you know that women either leave or boot out their men in nearly eighty per cent of cases?' I tried out on a yawning Roger who was at that moment eyeing up the girl behind the bar.

Strange, I had thought I was getting over all this and now I couldn't drag myself away from the subject. I read every newspaper or magazine article I could find, noticing things like how virtually every murder or suicide in the papers outside of those committed by armed robbers or the insane seemed to have a family breakdown at the bottom of it. Looking for role models in how to behave post-divorce I came to the conclusion that my sympathies lay more with Prince Charles than with Princess Di, who reminded me of Marie-Sophie; whereas Fergie and Andy both deserved praise for maintaining a co-operative front for the children, turning up together at sports days and the like and not fighting in public.

We were going to drive out to Italy, a long way maybe, but Roger had a large, powerful, convertible, stockbroker's Saab which he'd recently acquired. He was keen to test its top speed on the French motorways. Once there we'd join up with a bunch of other friends who'd decided to be more sensible and fly out.

On the day of departure I suddenly realized that work-wise, it was going to be a bit awkward to go and pick Pierre up from school, as I had a few things to finish off before I went. You always do have.

It was one of those occasion where self-representation in legal matters was not going to work so I had to ring up Sally the solicitor to ask Bonham-Lee to ask whether

Marie-Sophie would be prepared to deliver him to me in the former matrimonial car. I couldn't ring Marie-Sophie direct for fear of a row, and any last minute attempts to stop me taking Pierre. Best to take no risks: she could easily stage a life-threatening cold on Pierre's behalf, so tread carefully, don't grind her nose in the dirt that she was the only one not getting away on holiday. Marie-Sophie had just been given a high profile news slot which she couldn't really hide from me. For my part this was good news because it made her busy at work and she couldn't escape so soon after a promotion. A trip to France with Pierre would be off the menu for her for a good while.

I called Sally, asking if she couldn't arrange to have Pierre delivered just this once at 7 p.m. Sally rang Rachel and asked 'Could your client possibly deliver Pierre to the former matrimonial home at seven?' Rachel said she would ask her client. Marie-Sophie said 'He can pick Pierre up from me at seven-thirty'. Rachel rang Sally and would have said something like, 'If your client is in agreement and frankly he is already proving uncooperative about contact, then our client says he can pick Pierre up at around seven-thirty.' Sally called to ask me whether that would be acceptable, and I said 'Bit of a bore that I have to do the trek, but for the sake of a quiet life, yes'.

Sally called Rachel back, and Rachel called Marie-Sophie. Twenty-five minutes of solicitor's time. That's the way the money goes down. I resolved when I came back to knock these Chinese whispers on the head once and for all.

In the event, I reached Marie-Sophie's flat a bit after the 7.30 agreed, so I was a bit late. She was more than a bit cross. A bit rich, her being more than a bit cross. I'd had to trail across London. 'I'm late,' she said. A strange place to put the emphasis, because normally I would expect something accusatory along the lines of 'You're late'.

Late for what? I wondered. She was looking stunning in one of those designer numbers with a slit up the side which she used to wear with me in happier times. The idea was to exhibit a tantalizing glimpse of great leg. It had worked on me. But to stun whom now? I felt a pang of jealousy, quite needlessly, perhaps. Besides I should have been cheering the next bloke along from the sidelines. She might then call off her rottweiler lawyers, and busy herself with organizing the time and place for her next earth-moving orgasm; meanwhile I could have more access. She might merely have been off to some media party. Or out with Tiff for a moan about men.

Arriving at the door with his snorkel in hand, Pierre leapt into my arms and clung like an affectionate baby orang-utan. That annoyed her, I could tell. She gave me a bag of his stuff and copious instructions about not getting him too tired, and another large bag containing embrocations for different parts of his hide in case he got sunburn.

Amazingly, given the history of the build-up to the hand-over, we avoided having a row, even though we came face to face. Could this be a sign of what might be achievable in the future? We might even become friends again. More likely, it was just a sign that this was a very important date she had lined up.

Meanwhile back at the ranch, I still hadn't packed. The plan had been to depart and drive through the night in the multi-valved stockbroker-mobile. That way you get an empty motorway with no speed cops on it, and best of all Pierre would go to sleep and only start yabbering into the driver's left ear somewhere around Turin.

Roger arrived, bringing with him his latest female target: a pretty, young, naïve (ie. tragedy-and-baggage-free) 26-year-old. Fortunately Louise seemed to hit it off with Pierre almost immediately and since she was going to be occupying the cramped back of the car with him, this was important.

When I said baggage-free, I meant emotional baggage. She'd turned up with this vast portmanteau of spare swimming costumes which was going to cause problems in the boot. I decided to leave Pierre's bag of embrocations behind – he could scrounge off Louise.

He was thoroughly overexcited to see his dad, and to be off to the seaside, especially in Roger's convertible. He expressed this by milling around in my way, laying out his Scalectrix on the floor, that sort of thing. 'Can we take this Dad?'

'You must be joking.'

I had to have a few races with him to keep him quiet. I'd got him this set when he was three, in other words for me, really. I am sure many fathers do this. Pierre was Damon Hill to my Michael Schumacher, except that unlike the other Michael, I'm not allowed to win.

'Got the tickets, Michael?' asked Roger.

'Yep.'

'Packed yet?'

'Nearly.'

'Passports?'

'Yep. Oh damn, she forgot to give me his passport. I bet she did it on purpose.'

Just before a midnight departure was not a good time to make this discovery, although better than making it at Dover. I rang Marie-Sophie, but it was only the answerphone. As likely as not she was in the middle of an amazing orgasm with her very important date, Jasper perhaps. Probably she wasn't even at home. To get the passport there was no choice but to drive across London in the 2CV to Knightsbridge and camp outside until she arrived. Before I went I put Pierre to bed, with instructions to an alarmed Roger to be the babysitter, and to take no lip.

By complete chance, as I turned into her road, the car in front of me was Marie-Sophie's. I pulled up behind her in front of her flat. The time was now 1 a.m. She got out one side and, horror of horrors, a man got out the other. But I had no time to worry about this now, I had Roger waiting. 'Hey, Marie-Sophie, the passport,' I shouted. She looked horror-struck.

'Wait there,' she said to the man and me, and dashed upstairs. The fellow was standing like a spare tyre next to her car, looking studiously the other way. He had a pony tail. Slightly paunchy. Dear me.

'Lovely evening, isn't it,' I said. I mean, it was, starlit, romantic. The man didn't reply, but remained silent, shifting from one foot to the other, hands in pocket, and looking off into the distance, insofar as it is possible to look off into the distance in Knightsbridge. The silence was deafening. You could have heard a hedgehog hump (on reflection, not in Knightsbridge).

Fancy going for a man with a pony tail, and an earring. Why one earring? If you are going to go for one earring, then why not two, and if you are going to look like a girl, why not have the hair permed and get some decent rocks for the ears – diamonds, say?

Marie-Sophie came out again and handed over the passport, and then went over to her friend with a pile of books. 'Here are all the books I was going to lend you,' she said, and made a great show of presenting them to him. He looked puzzled.

I got back into my car and screeched away. You can screech away in a 2CV. A little known fact is that because of the gearing the acceleration in the 0–20 range is probably as good as a Saab convertible. It always surprises the GTis at the traffic lights.

I wondered if this bloke was the 'Jasper' Pierre talked

about.

Back home we all decided it would be better to go to bed for a few hours' kip before what my military father would refer to colloquially as a sparrow's fart departure. I didn't sleep though. I was strangely excited by the idea of my ex-wife and this man.

There was also a feeling of a boil being lanced, a cord being cut.

<< >> << >>

The holiday was everything you expect from a holiday. I managed to put all the unfolding horrors enveloping me at home on hold while spending hours building sandcastles and swimming and drinking and eating too much in the evening. The only frustration was watching Roger move in on Louise who I really quite liked, she was the best fun of all the unattached girls in the party She looked great in a bikini and even better without the top bit and was also very solicitous in her handling of Pierre. After a couple of days I gave up on sun-tan oil (filthy slimy stuff), but she took it upon herself to keep Pierre's hide in order, something Marie-Sophie was paranoid about. I could just see a future court welfare report with five paragraphs in it about sunburn and what an irresponsible father I was.

There was the opportunity too to do things with Pierre which Marie-Sophie would have had a fit about. I had a patch as a child living in Malaysia where we children swam all day every day. As a result I swim well, and I've had so much fun over the years jumping off high cliffs into the sea, hurtling down rapids in a canoe and generally doing things which involve having no fear of water, that I felt a duty to demonstrate this potential source of enjoyment to my young son – especially as British pools these days ban diving, bombing, splashing, ducking and all things which are fun (including petting). Swimming pool attendants with whistles are a class of people I'd like to see collectively drowned.

The group of us established a favourite picnic spot round the corner of a headland only reachable in the rubber dinghy with an outboard we'd hired. I liked it because it had a beach on one side with perfect sandcastle sand and cliffs on the other. The cliffs had very deep water under them, were sheer and rose out of the sea at angles which gave us a great choice of spots to dive off – from one foot up to Acapulco height. Even so, I am a responsible parent. I made Pierre put his snorkel on and swim with me while I checked that it was deep enough. The test for this was whether it was three of me deep or not, which it was, comfortably.

'No sharks, Pierre,' I said as I encouraged him to try increasingly high launch points. I got him up to about five metres, not bad for a six-year-old (half the top Olympic board). His mother would have disapproved massively, and it was higher than Roger and Louise managed, even when drunk. I went off fifteen metres, I reckon (what a stuntman – feet first though).

I must say, I did enjoy the company of baggage-free Louise. I couldn't help comparing her with Marcia who, whilst kindness itself, was just a bit too worldly, as well as being baggage-laden. The trouble was that it was Roger who had the fancy convertible automobile. My accessory was a winsome urchin of a child, scarcely a big pulling factor. Although Louise did seem to have taken a shine to him.

We swam out to her while she was sunbathing on her lilo. I couldn't resist doing my shark act, coming up from under the water and tipping her over. Unfortunately, I hadn't spotted that she had had a fat novel beside her. She suffered an uncharacteristic sense of humour failure as the lilo floated off in one direction and Jilly Cooper in the other. I did my best to resuscitate the pulped fiction but . . .

Been there, blown that, over to you Roger, I thought.

And so the holiday wended its happy way. On a clear day we could even make out the hills on Corsica from where not even my in-laws would have a telescope trained on us.

<< >> << >>

A T the end of the holiday I thought it better to write a pre-emptive letter to cover myself against accusations of handing Pierre back in flawed condition.

Dear Marie-Sophie,

Pierre had a lovely time, and I think the time away with me has done him a power of good. I managed to keep him from getting sunburnt and I am returning him to you in perfect health. Incidentally his tic appears to have gone. Let's keep it that way.

Love,
Michael

I knew this letter would wind her up a bit but, what the hell. It is sad when you come back from a great holiday even when things are normal. The bit about the tic might seem pointed but it was true.

After a night back at my house I had to return Pierre to his mother, to be left with the mess of his Scalectrix and semi-unpacked holiday clothes. It would have been good to have held on to him for a bit longer. Why not? She wasn't going away, she'd got too much work on. My house was so

untidy – get a grip? Discipline? Self control, etc.? Naah.
Anyway, on holiday I'd read the following article in *The
Times*.

Clean Homes Could Cause Child Cancer

Scientists are to examine whether cleaner homes associated
with rising living standards are responsible for the increase in
leukaemia among children. The investigation will be part of the
world's biggest study of the causes of childhood cancer.

The five-year £6 million study will gather information on
4,000 children with cancer and on a similar number of healthy
children.

Professor Sir Richard Doll, emeritus professor of
epidemiology at Oxford University, said that the virus theory
was 'the most exciting hypothesis we have to test. It could go
a long way to explain a high proportion of childhood cancers'.

It is nice to have the backing of science for being a
complete slob.

<< >> << >>

A month or so later, towards the end of August, Roger
wandered over to my desk. 'I have some inside
information which might be of interest to you.' I
looked at him with as much cynicism as I could muster.
Once or twice I had followed his stock market
recommendations, and they had never worked out for me.
'You didn't buy when I told you to,' he'd say.

'You didn't tell me to buy when you should have told
me. Now what completely worthless inside information do
you have for me this time?'

'Louise has got the hots for you,' he said. 'You're
coming to my drinks party next week aren't you, she'll be
there, get stuck in.'

There was a surprise. We'd got on well but my enduring

memory of Louise was of her incandescent and spluttering about her soggy Jilly Cooper book. On the other hand I was intrigued. It is flattering to think that someone might fancy you from afar.

'Roger, are you being serious for once in your life or is there an ulterior motive somewhere that I'm missing? Have you tried and failed and are you now offering me your left-overs?'

But Roger had an answer for my scepticism. He had taken Louise out to dinner a few times since we'd got back (incidentally, he'd kept this very quiet) but nothing much had come of it because instead he'd got off with Louise's best friend – an affair, which by Roger's standards was showing some legs (three weeks so far). Thus Louise's best friend had told him during pillow talk that Louise now fancied me. 'Now that,' said Roger, 'is inside information. I got inside her to get that information.' Disgusting to the last.

I told Marcia that I had to go to a boring work leaving party for someone, but in fact I needn't have said anything. We had an unspoken rule that we didn't quiz each other about unaccounted for time. We had our little rules and territories, and compartmentalized social lives. There had never been any discussion of her coming on holiday, for example.

This way, I had both the bird in the hand whilst being free to keep an eye on those in the bush. Marcia was great in that she had no jealous streak – or maybe she didn't feel strongly enough about me to feel jealous, not something I questioned at the time.

Nonetheless, something in my manner might have alerted her because she asked, 'Will I see you tonight? The kids are away.'

'I'll see how it goes,' I replied, 'I think there is every chance I will be pretty pissed. I will be doing you a favour if I stay out of your bed. You wouldn't want me there.'

'I like you in any condition,' she said, which was unnecessary but nice all the same.

Roger's was a filthy plutocrat's house in Chelsea, and it was already heaving with Sloany voices by the time I arrived. Louise seemed pleased to see me.

'Still acting hard to get?' were her first words to me. We had a good yabber in which I was largely oblivious to the other people in the room, apart from sticking out an arm occasionally so that Roger – flash git, excellent host – could prime my glass with more champagne. Louise and I even had a laugh about the lilo. Really quite a nice girl.

Anyway, I didn't act hard to get. I am easy to get – she, or anybody else, just need ask. It is a well known fact that all men are interested in one thing. Sigh. Love. Two things. And commitment. Three things. Bugger you, Marie-Sophie.

I flitted around the party, every so often redirecting myself towards Louise to see if I could advance things further. Towards the end of the evening my *methode champenoise* confidence began to flag. A worse for wear couple wedged between us and before I could do anything to prevent it, the bloke had successfully annexed Louise. I was lumbered with the spare girl, who was very pleasant, but that was not the point. I found myself talking over her shoulder. Shortly afterwards the bloke marshalled Louise across the room, making some point about modern British painters with reference to one of Roger's tackier daubs bought off Hyde Park railings.

I decided to cut my losses and head for home. I couldn't avoid Louise and bloke on the way out, so I said a bit sharply, 'See you, Louise.'

She almost leapt at me. 'That thing we were discussing ...'

What thing? Once out of bloke's earshot she added,

'Thanks for rescuing me, God he's *so* boring. And ignorant. Are you really off, will you call me? You've got my number haven't you?'

I felt all tingly. If I'd had my wits about me, I'd have taken her on to a restaurant at the very least, but I am basically risk averse, a coward. I promised I'd call.

Marcia's home was en route to mine so, feeling guilty, I popped in there on the way back.

'You seem a little distracted,' she observed.

Damn female intuition. 'I am,' I said. 'I wasn't really in the party mood, it's the bloody divorce, can't get it out of my mind.' I was learning that divorce was a handy excuse for surly behaviour on all sorts of fronts.

She looked a little sceptical but said: 'Come to bed, I know what you need.'

She was right about what I needed and she was wrong. But where she was wrong I wasn't going to put her right. Somebody to love not just to spend the night with.

<< >> << >>

THE relationship with Marcia had served its purpose, therapy at every level, but somehow I failed to see what future it could have. Time to move on, cut loose. I liked her, but I found my eye wandering off on to some girl on the table off to the left in whatever restaurant we went to. 'She looks nice,' I'd think, and wish I could be chatting her up.

I wondered if there might be a chance that we could part on good terms. This was my first break-up in years and I wasn't looking forward to it. My father says that in his day he used to say, 'Prudence, I fear I'm growing too fond of you. I think it might be better for both us if we saw less of each other for a while.' Quite why, in the late 1940s this was effective is not altogether clear. If you are growing increasingly fond of someone surely you should be considering means of seeing them more, or even asking them to marry you.

I hung off calling her for a bit and ignored her answerphone messages then finally told myself that this wouldn't do and went round to see her.

I said, 'Marcia, I think it might be time for us to go our different ways. You've been good to me, but you deserve better than me. With all this litigation hanging over me, I don't think it is fair to have a girlfriend. I can't give you the attention you deserve. I'm very fond of you but there isn't space in my life for you. It's not your fault. It's mine.' That was roughly what I stammered out.

Funny, but she didn't seem distraught at all. In fact, as usual, she seemed very understanding. Perhaps she had been agonizing over how to give me the boot.

'I knew this was coming. It was very nice while it lasted. But we'll stay friends, won't we?'

I was too confused to contradict her and indeed I hoped we would. 'Yes, of course we will.' I got up to go. At the door I turned to kiss her goodbye, she was understanding to the last.

'Goodbye, Michael. It was fun, but I knew it couldn't last.'

I suppose I did, too. I didn't know whether to think 'Blimey, that was easy' or to be profoundly miserable.

<< >> << >>

AFTER my outing at the end of the last season, one of the things I was getting back into was rugby. This was something which Marie-Sophie couldn't interfere with, although believe it or not she tried. 'You mustn't play rugby, you'll get hurt' she said as I handed Pierre over one day. I did a double take for a moment. Was she starting to be concerned about my welfare? Bit late for that, I thought.

Anyway, there was no danger of me getting hurt, I keep out of danger (the master of the despairing tackle which just misses) but I liked playing rugby because it was one of the few areas of my life which was truly divorced from divorce. The club I play for is peopled mainly by golden oldies and so there aren't even any female groupies to turn one's attention to. Marcia had come to watch me that once, but once had been enough.

An exception to this might have been our prestige fixture against the Lords and Commons XV. I did consider inviting Louise along instead, but then reasoned that it was asking a lot of a first date to make a girl spend all the time on the touch-line getting cold and bored while I had all the fun. No, Louise had better wait.

Having said that I was keen to play not so much for the opportunity for some discrete lobbying about the Child Support Agency but because there was bound to be a coterie of attractive 'research assistants' on the touch-line. Even the dimmest Tory MP will have worked out by now that the wrong kind of girl consort is bad for a political career so I reasoned there should be at least one decent one going spare for me.

It is amazing that MPs have the energy to play rugby after all they are alleged to get up to at night. Nonetheless, they put on a good show on the pitch, won, and what is more were very generous hosts at the subsequent lunch, or at least their sponsors were. Sponsoring a parliamentary sports team may be one of few ways to bribe an MP these days. Now that 'Cash for Questions' has gone out of the window the various parliamentary teams, clubs or whatever are going to become very wealthy.

There did indeed seem to be more female hangers-on than is usual in my type of game so I thought there might be a chance to chat a decent one up but they all said discouraging things like 'That was my husband on the wing'. I failed to find a single research assistant of the right voracious specification. All the women seemed to be spoken for. What chance an impecunious near divorcee bereft even of a Will Carling cleft chin?

Somehow I mismanouevred myself onto a table with only one woman on it, attractive, but out of reach. As a predatory male, I'm hopeless. The man I ended up next to looked like an MP, if not a Peer of the Realm, and I was surprised at how much interest he seemed to take in my conversation, an insincere interest I immediately assumed. Greasy palm pressing politician I thought, because I was of no significance to anyone.

Some wine inside us and he became chummier still. Rugby, of course, is a blokesy contact sport, but nonetheless I recoil a little when an arm wraps itself uninvited around the back of my chair. It might have been my imagination but I thought I sensed a knee colliding gently with mine. My knee I removed from danger, but it might have seemed churlish to remove the arm publicly so I had to let it stay there.

'Would you like a tour of the Houses of Parliament?' he asked. He requested my telephone number. I did what women do in such circumstances – I gave him a false one. He turned out to be something in the catering department and not a politician at all. I would be glad to accept a tour of the Commons, but I was going to be avoiding the kitchens.

<< >> << >>

THE rugby reminded me that I was going to get Pierre going on team sports and organize a bit of football on Thursday contact days. Michele, with whom I had been more or less successful in becoming 'just good friends', did a recruitment drive amongst Jake's (and Pierre's former) school-friends.

It was a great success. The bunch of six- and seven-year-olds in my care had little clue about the rules, showing how little they'd learnt at school. The concepts that there are two sides, that you have to score goals, make space, pass to each other, etc., had clearly never been inculcated, and so to begin with it was more like a rugby scrum than football. One or two little boys did understand and were perfectly happy to score six goals each. The others would soon catch on and realize they were being plundered.

I decided to institute the thing as a regular access Thursday event. The trouble was that my mid-week access with Pierre was only every other week. It seemed hard on Pierre that all his friends would be there the following week and not him, but for the sake of continuity I'd have to do it every week otherwise the parents of the other children would get confused and it would never take off.

I decided to write a letter to Marie-Sophie – direct, I was still sticking to my resolution to avoid the Chinese whisperers. Surely there could be no objection to my having Pierre every week for football? The request was so reasonable. It had nothing to do with law, and affidavits, judges or court welfare officers. Only common sense. Surely. It would benefit Pierre and take some strain off Marie-Sophie. It would use his pent-up energy from doing no exercise at school. He would keep up with his old friends from Clapham. He'd see me more often.

Actually, I didn't add this last point. Or that six months on from that second court hearing, I still hadn't come to terms with seeing Pierre so little. I found the non-Pierre week agonizing and I couldn't begin to understand how such an arrangement could be to his benefit. If going to Dad's is going to be a patch of high excitement followed by the let-down of returning to Mum's and disciplined bedtimes, homework and all the rest, no wonder the process is destructive for children. In my divorce trainspotter mode I'd come across loads of academic research, a consensus even, that dads should be more involved after divorce and yet the system remains stacked against you.

I sent my letter but didn't have much confidence that it would be treated favourably. I could imagine only too well Rachel Bonham-Lee's advice on the subject once she'd told Marie-Sophie how to reply. 'Pierre already returns over-tired and over-excited from access visits with yourself. I reiterate that my client feels you are ruining his good health.'

<< >> << >>

PREDICTABLY, we had an access crisis over the half-term holiday. I'd promised Pierre that he could go and see his grandparents but as soon as Pierre started telling his mother that he was going to see Granny and Grandpa, up went her hackles, and on went her answerphone.

'Marie-Sophie, this is Michael speaking. Would you be so kind as to tell me when I can have Pierre over half-term?'

'Marie-Sophie, Michael again, I left a message a couple of days ago, and I wonder if . . .

'Right, I'm going to take you to court about this.' And I meant it.

At this moment I had two strong factors which to me justified an argument for going to court. The first was this buggering around every time it was my turn for access. Plus I'd had no response to my letter about football. I thought the courts would listen about the extra Thursday when I explained my reasons, even if my wife would not. The second was that Marie-Sophie's threat to take Pierre back to live in France had resurfaced. Pierre had recently let slip something about going to live in France at Christmas. I didn't know if he meant 'live' or 'visit'.

'What do you mean? Just for Christmas? Like when we went for New Year last year? Paris or Corsica?'

'I don't know. Mum says it's to make me better at French.'

'Do you want to go?'

'Yes, silly, I like *Grandmère* and *Grandpère*.'

'What about me and Granny and Grandpa.'

'I like you, too.'

I let it rest there with Pierre, but I certainly wasn't going to do so when it came to his mother. I found the way she made plans without discussing them with me very high- handed. I had this image of a replay of the legal mugging they hit me with when she first removed Pierre, but this time on a larger scale: France not the other side of London.

I had no way of knowing what Marie-Sophie was really thinking, which was what made the whole thing so frightening. Her last spoken words to me had been about the rugby but if I'd hoped for a slight softening towards me, I'd have been wrong. She and I had since only communicated by letters. As she wouldn't answer the phone, I had no way of knowing whether she was in the house or away on some freelance assignment. Short of sitting outside her house every day to catch her and plead with her for an understanding, there was nothing for it but to force a hearing.

The upshot of my last meeting with Muriel and Sally had been that we might have to have seek directions for a full hearing to protect my current access. A directions hearing had been described to me as more or less routine, nothing to worry about, but as it approached, memories of the last trip to court filled my mind. Even now, most of my waking moments were filled with rehearsing replies. I was on a nervous high again. The last time it had taken at least a month to come off it, night sweats and all.

Hank said that my directions hearing should go OK, but I should still be on my guard. Judges can spring surprises on you. It was at a directions hearing the judge had suddenly decided to make his Christopher into a Ward of Court and assign the handling of his best interests to the Official Solicitor. Neither side had asked for this, but the judge had clearly decided that it was the moment to exercise a bit of imagination and flair to break the deadlock.

<< >> << >>

O N the day itself, the same cast of characters (with the exception of Judge Stern) assembled – including Mr Wheedle. Same place (Somerset House), same slightly surreal feeling of meeting someone with whom you have enjoyed every intimacy and finding her protected by a phalanx of rather unpleasant strangers. 'Leave her alone, mind your own business,' I wanted to say.

There are few places where sex is further from your mind than Somerset House, but I confess to a slight frisson on seeing Marie-Sophie. It would really have made things a lot easier if in addition to acting like my mother-in-law, she had begun to look like her, but no, she still looked nice. I noticed that she was still wearing her usual perfume. Jasper obviously wasn't a perfume buyer, then. Confusing.

Muriel was yet again a disappointment. She was very forthright in the corridor that we must get the CWO changed but in court the strongest argument she could come up with was 'We don't think Mr Wheedle is very appropriate'.

James de Vere Crispe said he thought Mr Wheedle was very appropriate, and the judge agreed. 'Mrs Leach, he is a man of very great experience, and he does know the case . . .'

Mr Wheedle himself was sitting to one side of the court. The judge asked him what he would need to do to reassess the case.

'I have already made one report in this case, I am not sure if another would be needed,' he said. He seemed to want to worm his way out of any further involvement. This was the point at which Muriel might have leapt to her feet and said, 'See, Your Honour, he's already made his mind up, he's biased, have him strung up and skewered with hot pokers.' But she didn't. She just sat there.

'Yes, but Mr Wheedle,' quoth the judge, 'that report was done in some haste I believe.'

'Your Honour, in view of the reservations expressed about me, might it not be better if this case were assigned to somebody else?'

'We have every confidence in you.'

'Well . . .' he began. Having tried to get away with a minimalist approach, with the suggestion that the existing report would do, he tried the opposite tack. He seemed willing to try anything to be shot of the case. 'At the very least, in a complex, highly charged and acrimonious case like this one, I would need to see both parties in my office separately, and then I would need to see them in my office together. Following those meetings it would be necessary to see the child in the company of each parent separately at their respective homes. It might be sensible to interview the headteacher . . .'

'Mr Wheedle,' said the judge. 'A moment ago you suggested that the existing report might be adequate. I did not agree with you. Now you are suggesting that no fewer than five meetings are necessary. Is that what you are saying?'

'Er, yes, Your Honour.'

'So be it, but I think we should try not to involve the school. I will bow to your superior experience.' My immediate thought was that the judge was the last person who should be bowing to his superior experience. 'How long,' he continued, 'do you anticipate all this will take?'

James de Vere Crispe interjected. 'Your Honour, I should like to inform the court that my client intends to take the child to France for the Christmas holidays, and so we hope it will be possible for the work to be done before then.'

That put the frighteners up me. Just the Christmas holidays? I needed to know. Go on Muriel, I thought. But the judge was still addressing Mr Wheedle and she obviously didn't think it the moment to interrupt.

'Mr Wheedle what do you say to that?'

'I myself am going on holiday shortly, and,' he thumbed through a large desk diary, 'I have a number of other pressing cases in hand. I do not think I could compile a report much before the end of November or early December.'

'Mrs Leach, is your client happy with early December? Have we a time estimate on the hearing?'

I wanted her to say that we had not been consulted about Marie-Sophie taking Pierre for the Christmas holidays. When would I get to see him, give him his presents, etc? I must get assurances that she would be coming back.

'Muriel . . . we must address the France issue,' I began. But Muriel whispered to me to be quiet. Sally could sort this out for me later. There really was not a great deal that she could do about it right now. Why not? I was furious and on the edge of my seat with worry. Meanwhile the judge was droning on.

'Yes, I think last time matters were rushed and that it might take two days to hear all the evidence.'

The issues as far as I was concerned were simple: one day extra of staying contact a fortnight and a bit more clarity over the length of holidays, plus some means of binding Marie-Sophie into not departing these shores. Not massively complicated.

'Your Honour, I am bound to say that this matter has become very highly charged. Our client is concerned that a number of issues should be examined, and she may call several witnesses. You have heard the views of the court welfare officer, who clearly believes this to be a complicated case.'

What was so complicated? Things were acrimonious, but to nothing like the extent that everyone was trying to make out. They all seeemed to be hamming it up massively. Doubtless they would find things to fill the time.

Mr Wheedle nodded his assent. Crispe continued, 'With the greatest of respect to my learned friend, two days is a very optimistic time estimate. We think that a time estimate of three days would be far more realistic.'

Finally the judge gave his directions. 'I do not entirely share Mr Crispe's pessimism. I accept that one day might not be enough, but am confident that two days should be more than adequate.' He had a brief conversation with his clerk. 'I have found a date in early December. I realize that this is some way off, but it is the best that we can do given the circumstances.'

'We are very grateful, Your Honour,' said Muriel. Are we? I wondered. What for, exactly? Once the judge had finished ordering the timetable he turned to Marie-Sophie and me. 'You have time to come to some understanding about arrangements for yourselves and your child. It really would be better if you could agree things before you come back to court. Please do your best.'

'Hear, hear,' I thought, you tell her. 'She's the one who doesn't like contact.' Except at that point he seemed to be talking more to me.

So there it was. A final hearing in approximately eight weeks' time. Muriel had done nothing to make me think she was worth the £500 or so that she and Sally had cost that morning, so I made my mind up there and then.

'Muriel, it's nothing personal, but I think I've decided that I might as well go it alone. I'll have a patch of representing myself. It will save me a good deal of money, and if I get cold feet at the last moment, I can always use your services again can't I?'

I thought she was hopeless, but there was no point in parting on bad terms. It would have been wrong to personalize her uselessness; it was more a case of divorce lawyers in general being useless.

There is the old proverb, 'It is a foolish lawyer who has himself for a client' and so I thought she might try to dissuade me, but she didn't. She was very pleasant about it. 'I think that is a very wise decision you have made, Michael, and I think that you have the right personality to represent yourself very well.'

I thought she might have told me that before. I'd be £5,000 richer (or less poor).

<< >> << >>

WHEN I got home, I was still reflecting on that one particular phrase: 'My client plans to take Pierre to France for the Christmas holidays . . .'. Supposing she didn't come back as she had threatened? What price access then? I'd spend my life on the Eurostar. That's if Marie Sophie didn't decide to go back to the family home in Corsica.

I decided I'd make this holiday my test case. If I was to represent myself in court it would be as well to get some practice at challenging her lawyers direct. I would probably lose – after all, Pierre had been to France every year since he was born. It would be unreasonable to succeed in stopping him from seeing his grandparents, but my fear that he'd stay was a genuine one. Mainly I wanted to send out a firm long-term message that any attempts to emigrate with or abduct my son would be met very vigorously.

So I started to a hostile letter to the other side's lawyers.

Dear Miss Bonham-Lee

Please note that I am not happy to have heard during the course of today's hearing that Marie-Sophie intends to remove Pierre to France. In the months before our break-up she made no secret of her intention of moving to France and has given me no indication since that she has changed her mind. I hereby give notice that I will not tolerate her going abroad anywhere with Pierre without first consulting me. I think it an outrageous liberty even for her to think that she can dishonestly get away with taking Pierre off to France for Christmas just like that . . .

Before long I was really getting into this lawyerly lark. I nipped down to the deli to show Hank the letter before I posted it.

'Sounds a bit shrill, Michael. Take out "outrageous" and "dishonestly get away with". Tone it down a bit. Remember that a judge might get to read anything you write and you don't want to appear too petty and obsessed. As a general tip, never send a letter the day you wrote it and always take out the adjectives, you know, things like "blatant", "contemptible" or "hysterical". Do your best not to accuse her of lying directly. Still, good to lob a few shots across her bows. Remember Chamberlain? Appeasement doesn't work.'

The letter I got back said:

Dear Mr Henry,
Your Matrimonial Affairs

I am unable to enter into direct correspondence with you except through your solicitor. If you have decided to represent yourself please be so kind as to send us a Notice of Acting in Person, a form for which purpose can be obtained from the court.

Yours sincerely,

Rachel Bonham-Lee

Back to Hank who said in his best British accent, 'Bollocks, you don't need any form. Just send them a letter saying, "I'm now acting in person. Don't be so difficult. Please correspond with me and take my telephone calls. And don't ask me the address for service, because as you well know, asshole, it is the former matrimonial home." On second thoughts, remove the word "asshole". They're just trying to mess you about. If you start to use yourself you are using non-union labour, you're taking work away from lawyers, and they don't like that. They are the last big closed shop and the most powerful. Forty per cent of MPs are lawyers. But you should write to the court, too, so that they know where to send any documentation.'

The whole divorce thing was beginning to take over my life again, but representing myself made me feel I had more control over events. Well, on the legal front. Other things were slipping. My driving for example, was falling apart. It was not that I was becoming aggressive or reckless, only that as I chuntered along I conducted endless dialogues with myself, which meant I didn't pay as much attention as I should to the car in front. I managed not to hit anything, though, perhaps because certain reflexes took over. I did catch myself several times nearly pulling out into the path of an oncoming dust truck, and once came within a hair's breadth of jam-tartdom when crossing the road on foot to buy a newspaper. Don't Drink and Drive campaigns should be replaced with Don't Divorce and Drive ones, but quite whether the medics would be able to develop a blood test for it to help the police secure convictions I couldn't say.

On the way to pick up Pierre, I found myself rehearsing speeches before the judge. I was practising my own form of road rage.

'Your Honour, it should be made crystal clear that my wife is a congenital liar. And Mr de Vere Crispe is a congenital lawyer. Believe me, she shouldn't be allowed to take Pierre to France.'

'Mr Wheedle, you say you have been qualified a long time?'

'Yes it has been twenty-five years since I received my social work qualifications.'

'And you would say that you have had a great deal of experience with children?'

The judge would leap in at this point in defence of his minion. 'Really Mr Henry, I fail to see where this line of questioning is taking us.'

'Your Honour, I would ask you to be patient. You'll see.'

I would bite my tongue and refrain from calling him a thick git.

'Mr Wheedle, would it not be fair to observe that you are a bachelor?' I would apply theatricality to the pause on the word 'bachelor'.

'Well . . .'

'Perhaps one of life's natural bachelors?'

'Really, Mr Henry,' snapped the judge, but the toothpaste was already out of the tube. He'd got the point. (They'd probably be swopping phone numbers after the hearing.)

Tactically I hoped that if I accused Marie-Sophie of planning a move to France, firstly she would deny it, and then secondly I would wring arguments out of her as to why she would never want to. These could then be thrown back in her face if she ever changed her mind. But right now, while she was feeling a little insecure about her hold on custody, only having the interim variety, she might well insist that she loved Britain, its weather, its cold unfriendly people and disgusting food.

I sensed that the main quality her tactical adviser, Rachel Bonham-Lee, brought to the party, was a knowledge of the law combined with nastiness – witness those mindless violence accusations (the accusations being the mindless bit). That's why she was in family law, not earning £250,000 a year drafting City takeover documents. Not that drafting City takeover documents is a noble calling, only that family law, it's where the dross ends up.

It would be good to have it in writing that she never intended to return to France, and how advantageous to her it would be to stay in England. Having despatched the court welfare officer to the boundary of my imagination, I began to compose the letter which would elicit the denials I needed. I shouldn't have been allowed on the road.

<< >> << >>

I had a rather worrying phone call from Michele. She'd been rung up by Rachel Bonham-Lee and asked to visit her offices to help file a further affidavit concerning Marie-Sophie. 'I said I would, Michael, she was a friend of mine, too. But don't worry. I said I'd only do it on one condition. That while I'm happy to confirm that Marie-Sophie is a good mother, I insist on you being put down as a good father. I don't want to take sides.'

I was a bit surprised both at this latest move by my enemies and at Michele's consenting to help them out. But I couldn't deny that she had been on good terms with my wife and, after the way things had turned out with me, I was lucky that Michele was behaving so decently. This could have been her opportunity for a very sweet revenge if she'd wanted it. But no. Not only was she honourable enough to warn me, she was also the lynchpin in the success of my football games. I trusted her to keep her word.

Still, reassured I was not. There was a slight worry that something about Marcia might leak out. Would it matter? Perhaps I was just being paranoid. I hadn't been in contact with Marcia since the break-up. It was lonely without her, not having someone to laugh with, cry with, eat with. If I was honest with myself though, it was the idea of her I missed not the reality. I determined not to go round and beg her to have me back. Even if she was daft enough to still want me, I couldn't see that I had anything to offer her really.

I became tempted by the dating columns. Dating columns are fascinating whatever end of the relationship spectrum you are at, including happily married or happily single. I began circling a few entries: in *Private Eye* there was 'Tall, attractive brunette adventuress, twenty-five, seeks man to sate wanderlust' – sounded good; in *The Times* the typical advertiser seemed to be a widow in her sixties – more Hank's stomping ground than mine; in the *Guardian* they carry a warning that you should take care to meet in a safe public place – this made me feel too insecure to read further. The filthiest entries were the ones in *Loot*: 'Straight, slim, young-looking forty-six-year-old male, own house, WLTM couple for adult fun, Chingford area. GSOH essential.'

WLTM? GSOH? I didn't do crosswords. But Roger was able to tell me. Would Like To Meet and Good Sense Of Humour.

Overall there were far more men advertising than women, presumably for safety reasons. But I did come across. 'Attractive single female, thirty, seeks honest, solvent, caring man with GSOH to explore finer things in life. Photo appreciated.' This sounded fine until I got to thinking that I wouldn't want my photo to fall into just anybody's hands. Besides, she would get about 60 responses and if I was one of the lucky few who got summoned for perusal, she'd probably turn out to be dumpy and hunchbacked with acne.

In the end I decided I couldn't possibly advertise and there was no point in answering. (Since, I have actually met someone who bought an ad for her older, nearly-on-the-shelf sister (age 38?) who actally got 60 replies. By the time she had filtered out all the obvious perverts and sad fuckers that still left fifteen to interview. She married one of them.)

I did answer one advertisement. It read 'Men wanted – we have lots of gorgeous women waiting for you at our dining club'. This reflected Roger's buyers' market, I thought, having heard that men were in short supply, and thus believing that I might be invited out on a jolly once every so often with her paying. But a letter came back inviting me to join the Janet Epstein Dining Club for the fee of £50. Forget that.

How about going on a computer dating database? The male half of one of the happy couples photographed in the ad had a bog-brush beard of the kind where you still have to shave. If you are the kind of person who has a beard and still has to shave no wonder you have trouble pulling women.

The form you fill in misses the point. Yes, I can tick the

boxes for 'countryside', 'classical music', 'cinema', 'sports', 'wining/dining', 'drinking', 'travel'. I can put a cross by 'smoking', 'pop music', 'watching TV' (unless it's sport). Then I can create some disinformation. To create the right impression, you probably need to tick 'romantic', 'reliable', 'considerate', 'warmhearted'. I could be totally honest about some other things that a woman might like to know – my age, gender, build (bean pole). After that it got difficult:

1. **Job**: freelance translator. (Without prospects.)

2. **Marital status**: up in the air. (Who wants involvement with someone in the thick of an acrimonious divorce?)

3. **GSOH**: definitely. (If you can stand endless wife and mother-in-law jokes.)

4. **State of solvency**: parlous. (Since my solicitor's bill for a custody case we lost, I'd be looking for any date of mine to pay.)

5. **Disgusting habits**: endearing, I think not. (I swig out of the cooking sherry bottle, and leave the loo door open. Fart in bed. Snore – involuntarily.)

6. **How filthy my fridge is**: very. (Some of the many exciting delicacies in my fridge waiting to be melded have mould on them. I believe that exposure to the listeria bacteria on soft cheese is good for you. Marie-Sophie, being French, did not give up brie when pregnant, for which I admired her greatly.)

7. **Physical health**: not bad. (Given that I hadn't slept properly since February. Except for brief patch when Marcia taught me the derivation of the expression 'shagged out'.)

8. **Mental health**: reasonable. (Unless can't sleep and the only things on telly at 4 a.m. are either cult bands from the

1970s with, if unlucky, previously unbroadcast footage, or porn dubbed into German. In which case, madness is only a short step away. Exacerbated by lying awake imagining murder scenarios for the wife, Rachel Bonham-Lee, James de Vere Crispe, Mr Wheedle, Judge Stern, Tiffany, etc.)

9. **Housekeeping**: passable. (Like the Hotel Metropole, Beirut, circa 1986, after a direct hit. Not a romantic spot to lure a catch back to. Might bring out the mother in the right kind of woman.)

10. **Emotional baggage**: items 1– 9 above.

So, there we are. I was faced with the divorcee's dilemma. To lie or not to lie? If, on the other hand, I were to take advantage of introductions by friends, I would carry the burden of responsibility. If you let a friend's friend down badly it doesn't go down too well. As with Marcia, I didn't want to feel guilty if – no, when – it all went wrong.

If I couldn't have immediate transport-you-to-the-stars love I wanted irresponsibility. Fear of the C-word, commitment? Of course not. I just wanted to sow a few wild oats while I had the opportunity, before my next marriage.

Caveat emptor – buyer beware. I wouldn't touch me with a barge pole. With the despairing thought that on paper at least I was not a very good bet, I went to bed.

<< >> << >>

I had an idea for some bridge building with Marie-Sophie. Pierre's seventh birthday seemed to me like an opportunity for a truce along the lines of Christmas 1914 when the British Tommies and the German Scuttle heads spontaneously stopped shooting each other and had a game of football in No Man's Land. Since the subject of Christmas promised to inflame hostilities, our equivalent would, I hoped, be a birthday party for Pierre.

I anticipated that there would be no chance of holding the thing in her flat, the inside of which I still had not seen, so I wrote her a letter suggesting the Former Matrimonial Home as a venue. In due course a polite but stilted reply came in Marie-Sophie's funny French handwriting saying that she had 'considered this matter very carefully, but the time was not yet right for a joint approach . . .' The English was stilted, but it was far too good for the letter to have been drafted by anyone but her solicitor. I noted the way it carefully avoided direct mention of a birthday party, presumably to avoid the risk of looking curmudgeonly if I displayed it in a bunch of documents for a judge. Never mind, I quietly abandoned the idea. Pierre and I would have a little celebration of our own. I'd take him out with Jake and spoil him a bit.

Shortly afterwards, I was picking Pierre up for weekend access one Friday afternoon and unusually there had been no communication that he had a cold or anything to prevent contact going ahead. I was a minute or two late, no more, and was surprised and a little alarmed to see Pierre and another child being led out of the school playground by a young bloke of about 23.

Pierre saw me and immediately shouted to me. I went over.

I turned to the young man and said, 'Where do you think you are taking my child?'

'I'm sorry, who are you?' The man looked confused and surprised.

'I'm his father. That's why he called me "Dad". That's usually why children call men dad.'

'Oh. I guess you must be . . . Hi, I'm Zack . . . Er, Marie-Sophie said you weren't coming today. I'm taking Pierre home for her.'

'You'll just have to tell her he's not coming home. It's

by court order.'

Zack shrugged his shoulders. 'OK. My girlfriend normally picks them up, I was just helping out.' I thought he was going to tell me to 'Mellow out, man' but he didn't.

'Who's he?' I asked Pierre once we had got into the car.

'That's Zack. He's Christa's boyfriend. Christa picks me up from school when Mum's working.'

'I see.' I didn't though. Shouldn't I know about it if complete strangers were looking after my child?

Pierre interrupted my choleric thoughts. The last thing you should do is take out your anger on completely innocent parties like your small son.

'Jasper . . .' he said.

'I am not Jasper,' I replied, too sharply.

'Sorry Dad . . .'

I softened my voice. 'Who is this Jasper? I want to know. Is Jasper your mum's boyfriend?'

'Don't be silly. She's married to you. She can't have a boyfriend.'

Well she was still my wife but only for a few months more. Obviously he hadn't understood when I'd spoken to him about divorce and the judge. Perhaps he was in a state of denial as I had been when first told of my wife's intentions.

'Can we go to Mark Donald's? Auntie Tiffany takes me there when she picks me up from school. She's got a BMW.'

This statement succeeded in annoying me further on four separate accounts: 1) mere mention of Tiffany; 2) her elevation to aunt status; 3) that 'Aunt' Tiffany was picking Pierre up from school when I, his father, was available and willing; 4) she had a BMW.

'Tiffany is not your aunt.'

'Mum says she is.'

'Tiffany is not my sister nor is she your mother's sister.

She is not your aunt. Aunts are members of your family. Tiffany is not a member of our family.'

'But can we go to Mark Donald's?'

'No,' I said.

Pierre used to go on about his friend Mark a lot, and it took me ages to work out what he meant; Mark sounded like a very spoilt child.

'You always get a present at Mark Donald's,' Pierre had told me. Mark sounded poisonous. It was a friendship his mother and I agreed we never wished to encourage. Pierre, however, had an unerring sense of his parent's frailties. He had the clincher argument. 'Mum took me to Mark Donald's.'

Right, I thought, I'll double the excitement. I parked the car at the first functioning metre I could find prompting one of Pierre's favourite observations, 'When a parking metre says "Out of Order" how does it know it is out of order?'

I ignored him and waved down the first black cab that came by. If he liked Mark Donald's so much, I would take him to a drive-thru one.

I hate McDonald's with its amazingly successful formula. The child is unfailingly delighted as he eats the chips and extracts the 'present' that costs 59p extra if you don't get a 'Happy Meal' (TM).

Pierre was about two and a half when he realized that the plastic toys come in sets of four, making at least four visits necessary. The sets change often, and the word goes round like wildfire in the school playground, where children discuss these things, and the cycle restarts.

The taxi driver said, 'You're not going to eat that lot in here are you, sir?' That had been the whole idea. Pierre loved black cabs and he loved McDonald's – the juxtaposition would have been a winner.

Back home, I rescued the now limp chips, and restored

the crispiness by frying them in a bit of olive oil, adding a touch of soy sauce and some garlic to give them a bit more bite. I can recommend this. McDonald's chips on their own are a trial. They seem specially formulated to stick in your throat and make you buy a drink. I had a Big Mac, tastier, I think, than Kentucky Fried, but the '100% beef' promise? I'd settle for less beef, and some herbs and spices, even some padding.

Pierre doesn't like pickles so he gave me his. I binned them and poured some of Mrs M's Jamaican Pickle and sliced in some of my home grown tomatoes. At last, my idea of a bit of flavour.

Marie-Sophie and I had big disagreements during our marriage, but she was right about some things. In France, most restaurants will welcome children, but here we have a children-should-be-seen-and-not-heard culture and only the fast food chains take them seriously. We get what we deserve.

'Dad,' he said as my mood recovered, 'I wanted to go and stay at Mum's work, but not for ever. Why can't I stay at your house more?'

I'd had this sort of questioning from Pierre several times and it had always been difficult to know what to say. On the other hand the Children Act allows for the wishes of the child to be taken into account so I didn't see how I could be criticized for explaining things to him as they were, so I did, reminding him about judges and Mr Wheedle. 'Mr Wheedle might be coming to see you again, so when he does you just have to ask him.'

He looked very thoughtful and then repeated back to me what I'd explained to him. 'So if I tell the judgeman I want to stay with you more he'll let me?'

'I think so,' I said.

<< >> << >>

O NCE I'd got Pierre to bed I rang Marie-Sophie to ask what she'd been playing at and to demand who Zack was and why, if ever she couldn't pick Pierre up from school, she didn't let me. I shouldn't have called. I'd expected to get the answer machine but evidently my wife had some explaining she wanted to do on this one. The conversation soon spiralled out of control and probably with it any chance of a positive answer to my request for football every Thursday.

I'm not sure which of us put the phone down on the other, but I decided this Zack incident was the occasion for one of my stiff solicitor-style letters to R. Bonham Lee rather than M-S. Dufour. The equivalent of a disgusted of Tunbridge Wells to the Queen.

Dear Ms Bonham-Lee,

1. Today I was due to collect Pierre from school. I was surprised upon arrival at the school to find Pierre being escorted away by a young man who told me his name was 'Zack'.

2. Pierre informs me that 'Zack' is 'Christa's boyfriend'. I would like to know by immediate return the full identities of 'Zack' and 'Christa'.

3. I would like to be informed whether or not Christa is a registered child-minder.

4. I may say that I mentioned this in a telephone call to my wife. I forget the precise formula of words she used in turning down my request for information, but suffice it to say that her choice of words was both abusive and dismissive. She might have said 'fuck off'.

5. I would take the opportunity to remind you also that neither you nor your client has yet replied to my letter(s) about football.

6. **I would take the opportunity to remind you that neither**

you nor your client has yet replied about her wish to take Pierre away during the Christmas period.

Yours sincerely

Michael Henry

<< >> << >>

I finally got a letter from Rachel Bonham-Lee confirming that their client planned to take Pierre to France for the whole three week holiday to see *Grandmère* and *Grandpère*. Marie-Sophie obviously seemed to envisage me not having him to stay at all. The trouble with Judge Stern's original order was that it didn't specify anything on the holidays. It only said '. . . and such reasonable additional contact as can be agreed between the parties'. 'Reasonable', I have since discovered, is a word which crops up in many areas of law, not just the Family Division. Lawyers love it because you can litigate about what the word 'reasonable' means for ever.

I went round to Somerset House in my lunch-break. I needed to swot up on the best form of defence. The clerks were very helpful, giving me the correct forms, telling me where to go to pay my £35 and so on. Okay, I thought, if my wife and Rachel weren't going to play fair then neither was I. I applied for a Prohibited Steps Order to prevent Marie-Sophie from going to France at all. I thought there was no chance of such an application succeeding, indeed I wanted Pierre to keep up with his French relations, but as Hank had advised, I was going to lob some shells.

To keep me focused, I kept reminding myself of that poor unfortunate at Families Need Fathers who had had his children taken to Australia. The judge said 'Fine, go to Australia'. No matter that the father now would be faced with an expensive flight, and nowhere to stay and entertain his kids on the other side of the world when he arrived. It must really hurt. And if that was Australia, how much easier would it be for a judge to say 'Fine, go to France'.

I brought my application *'ex parte'*, as advised by Hank. It is a way of jumping the queue for emergency cases. I had actually chosen to go *'ex parte* at notice', which allowed my opponents a week's notice to back down and be 'reasonable'. In fact, looking back on it, this must have been the procedure with which Rachel got us all into court so quickly when Marie-Sophie first abducted Pierre.

Unfortunately, they wouldn't be reasonable, so we found ourselves back in the courtroom for the second time in three weeks.

James de Vere Crispe with his pale skin and purplish lips stood up before the duty judge and made his deposition. Really it should have been me talking first because it was my application, but the judge explained that 'it would be better if Mr Crispe speaks as he is more accustomed to our procedures, and I assure you I will not allow that to disadvantage you'.

'My client's mother is dangerously ill in France, she has a brain tumour,' Crispe said.

This was not a surprise exactly. Just something of an exaggeration. She'd had several before – of the imaginary kind. Actually she did have a growth in her head – it had been discovered years before and had proven benign, indeed was possibly the only benign thing in her head.

'Well Mr Henry, that does sound very serious to me,' said the judge.

What could I say? I could hardly explain that like most French women my mother-in-law was a hypochondriac, never happier than when administering a fistful of suppositories. Or that while I was aware of the growth in her head I did not believe she had a brain tumour. I'd just appear completely heartless and hate-filled and, knowing my luck, this would be the occasion on which she wasn't crying wolf.

A decision was rapidly arrived at. Pierre to France for the first two weeks of the holiday, me to get him for one at the end, the sort of equitable distribution I was becoming accustomed to. Plus the December court hearing would now be postponed until the end of January. If I hadn't won, I had at least bought myself a bit more time before the big one. Meanwhile, I had also garnered a bit of experience of representing myself in court. I'd not done too badly. Next time, and it didn't look as though we were going to avoid my big hearing, I'd do better.

<< >> << >>

NEXT time, sigh, the whole thing was relentless as yet another letter arrived.

Our client feels that the former matrimonial home is far too big for the respondent, it must be put on the market and sold immediately . . . Our client feels that her increased responsibilities towards the child are affecting her income and that the respondent must make her welfare his concern . . .

It was not my fault that the house was far too big, she made the space. Besides, if she wanted the benefits of the sale, she could pay me half the monies I'd invested in the mortgage. If it was fine for her to have a flat in Knightsbridge, it was bloody well fine for me to have a house in Clapham.

I needed a big mortgage, too: high financial outgoings mean low maintenance because your housing costs, however big, are one of the things that the Child Support

Agency's rigid formula takes into account. Not that I wanted to duck my financial responsibilities. But Marie-Sophie was employed and, evidently, adept at stashing cash. I didn't see why I should I pay for her at all.

I wrote back a letter saying that I needed the space. Pierre needed a room, I needed my office. Plus there was no point in selling the house while the equity in it was negative. I'm not sure it was but I wasn't going to let them take my house away from me. No chance.

Unlike conventional householders, I suddenly had every reason to make the house look as tatty as possible. Helpfully, the near-identical house opposite had been repossessed by the building society and knocked down at auction at a price which gave a great deal of credence to my protestations that selling would not improve the combined family finances. I thought it was funny how in a court of law they talk about 'family finances' after a divorce.

I wrote another letter to put in the same envelope to say 'How about responding to my letter on football?' and a third saying 'Did you get my letter about Zack?' Perhaps separate letters on separate issues was the way to go.

Meanwhile, I rang Hank who advised me to spin things out for as long as possible on the money front. 'Let her build a track record for paying for herself. She can afford to, can't she?' She certainly wasn't likely to starve. Anyway, she had cited her earnings stability as a factor to get Pierre. Yep, on matters of 'ancillary relief', delay and obfuscation was the way to go. I'd answer on the third request and, when I did finally, I'd ask lots of obscure and detailed questions. Rachel would love the detailed approach; we could get hopelessly bogged down and she'd earn a fortune in the process.

<< >> << >>

I decided to pick Roger's brains about my potential financial problems over a lunch-time pint. I figured it would appeal to his vanity. Vain people love giving advice and people in high finance love applying their insights into low finance.

I thought the great thing about my firm was that it had an understanding of the personal needs of its employees. It was true of stockbroking in general that many employees needed their pay structured cleverly, usually for reasons of 'tax planning'. Divorce must be a factor too, I surmised. Most stockbrokers became stockbrokers in the 1980s. In the mid-1990s the median description of a stockbroker is age 35, married five years, two children. Wife pissed off with stressed out workaholic husband she never sees. Likes the money, though. Works out that if she leaves him, or better still boots him out, she'll get the house, an income and the kids.

Broking firms, for their part, don't want to lose experienced staff, so the personnel department is used to constructing pay packages to help hang on to them. The trick is to get the variable portion of the earnings – aka the performance related bonus – as high as possible in order to keep the rapacious hands of the ex-wife off it. Shame I wasn't going to get one.

'Resign,' said Roger.

'Resign?'

'Go freelance. Then Marie-Sophie can't accuse you of being on a salary and you can say you've got more time on your hands for the sprog . . .'

'But I already work at home quite a lot.'

'You're telling me and you're for the chop unless you're careful. All this divorce crap is doing us all in. She's left you, so what? Hundreds of fish in the sea. Why can't you get shagged? I mean, why didn't you ring Louise? A bloke couldn't be more generous, invites you to his party, provides the girl even though he has an eye for her himself. I don't know what the hell's got into you Michael? But the boss is worried that you spend your whole time writing letters or on the phone to your solicitor. You're addled mate.'

I took a good swallow of my pint. Why didn't I think that Roger was winding me up? My plan was not exactly on course. Was he indirectly telling me I was for the push? Somehow I didn't think now was the time to broach the subject of Marcia or Michele.

I did a quick calculation. Freelance? Maybe, but what about the risks? Stockbroking firms are notoriously cyclical; you can be rushed off your feet earning good money for six months as markets go berserk, then suddenly find yourself with nothing to do at all. But then if I was to set up on my own, now was the time to do it. As I saw it, year one in self-employment would see me earn very little indeed. I had loads of off-settable setting-up costs to be taken into account: new computer, angle-poise lamp, reams of A4, paperclips. It could be made to add up just as it does on Visa bills. I can never understand how all those disparate items for £10.53 and £17.36 add up to £633.91 each month, but when you reach for the calculator in disbelief, they always do. Expenses big, income small. The latter would be easy: either work less hard, or get really sloppy about invoicing; do a bit of stuff for cash as well.

'Do your homework. Seriously Michael, think about it. I can't keep covering your arse for you mate. Got my bonus to think about. You can't keep bringing your homelife into the office. They don't mix. You gotta get tough. Love 'em and leave 'em that what's I say . . . My round? . . .'

<< >> << >>

I went to see the personnel officer and it was all settled that I would go freelance immediately (at their suggestion). I didn't analyse this too much. I did my CV and sent the word out there that Michael Henry was now freelance. Not having to work out my notice period meant that I managed to earn double money for the first month which was a start.

As Roger had said, one positive spin off was that I could choose when I'd work more easily, which for a father bound by inflexible court orders as to when he could see his child was important. As Families Need Fathers said in one of their hand-outs, 'Never miss contact, never let your child down.'

I wondered how many other divorcing couples decided to go part-time or freelance, deciding that work is no longer worth the candle – especially if the price of work means not seeing little Johnny any more. The effect on the economy must be enormous. The real mystery though, is how people manage to hang on to their jobs at all during this period of emotional strain and time-consuming visits to solicitors, court appearances, marriage counselling, etc.

Michele also came to my aid. She rang to tell me that she had a friend called Rupert who needed a room for a few months. She'd actually met him through the dating columns and they'd got on well, though he'd not got on as well with Michele as I had. Not that I want to be competitive about these things. He'd been made redundant by the army in a round of defence cuts and needed a base from which to plot his assault on civvy street. Could I help him out by any chance? He'd pay generously. She had thought about it herself but . . .

The other interesting thing she had to tell me was that she had indeed gone to see Rachel Bonham-Lee and found it a very upsetting experience. 'I'd have been a very good witness for Marie-Sophie as a mother – whatever you may think Michael she seems perfectly OK to me – but they weren't interested in that at all. I went to quite a bit of effort to get there and then all they were interested in doing was getting the dirt on you and how wicked your family were to Marie-Sophie. Anyway I refused to do it. They haven't thanked me, and I haven't heard from them since.'

As a lodger Rupert was ideal, paid his rent up-front and in cash. He seemed to know instinctively not to talk to me at breakfast-time, usually left the bathroom clean, and after an early attempt at an omelette, only messed up the kitchen with polystyrene containers from McDonald's and the local kebab store. The spare bedroom had only a single bed so if he ever made any conquests, he couldn't ever realistically bring them home. I was glad about this as it would have been a kind of torture to hear gleeful grunting going on in the next room.

It was quite interesting to observe a fellow single man operating from close quarters. I quickly got the impression of a bloke who had not been in a long-term relationship for quite a while. Despite this, or maybe because of it, he seemed to have a stream of attractive sounding women phoning him up. Occasionally he would disappear for a few days and when he returned would explain cryptically that he had been 'off on manouevres'.

Since going freelance I was seeing less of Roger but he gave me a call one day to suggest I joined his team in a five-a-side dating match, a 'singles' party. I wasn't sure if it sounded ghastly or great. 'I've got some nice women lined up,' he promised. 'I'll give the opposing team captain your telephone number and you can organize our team. She's called Helen.'

Very soon afterwards Helen called. She explained to me that fixtures took place once every two months at a certain wine bar. Normally it is five-a-side 'unless,' she said, hope seeming to creep into her voice, 'you can raise more'. So I got Rupert and then roped in a few of my sadder colleagues from the rugby team.

The night of the great dating match came. Helen was in PR. They always are, this kind of girl. She had given very precise instructions of where to meet, at what time and how, and was clearly used to organizing events, marshalling troops. How Margaret Thatcher might have been if she had been preoccupied with procreation not politics.

Our team formed up at a pub beforehand for some Dutch courage. I wasn't quite sure whether she'd said 7.30 or 8.30, but plumped for the latter as being more probable. Keep them waiting a bit and the sense of anticipation high. We moved on to the wine bar at about half past eight. There was a gaggle of women the other side of the room with drained gin and tonic glasses. They'd even chewed the bits of lemon.

'Helen?' I ventured.

'Thanks for turning up,' she said looking at her watch. I was surprised by her tone. 'You must be Michael.' She said she hadn't been sure whether we were going to stand them up or not and had left a message on our answerphone. She seemed embarrassed about this. 'If you are a real gentleman you will ignore it.'

The meal passed without incident, which was a shame. I was sat at the end of the table next to a plumpish girl, whose body, I imagined, was like the one attached to the telephone voice of Rachel Bonham-Lee's secretary, Jacquie. She was sweet but painfully shy, and went red every time I spoke to her. By the time we'd asked each other what we did, and had had a halting conversation about what we got up to at weekends, it was clear that opposites were never going to attract.

Maybe not so. At the opposite end of the table there was one girl I very much liked the look of. Typically, she was sitting next to Roger. I kept hoping that Helen would blow a whistle at the end of each course and we'd move round a couple of places to test the chemical bonding elsewhere, but it was not to be. Helen herself wasn't bad, but a bit hard and brassy for my tastes. All that being nice to her PR clients down the phone. She'd had a lovely telephone voice but the reality was disappointing.

When the dinner came to an end Helen suggested we move on to a nightclub. I hate nightclubs. You queue to get into a smoke-filled place, pay to get in, drinks cost double what they do elsewhere, and you can't talk because the music is too loud. If I could dance properly, the tango say, then I'd see the point of it. I decided it was time to cut and run, leaving Roger and Rupert to it.

Once I got home I went straight to the answerphone message I'd been told to ignore.

'This is Helen, it's ten past eight, and I am here as arranged at the wine bar with a group of friends, erm, I understand that we had an arrangement to meet at 7.30, erm, I have to say, that I really thought from the tone of your speech last week that I was dealing with a really intelligent and articulate gentleman, erm, obviously I was mistaken. If by any chance, erm, somebody got cold feet and called the whole thing off, I think it would have been polite if the bastard had let us know.'

Talk about crabby. No wonder she was not married – doomed to a rounds of eternal blind dates.

<< >> << >>

PICKING up Pierre from school one Thursday afternoon I bumped into Christa outside his classroom. I knew it must be Christa because she was with Zack. I had never met her, but Christa had become something of a hate figure in my imagination. She was doing my job. As hate objects go she was rather a disappointment. I wanted her to be shaven-headed with multiple nose rings . . . but she was nothing like that. She was young, fresh-faced and exuded maternal goodness, with the kind of soft, ample bosom small children (inter alia) should be allowed to sink into.

I could hardly ignore her and went over to speak to her. I don't know what words of warning Marie-Sophie had given her about me but I could see she was nervous. Sweat broke out on her nose and her words came out haltingly, in an East European accent, Hungarian possibly.

I asked her about Pierre, how he was doing. I was gathering evidence, I admit, putting her in an awkward position; she would not want to say anything against Marie-Sophie if that was who was employing her. It immediately became embarrassingly obvious that my hate figure was a completely honest person, innocently caught in the crossfire while doing her job. She even seemed to disapprove a little of Marie-Sophie. She told me that Pierre was mainly fine: 'He talks about you a lot. He's crazy about you. It's Dad this, Dad that. He never talks about his mother like that.' I was very touched to hear her tell me this.

One of my biggest anxieties had been that a distance might develop between Pierre and me and she seemed to be saying I had nothing to worry about. I didn't for a moment think that he was crazier about me than about Marie-Sophie, only that Marie-Sophie was making life difficult for herself in believing the orthodoxy about a dad's involvement being better if minimalized. If what Christa said was true, Marie-Sophie must find it maddening to have Pierre going on about his dad in this way, but the cure was obvious. Let him see me more.

'Do you mind if I have your address and telephone number? I think as the father it might be useful to have it. In case something happens,' I said to Christa.

'Of course you can have it,' she said, which was naïve of her. I jotted them down.

'Me and Barbara, [I didn't know who Barbara was but nevermind] we think you must be a very good father. You're always on time. I feel I must tell you that quite often Marie-Sophie is late. Often Pierre is the last child to be picked up although we usually stay to check that someone is coming for him. Your wife usually lets us know if she can't make it at all. But we are worried that one day Pierre will be left by accident. We are very impressed that you are always on time, though . . .' If she went on like this any more I would be in severe danger of falling in love with her.

Pierre came out of the classroom in the middle of a stream of children. Excitedly he introduced me to Christa. 'She's my child-minder. She's very nice.' Damn it. It was impossible to hate her. I even thought I might recruit her as a behind the scenes witness for our looming court hearing. There were only two weeks and I was puzzled not to have heard anything from Mr Wheedle about the multiple meetings he'd said were going to be necessary. I'd checked with Sally and she said it was unusual, too.

In the car on the way back Pierre was on at me about having another baby.

'How old will I be before I get a younger brother or sister?'

I had to explain to him that it would be a half-sibling. Although schools these days get on to the facts of life very early, as far as I could make out he didn't know them yet or that babies were slightly more complicated than a 'just add water' sort of thing.

'Can't you give a seed to Mum like you did when you had me? She can put it in at her house, then we can have a baby.'

'I don't think Mum would agree to that Pierre.'

'Can't you give one to someone else then?'

'You have to be married to have a baby, Pierre.'

'Darren's mum and dad aren't married.'

I ignored this. My comfortable world view had received enough blows this year without yet more.

'You've got to find your mum a nice boyfriend then she might be able to have a baby. What about Jasper?' I asked, unable to resist.

'Mum and Jasper always argue. I haven't seen him for ages,' said Pierre.

'Why is that, Pierre?'

'He's away filming.'

Ha! I reckoned she had broken up with the bastard. Pierre went quiet for a bit, then he said something which surprised me a lot. 'When I go to Corsica at Christmas I'm going to light a candle and say a prayer.'

'Oh, yes, Pierre, what about?'

'I'm going to ask God that you find a nice new girlfriend, get married and have some more babies.'

What could I say to that?

<< >> << >>

I got a letter from Mr Wheedle's office saying that he had been taken ill so would have to delay his visit into the New Year. So that explained that. It actually quite suited me – 'Last Minute Reprieve For Condemned Man'. With a bit more time Marie-Sophie and I might be able to come up with an agreement of some kind which she could live with and which made me feel more secure about France.

For once, Rachel and I managed to agree about something and she got her clerk to go down to the court and shift the whole hearing back to the beginning of February. I was glad to have someone else organize this. It's all very well representing yourself but I was beginning to find the whole prospect too daunting for words. I now seemed to be spending three-quarters of my life writing letters and plotting affidavits and if there was a chance of us all coming to our senses then so much the better.

BACK to more important things. Finding that elusive long-term replacement woman, the mother of my next batch of kids. Louise had said 'Call me' and I never had, so finally I did and she seemed pleased to hear from me. We arranged a date for that week. When I'd said 'What do you want to do?' she'd answered, 'You think of something. Surprise me.'

I was plagued with self-doubt. Where to take her? Roger had been the most recent of her admirers so she wouldn't be on for a take-away or something cheap. Should it be the Savoy with the option of a suite upstairs if things went well? Or, should we meet in a local wine bar, keeping the stakes low, our options more opaque, the pretence maintained that we were considering the 'good to catch up with you, just good friends' option. This might have been the gentlemanly way, putting her under less pressure.

Gentlemanly considerations aside, Louise and I had some knowledge of each other's feelings and so to some extent our cards were already on the table. If we were both really 'gagging for it' perhaps we could skip the date and I should be up-front and say 'Come to bed'. There are people who do this, and the hit rate is said to be excellent. A sharp slap from a woman doesn't hurt too much, though. Makes you feel all manly and Rhett Butlerish. I weighed all these things up and decided to go the route of the set-piece date by candle-light complete with unctuous but unobtrusive waiter in local Italian – plus me paying. So much for men's lib.

But what to wear? A jacket? Overkill. A pair of jeans and favourite sweater with holes in sleeves? Underkill, but warts-and-all honest at least. The blue double-cuffed shirt with yellow pin-stripes and the olive cords. Or the white double-cuffed shirt with red pin-stripes with the olive cords? I discovered to my dismay that I only have olive cords. Or tatty jeans. No pulling kit in my wardrobe at all.

All my shirts were sub-stockbroker work shirts. My leisure shirts were all ex-work shirts with frayed collars. A crafty way round the problem would be to wear a suit and pretend to have come hot-foot from a high-level meeting. Before long different combinations were spread over the Former Matrimonial Bed. I felt like Richard Gere in *American Gigolo*. Eventually I went for a newish pair of jeans (given to me by Marcia), a newish shirt, and a V-neck sweater from Marks and Sparks (also given to me by Marcia). The great thing about girlfriends is that they love to try to smarten you up; the relationship may die, but you get to keep the clothes (unless someone is particularly vindictive and cuts them up or takes them all to a charity shop).

All my ties had been given to me by Marie-Sophie, which is not why I rejected one for this date. No tie reveals the little hairy bit (which stops rather abruptly, should anyone get the second button undone). I also shaved – something I don't normally bother with of an evening, chiefly because I am not so hairy that it is really necessary – but I was taking no risks.

The dinner cost me one hundred and two quid. Blimey. By the tiramisu I think we were both a little flushed. I was describing a try I had once scored – probably the one Marcia didn't see when she came to my rugby match – or some incident at work. I can't really remember – but frankly neither of us was really interested in what I was saying. Pepper-pots, champagne glasses, etc., were marshalled, to illustrate some arcane point on Bill Clinton's leadership, so that our hands could brush lightly against each other. We were the last out of the restaurant.

There was some moonlight as I walked her home. The cold made it natural to put an arm round her shoulders and accept one back round my waist. She invited me in for a coffee. I still didn't presume to think I was home and dry. I remembered something Roger had said: 'She invited me in for a coffee, and what did she give me, bloody coffee.'

I did better than that. The coffee was never made. We had a long lingering kiss on her sofa. After a while I said I must go, which might have been a risky thing to do, but might not. 'Seems a shame,' she said, 'but perhaps you ought.' We had another long, lingering kiss by the door. Then I went. I think I did the right thing. This was love. Nothing must be nasty or smutty about this. Mustn't rush things.

<< >> << >>

IT was now approaching Christmas and it seemed to me things were picking up in my life. Obviously Christmas wasn't going to be quite the same without Pierre, but as a consolation I took him out and bought him the bike he'd wanted for his birthday but which I'd said he couldn't have until he grew out of his old one. He still hadn't grown out of his old one, but there you go.

Then a friend in the translation business came up with an interesting working holiday suggestion which, if not exactly lucrative, would allow me to break even, and you can't ask more of a holiday than that. It sounded a fantastic opportunity. He needed someone to stand in for him at a seminar in the Ugandan capital Kampala, translating for a French aid agency who were involved with helping out refugees from neighbouring Francophone Rwanda. There would be three or four days of work in the run-up to Christmas in a smart hotel, if they have such things in

Uganda, then I could go off and see chimpanzees in the rain forest, go on safari or whatever. It sounded brilliant. It would also be a good diversion from a lonely Christmas period. It would have been even better if I could have combined it with romance and taken Louise along too, but she was off for a week's skiing with three girlfriends on Boxing Day. Nevermind.

By the end of the flight I was already feeling ten years younger. I checked into the Lake Victoria Hotel near Entebbe airport, in a corner of which (the airport, not the hotel) still sits the Air France Boeing 707 disabled by the Israeli commandos freeing Idi Amin's hijacked hostages.

Uganda was in a recovery period after twenty years of civil war and terror under Idi Amin and Milton Obote. It was thus crawling with Land Rover Discoveries and four-wheel-drive Mitsubishis and Toyotas, with UNHCR, European Community Water Project, or Christian Aid written on the side. God knows what they were all up to. I very much doubt that the United Nations High Commissioner for Refugees did.

The Lake Victoria Hotel was the nearest thing you will get to a five-star hotel in Uganda. It had air-conditioning and souvenir shops which took Visa – very civilized. It was over-run with young American Peace Corps workers giving courses in business management to the locals. This seemed to me to be putting the cart before the ancholi ox, but then I suppose it kept a worthwhile proportion of rather earnest preppies off the streets. Their efforts looked a well-meaning waste of time, and I could see that the men being taught would go back to their villages, apply their new learning to the goat-milking rota for about a day and a half, then give up. In a way they would be right to give up. Uganda was so fertile that planting successful crops didn't seem to be one of their problems. Indeed it is said that together Uganda and Rwanda could feed the whole of Africa .

There was a definite buzz about Uganda, in-so-far as anything in this part of Africa buzzes other than with tsetse flies, termites and mosquitos. Locals and aid workers alike seemed quite excited about the leadership of President Museveni. In many African countries no one will say anything rude about the president in public, but over a beer you hear what a corrupt and useless bastard he is. Here, after Amin and Obote (not much better), Museveni was highly rated, even several beers down the line. I even heard the word 'statesman' used. He was said not to be quite in the Mandela class, but nonetheless a decent bloke. He had for example invited the Asians booted out by Amin to reclaim their properties and help kick-start the economy – a decision which had involved a courageous non-racist admission that the indigenous peoples did not yet have the educational wherewithal to do it alone.

I liked Kampala. The bananas tasted better than Sainsbury's. I was fascinated by the edible ants for sale in the market, some ready-fried, some alive-alive-o, but with their wings and legs removed to stop them doing a mass break out. These termites didn't buzz. Being a bit of a culinary stuntman I had a taste. You play with it on your tongue, then as the exoskeleton breaks and the guts of things splurge free of the carapace, flavours are supposed to erupt through your mouth. They are something of an acquired taste (I expect). Actually they didn't taste of much at all, although the fried ones were quite good. They could catch on as a snack, comparable in crunchiness to pork scratchings. I think the stallholder was probably a bit disappointed with me, in the same way as the Japanese get disappointed when you swear to them that you adore raw fish, or the French when one expresses a delight for snails.

Kampala, I was told, was very safe. Marie-Sophie could have wandered around in her Gucci with no fear of having any of it nicked. My interpreting duties were light, involving only a few hours a day, which was good, as the main purpose of taking this trip (for me anyway) was the holiday.

One evening, I'd finished my assignment, and I wandered down to the bar for a drink. I was too in love with everything to feel at all lonely but I felt that I needed to share my enthusiasm with someone. I spent an hour or so chatting to the barman and was perfectly happy when Colette, a translator from Paris I'd been working with asked if she could join me. She, like me, was there for only a short time. In fact, this was her last night.

We were discussing each other's lives in the way that can happen when you meet a perfect stranger in a foreign country who, the chances are, you will never meet again. She said she was a single mum, which raised my hackles. I reject the term. As far as I am concerned, there is no such thing as a single mum unless the father is dead. Still, she made up for it by remarking that she could tell I was a good father: 'I wish my boyfriend was like that.' I thought of my own fears of involvement with Michele or Marcia's children and found myself feeling a bit sorry for her. 'We are more or less separated,' she went on. 'We don't get on any more. If we got married we'd just get divorced again. That wouldn't be any good to me or my child.' I could see the sad logic in that.

Collette was a nice girl, but she was not particularly attractive. It's unkind for a man to comment adversely on the physical appearance of a woman, but I couldn't stop myself from thinking that if all French women looked like her, we might be justified in calling them Frogs. She was a chainsmoker, which I was not keen on. I can't stand baccyfascists who'd ban smoking completely. In fact I'd almost take it up myself in solidarity with smokers who wish to exercise their freedom to smoke. But there is no denying that it is smelly and does get up your nostrils.

She was maybe a shade younger than me and a foot or more shorter, with a round figure. Her cheeks were pouchy, although in her favour it has to be said that her skin was not green or pitted, and her feet were not webbed. If you were looking to flatter you might sum the whole package up with the word 'curvaceous' or 'comfortable'. If you were looking to be brutally honest then you'd say 'frog'. (I wish I wasn't lookist, that I went for women according to the contents of their minds and generosity of spirit, their good humour, but the fact is that a good body and face attracts my interest – at least to begin with.)

In addition, her armpits, visible below her sleeveless frock and hairy in the European manner, were not coping terribly well with the Ugandan humidity. In short, she was ugly and a bit smelly, but quite pleasant to talk to, and made a fine enough companion for the evening.

I mention all this because by the time we had laced various tropical fruit cocktails with strong liquor she had begun to look quite attractive. Not very attractive, it must be said, but quite attractive, and if she was finding me unattractive – as she had every right to do given my thoughts about her – she had a funny way of showing it. There was a lot of touching of hands going on and she had pulled her stool up quite close to mine.

By about half past ten she had begun to look not bad at all.

I was faced with a dilemma of sorts. A man with real moral backbone would have retired before it was too late, but having spent all those years living with Marie-Sophie in which I never strayed once, I seemed to be being presented with an opportunity to conduct an experiment in personal degradation and see whether I felt bad about it afterwards. I could find out 'what it's like', the 'what' being infidelity, a one-night stand with a complete stranger I'd never see again. It was not a particularly tough test in that I was doing well with Louise but not quite going out with her (or staying in with her, to be less euphemistic). I had never deliberately two-timed anyone in my life before and I am ashamed to say that the thought of it was exciting.

Could what I would do next could be described as part of checking out where I had been missing out on life? Perhaps not. It was a selfish gesture anyway. Colette seemed possibly to be 'coming on' to me and I read this as an opportunity for a bit of experimentation in promiscuity, what it would feel like to qualify for that cliché 'only interested in one thing'?

It would be safe sex as well. By this I don't mean HIV-worry-free – Uganda is rife with it – I mean safe sex as in the kind which no one else would ever find out about. The kind that executives are supposed to have when they are away on trips or conferences, or judges have round the back of King's Cross station. No one would ever know. I'd never see her again. Why not have a go?

Even more interestingly I had never slept with somone who was ugly and smelly. Did it matter? Thus I made a conscious decision to allow Colette to nudge up to me and after a short while, when she said, 'Come and see my room, I've got a balcony with a view over Lake Victoria,' I agreed. If you overlook the fact that we had been doing little else but look over Lake Victoria – a stretch of water big enough to have a horizon at the end of it – for the past few days, it was a good enough excuse.

The upshot of the situation was that I believe I rose to the occasion with absolute adequacy. Indeed, so successfully did I overcome my moral scruples, a certain incapacity due to alcohol and a lack of fundamental desire for Colette, that we managed to do it twice. I didn't linger that long in the clinch afterwards, though.

By one in the morning I was back in my own bedroom

and in the shower. Before going to bed, I remembered to put the slip outside the door that tells the cleaner not to come in and, if you're lucky, gets you an English newspaper. Just then, a young attractive Ugandan girl in hotel uniform turned into the corridor.

'Do you require anything, sir?' she asked.

'No thank you, I'm not in the mood,' I replied.

I don't think she knew what I was on about.

<< >> << >>

COLETTE came over to my table at breakfast-time, but I didn't gesture for her to sit down. I felt a bit mean, but the truth was that I couldn't face her. She took no notice and pulled a chair up as close to mine as she could.

'I have a plane to catch,' she said.

'I know,' I said.

She knew I knew, so I also knew that the subtext of this statement was, 'This is your last chance to make a fuss of me, unless, that is, we make arrangements for you to hop across to Paris for a filthy weekend.'

I felt I could add non-committally, 'Have a safe journey. See you sometime,' although this was said with complete insincerity.

'Shall I give you my address?'

I didn't want it, but it would have been rude to say no. I nodded and she wrote it out for me on the back of one of her business cards, so I now had all her co-ordinates and no excuse for arrangements not to be put in place for the Eurostar to scorch between London and Paris.

'Don't you want to give me yours?'

'I haven't got a card,' I lied.

'Here, write it on the back of one of mine.'

'It might be better if I didn't. There are things about me which I haven't explained.' I left the implication of

269

complicated love triangles hanging. I hoped this would make her feel more important, and she'd be satisfied to leave it at that. He's in love with somebody else, but he just couldn't resist me.

'So was that what you English call a "one-night stand"?'

'I'm sorry. Something like that. Look it would just be better if we didn't see each other again. I'm sorry.'

'I think you don't understand about French women,' she said. 'Goodbye.' She turned away with a slightly dramatic flourish and walked off.

'I think I know all about French women,' I said to no one in particular.

'What's a one night stand, Mum?' asked a small boy of about Pierre's age at the next table.

'Just hurry up and finish your breakfast,' she replied.

<< >> << >>

ONCE back in England I rang Pierre in France and he appeared to be having a thoroughly good time, slightly to my chagrin, but I couldn't begrudge him that. It had been a good thing that I had failed at court to stop them going.

'We'll bring you a present back, Dad,' he said. Fat chance, I thought. But at least he'd be home soon.

'I said my prayer in church, Dad.'

'What prayer?'

'I told you. I lit a candle as I did it so it will go up to God. I wished that you could find a nice girl so that you can marry her and I can have some brothers and sisters.'

All this religious stuff made me think that perhaps his grandparents were trying to promote his Catholicism. Meanwhile it struck me that the Pope would be appalled at Pierre using the Church to promote his dad's remarriage before the last one had officially finished. Also, on recent form, it would be severely unlucky for any 'nice girl' to fall into my arms. Louise had sent me two postcards from Val D'Isère of the 'wish you were here, missing you heaps' variety. I hadn't been able to face sending her one, even to tell her about the safe things, like getting rained on in the rain forest while looking for chimpanzees.

Being New Year, I once again addressed the making of resolutions. Perhaps I would make some more definite ones this year: (1) child – get access increased, regularized, stabilized; (2) woman – fall in love with the next Mrs Henry; (3) have fun finding her; (4) but not with anyone ugly or odiferous; (5) get money sorted so that Marie-Sophie could have as little of mine as possible.

Louise was the obvious front-runner for (2). She'd bought me an expensive looking jumper for Christmas and a huge smelly fromage from her skiing trip. I decided I'd be a fool to confess.

<< >> << >>

I was at home one day in early January, slogging away at a particularly dull but urgent translation, when the telephone rang. I decided to leave it. I had to get the translation finished. However, Rupert picked up the receiver upstairs.

'It's for you Michael,' he called down.

'Ello Michael? Is zat you.'

At the other end of the line was Colette.

This surprised me, because I had been careful not to give her my number. This wasn't supposed to happen. The plan had been to conduct my little experiment in personal depravity then never see her again. There had been no plan to create a real love triangle for added excitement and danger. The only thing I could think of was that she had obtained it from the receptionists at the Lake Victoria Hotel, or by careful detective work backwards through the aid agency and thence to the translation agency. Neither method would be that difficult.

Luckily, Colette purported the call to be about business – could I help her for a few minutes with a translation of a letter which she had to write, applying for some European Community money for a project to build wells in Chad? I sensed a larger agenda. The letter was well within her own linguistic grasp and Paris had plenty of Englishmen with linguistic abilities greater than mine roaming the streets. She did not need to go to lengths to track me down if all she wanted was a competent translator.

Being a courteous kind of person and not wanting to compound the meanness of which I was already guilty, I helped her sort out a couple of minor grammatical points and clear up one spelling mistake. Once we'd got that out of the way the conversation got to that awkward 'What shall we talk about next?' phase. I was all for putting the phone down, but I felt I had a duty to chat inanely for a while.

'So, how are you, Michael?' Colette was saying.

'Oh, not too bad.'

'Work going well?'

'OK.'

'Uganda was interesting wasn't it? How did ze rest of your trip go?'

'Oh, fine thank you. I enjoyed the zebras and the crocodiles.'

'Not at too close range I hope. Are you planning any trips to Paris?'

'Can't say that I am. Don't have any family there anymore.'

'That needn't stop you. I have a spare bed. I could show you some sights.'

At that moment Rupert came into the study. I started to

272

roll my eyes at him and began hunting around for a pen and some paper. I scribbled him a note: 'Ring the front doorbell'. He looked puzzled but much to my relief disappeared.

'That's too kind, Colette, but really, I'm a bit strapped for cash at the moment, there's not much of Paris I haven't seen already, about the only bit I haven't seen is the catacombs. I've got no particular plans to go there at the moment.'

'I can guide you round the catacombs.'

'I bet you can. But I'm really tied up here. I've got a court case coming up and really I haven't a weekend to spare.'

'Never mind. I'm coming to London in the third weekend of February, we can see each other then.' She was so thick-skinned. Couldn't she get the message?

We? Help! I paused. 'Bad weekend. I've got Pierre and I'm not very free.'

'That's nice. I can meet Pierre.'

'It would be nice,' I said uncertainly, 'But, I'm taking him off to see his grandparents in the countryside, so we won't be around, what a pity.' This last was added with more certainty.

'What about the weekend afterwards? I could change my plans.'

'I'm playing rugby the next weekend,' I said. 'In Scotland,' I improvized.

'Oh I've always wanted to go to Scotland.'

'Look do you mind, I'm very busy, could I call you back?' At that moment Rupert rang the doorbell. 'My doorbell,' I said. 'That'll be the bike. Urgent translation, I'd better go and sign for it.'

Of course I'd never ring her back. Blimey, I thought, I must have shown her a really good time. Dead grateful as Benjamin Franklin would have said. She was in Paris, I was in London, we'd had Ugandan discussions in Uganda. I'd have thought I'd have been safe.

<< >> << >>

I picked up Pierre from school. Seeing him again was great. I still resented the journey between Knightsbridge and Clapham, but in a way it had become slightly special because he was always so excited to see me, and our conversations had become far more wide-ranging – anything from religion (candles in Corsica), politics (why does John Major have square glasses?), science (gasometers remained popular), love (how do you make babies?), to sport (I can run faster than anyone in my class except Natasha).

I noticed his tic had returned. It was unsettling to watch his little face screw itself up in that involuntary way. I asked him how Corsica had been, how his grandparents were. He paused briefly but then just abruptly changed the subject. I'd love to know whether he did exactly the same when he was with Marie-Sophie, whether there was some kind of in-built loyalty mechanism whereby he protected his parents from each other. Or whether he was just under orders. I did genuinely care how her family were. It could never be said that her mother had a heart of gold from my point of view, but she wasn't all bad and, after all, she was supposed to be suffering from a brain tumour. To ask how she was was a natural question. Suppose she needed a lot of nursing. That would affect me, because Marie-Sophie would end up doing it. Instead Pierre switched the conversation to religion. 'Dad, how big is God?' We eventually settled on larger than the sky, bigger even than space. I loved these conversations and the mad way in which they lurched from subject to subject.

The 2CV was stuck behind a couple of caravans, and held up at roadworks. I raised the problems of traffic flow, which had an abiding fascination for Pierre. An enterprising

274

toy maker would market a police speed-trap scene. Speeding is bad: uses fuel (pollution), is dangerous (causes death to innocents). The toy could have 'Non-violent, educational' on the box. It could even satisfy the desire of small boys for guns and have a non-violent ray-gun for recording the speed of rich bastards in flash, environmentally unfriendly sports cars.

'Why are all the cars going so slowly, Dad?'

'Because they've got caravans.'

He went quiet while he digested this. 'But Dad, we're going slowly, too. Why haven't we got a caravan?'

He was a bright lad, but he still had some way to go on logic. 'When they dig up the road, they always put it back worse, don't they Dad,' he observed wisely, sensing my mood. A good metaphor for a broken marriage, I thought.

We still weren't through the dug up bit and I looked at him in my rear-view mirror. Pierre's face was doing its involuntary blinking. I didn't think I should have a word with Marie-Sophie about it, she already blamed me and the thought of some bum-probing child psychiatrist was too horrible for words.

But it broke your heart to see your child like that . . . or – I watched a bit more. The little swine. He was practising it. I watched a bit longer – definitely trying out different ways of screwing his face up. Even so I didn't think it was a complete put on, it was without doubt a genuine nervous twitch but equally, at some recent point in time, Pierre seemed to have worked out that it was a good device for getting attention.

A loud beep came from the car behind. The road ahead had become clear and a 200-yard gap had opened in front of me. In a way I was reassured that Pierre himself was aware of his tic. He still hadn't quite got to the bottom of God, so I didn't broach the matter with him.

'Where is God, Dad?'

'In heaven.'

'So if I say a prayer how can he hear me?'

'Well, God can be all over the place at the same time.'

'In the car?'

'Yes.'

'In that car?'

'Yes.'

'In the radio?'

'Yes.'

'Even in the ashtray?'

'Er, yes.'

'Why can't we see Him then?'

Fortunately, I managed to get him to accept that God could be invisible by reference to the the number of cartoon characters on telly who have the power to become invisible. That was one lesson in theology easily dealt with.

As we finally cleared the obstruction on Chelsea Bridge, Pierre asked, 'How can God be bigger than space, and fit in the ashtray?'

After football I took Pierre home to feed him and ready him for bed. There were a few new messages waiting for me on the answerphone. The first must have been left just after I left the house to get Pierre. It was a cheery message: 'Hi, Michael, Marie-Sophie here. Pierre's got a bad temperature and I'm taking him to the doctor. I'm afraid he couldn't go to school today, so no need to pick him up.' About three messages further on there was another message from Marie-Sophie. This one gushingly apologetic: 'Michael, it's me at 4.39. Sorry I didn't have time to call you earlier. Pierre is fine, he just seemed a bit hot when I got him up. I took him to school a bit late. Anyway you got him. How was football? Bye.'

Caught with her pants down. I removed the tape and filed it in my 'Evidence' folder.

<< >> << >>

I was getting a bit nervous about my upcoming court hearing. Further meetings at Families Need Fathers had made me think I should have a go at settling this out of court. If other people could manage it, so could I. If I wrote a suitable offer letter with compromises in it designed to head-off the court hearing, Marie-Sophie might consent to football every Thursday and something concrete on the holidays – like half of them – rather than what she thought it 'reasonable' to bestow. Then I'd feel more secure about her intention to return to France, and I could drop the application for a residence order and we could skip the going to court.

So that's what I did, but I marked the letter 'Without Prejudice' which means 'off the record' in the context of legal negotiations. That meant that they could hold me to the detail of my offer, but if they rejected it they could not use the letter in any court proceedings as a sign of weakening of position on my part. It would also give them scope for negotiating which they might like.

I also wrote an open letter restating my request for football every Thursday. Both letters went direct to Marie-Sophie. She could show them to Rachel if she wished, but I had the hopeless hope that she might actually make a decision without having her solicitor hold her hand. It seemed such a little thing for them to concede and would go such a long way to clearing the air between us.

PARTLY because things were getting on top of me and partly because the phone-call from Colette had frightened me, I'd only seen Louise the once since I'd been back. I was in danger of letting the momentum slip a bit again. I needed to make more effort to get on top of things (*double entendre*, unintended).

I decided that I could do with some female advice. I thought about ringing up my sister Katie but in the end plumped for Michele. I could now do so because she was firmly back on side as just good friend; you see, having palmed Rupert off on to me in case he tried anything on, the pair of them had started to go out with each other. Funny old world really.

'Michele, I had this date with a girl I met on holiday [I didn't say which holiday], I think she might be just right for me but the trouble is I've left it a couple of weeks without calling her again and she hasn't called me. I forgot to get her a Christmas present which might have something to do with it, I just didn't know what to get her . . .'

'Michael, you are hopeless,' she said with some feeling. 'For goodness sake, get a grip, ring her up immediately. You shouldn't leave these things, she'll think you're just a chancer.'

'You're right. It wouldn't do for anyone to start thinking that.'

I called Louise and grovelled appropriately. I told her I had a present waiting for her but just hadn't had a free moment to get round and give it to her. 'I'm sorry I haven't called you, I had to have Pierre for a week, and then I've been preoccupied with my court case.'

Against the odds she sounded pleased rather than angry to be hearing from me. I felt forgiven. 'I'd love to see Pierre again,' she said. 'Anyway, if we're going to be seeing each other a bit then you're going to have to fit us both in. By the way, when are you going to get divorced?'

'I don't really know to be quite honest. This coming hearing is about access, I think the divorce is a bit of paperwork which you do later on. I've got a decree nisi and I think the decree absolute happens when you want it to. Or rather when my wife wants it to. Originally she wanted it sorted quickly but it's got put on the back burner for some reason known to her. I'll ask her lawyer shall I?'

Funny, I hadn't thought about this much. Anyway, it was one bit of admin they could pay for. I'd just sign along the dotted line. Anyway, we agreed, a low-key date in which I cooked her something wholesome avoiding ingredients like oysters, asparagus or ground rhino horn. Pierre would do his winsome urchin bit then be put to bed after which Louise and I would have a little kiss on the sofa, and then she'd go home, impressed by my domesticity, aching for more, thinking 'This man should be the father of my children.'

Pierre must have guessed something was in the air when I told him, shortly before she arrived, who was coming to supper. 'Are you going to snog?' he asked. The dreaded 's' word. 'It's disgusting,' he went on. 'Did you snog with my mum?'

I ordered him sharply 'into the bath or else', fearful of more dangerous topics. I had him in his pyjamas when the doorbell sounded. She had a large bunch of flowers for me, a toy car for him. I cringed at the flowers. Not In Front Of The Child, I was thinking. Fortunately Pierre was more interested in the car, an MG with wind-up back wheels.

I failed utterly to get him to bed. Three times I read him a story and put his lights out, three times he could be heard creeping down the stairs again. He knew he'd got me by the whatnots.

Neglected under the grill, my delicately marinaded pork chops had shrivelled into tough little bits of shoe leather. Eventually, Pierre was plonked in front of a Tom and Jerry video in my bedroom and Louise and I shared a tin of ravioli. The salad was good though. When she left she gave me a kiss and said what a sweet boy I had and what a sweet boy I was. Perhaps not all was lost. Not such a bad date then.

<< >> << >>

I wanted to have a chat with Rachel about my 'Without Prejudice' letter suggesting that we call the whole hearing off in exchange for the extra Thursday night and half the hols. We could have an off-the-record discussion and see what could be sorted out. I got through to Rachel at the third attempt, having been fended off for a while by her secretary Jacquie with a selection of 'She's in court this morning', 'She's in a meeting', 'She's at lunch', and finally, 'If it is not urgent could you write it in a letter?'

'I have written a letter,' I said.

I finally got through to a weary and wary sounding Rachel. There was an immediate misunderstanding. She thought I was going to go on at her about not answering my letter about football, as well as a general ear-bending about her failure to communicate with me.

'Yours isn't the only case we have, Mr Henry, I have drafted a reply to your letter but it's still in typing.'

'Right, now that's fine. I don't want a letter I just want to know . . .'

'I think it would be better if you wrote to me with your concerns, I can't be taking endless phone calls.'

'It's your job.'

'Mr Henry, you must only phone me when something is urgent.'

'Who's to say this isn't urgent, she never . . .'

'Mr Henry, if you phone me about every little thing I am going to have trouble getting paid My client is legally aided.' Music to my ears. I liked the sound of her not getting paid. I could see a guerilla strategy developing in which I took up lots of her time in ways that she would have difficulty billing. The trouble with lawyers is that they have an irreconcilable conflict of interest between finishing a case quickly and earning fees.

'That's your problem not mine. I just wanted to find out . . .'

'Mr Henry, I'm very busy, I've just spent the morning at court in a very complicated abduction case.'

'You know about those I suppose. Did you win this one?'

'Mr Henry, you don't win cases in family law.'

'Touched on a raw nerve have I?'

'Mr Henry, I find it very difficult to talk with you. I think you should get a solicitor . . .' At my end the phone went click, indicating that at hers it had probably been slammed down.

I hadn't realized that Marie-Sophie was on legal aid. She probably thought she was getting her legal advisers free. I wondered if it had been spelt out to her that legal aid is just a loan and that if she ever raised any money through her litigation its first port of call would be to repay the Legal Aid Board.

This tiff with Rachel, while fun, worried me a bit. Part of my idea in going it alone had been to strip the Chinese whispers effect of talking through too many middlemen. Now, I'd got a hateful secretary to deal with. Things were spinning gently out of control on the acrimony front.

I got two letters the next morning in separate envelopes from Bonham-Lee and Baldinelli. One said, 'In view of the highly charged nature of this case it might be better if we communicate only by letter or by fax. In emergency it will be possible to leave a message with my secretary Jacquie.'

The other said that 'her client' did not think it would be appropriate to increase mid-week access so that I could play football with Pierre every Thursday as opposed to every other one. Indeed, my hate figure 'questioned the motivation for instituting football at this stage . . .' the thought presumably being that it was an excuse for getting extra access.

<< >> << >>

OUR court case was now booked for the February 3. Mr Wheedle was to come round on the January 25. I had to wonder whether this was not yet another attempt at making sure that I had no time to read his report before the court case.

Mr Wheedle's original plan, as stated to the judge at the directions hearing back in the autumn, involved him mounting an inquiry on the scale of Mrs Justice Butler-Sloss's inquiry into the Cleveland child abuse scandal. Now because of his illness and lack of time he'd had to cancel our individual visits to his office, plus our combined visit, and had decided that it would only be necessary to see us in our individual homes once more with Pierre. This time round I made sure that I had Pierre sufficiently in advance to get him well settled with strict instructions for nothing athletic. I also told him that if he wanted to spend more time with Dad now was his chance to tell Mr Wheedle.

I didn't buy éclairs to get stuck in Mr Wheedle's moustache, and I got hold of a decent teapot. I borrowed Jake to keep Pierre occupied and to show Mr Wheedle an example of the extended community in Clapham.

Mr Wheedle commented that I looked far better this time, much more relaxed. Since one of the things he'd had against me last time was that I had clearly failed to come to terms with the end of my marriage, my new relaxed state seemed like it might be a plus point in his assessment of me.

He took Pierre off to Rupert's room to interview him privately. Rupert had agreed to make himself scarce for the day at Michele's – I didn't think a lodger would go down too well. I hovered at the bottom of the stairs trying to listen to what Pierre said wishing that I'd wired the room for sound. I was trying to get a cup of tea ready at the same time as catching the more important bits of interrogation. I heard him saying that he wanted to see his dad more, quite a brave thing because he was defying his mother. Then Mr Wheedle started to ask him which he considered to be his real home.

'I've got two homes, my mum's and my dad's.'

'No, but which is your real home?'

Pierre paused and I could imagine the look of puzzlement on his face. 'I've got two homes . . .' he repeated in the tone of voice a child has when he has just said that $7 \times 5 = 36$ and can tell from teacher's voice that he isn't quite there.

'No, your real home, Pierre.'

'Mummy's,' he said. And then the conversation moved on to other things.

Before he went I gave Mr Wheedle a copy of the 'Without Prejudice' letter I'd written to Marie-Sophie and Rachel. I wanted to show that I was in the mood for compromise I thought it would go down well. I showed him out. 'Goodbye Mr Wheedle, good riddance, don't come again' I said as soon as his reteating form was out of earshot. As his car drove off I banged the front door firmly shut.

'Pierre,' I called 'It's safe to go to McDonald's now. Come and get your coat on.' The phone rang. 'Hi Michael, how did it go,' Louise said.

It was a bit too soon to have digested the situation but I said that I thought I had got much closer to Mr Wheedle this time. 'He was very friendly. He said that I looked much better than before. I think I got the message across that although I didn't agree with his last recommendation, I think contact with Pierre as recommended by him has been so successful that he should build on that success and recommend more.'

Louise laughed. 'Well I hope it works out for you this time. Damn, got another call on my line. I'll ring you back later. Miss you. See you soonest. Lots of love. Bye . . . Au revoir . . .'

As I replaced the receiver I caught sight of myself in the hall mirror. I was grinning broadly.

THE report arrived a week later, on the Thursday of football, but on the off-week when Pierre wasn't there. The dreaded A4 envelope with 'Lord Chancellor's Department' stamped on the outside was delivered at about 4 p.m.

I tore into it. There was the usual blurb about showing it to no one except a legal adviser, and a history of the case. A few paragraphs down came the onslaught. Obviously Mr Wheedle still didn't like my tea.

It will be clear from the evidence filed by the father that he has maintained an attitude of almost unremitting hostility towards the mother throughout these proceedings. He questions her good faith at every turn, he is suspicious of her intentions, and he has acted in a way likely to undermine and frustrate what she is trying to do for the benefit of their child. Indeed it is symptomatic of this father's highly obsessive attitudes that anyone who takes a different view to his own is considered by him to be guilty of bad faith, mendacity or incompetence. This appears to be his view, inter alia, of His Honour Judge Stern, myself and the mother's solicitors.

When I produced my first report a year ago the parties had only recently separated, and I considered that at that stage Mr Henry seemed 'more vulnerable, emotionally, than his wife,' and less able 'to think clearly about Pierre's future needs' than I hoped he would in time be able to do. I was also of the view that he seemed 'disabled by the trauma of marriage breakdown'. Almost a year later, I am sad to say that he appears to have made little or no significant progress towards accepting that Pierre should live with his mother. He is still embattled and embittered, and his now very close involvement with the pressure group 'Families Need Fathers' seems only to have reinforced his resolve to fight his wife at every turn over almost every inch of disputed territory. I consider that he is putting his long-term relationship with his son at risk by such behaviour.

When I spoke to Pierre on his own at his father's home he was quite relaxed and friendly. He told me that he now likes his new school more than his old school.

We spoke about his two homes, and Pierre told me that he 'works' at his mother's and 'just plays' at his father's. It is clear, though, that Pierre does also play a lot at his mother's, and I am sure that some of the play activities organized by his father are, as he says, geared to learning.

Pierre told me that his mother's was his 'real home'. Pierre told me about his Christmas holiday in Corsica, and he also spoke some French with his father while we were all having tea together.

Pierre still sleeps in his bedroom on contact visits, although he also sleeps in his father's bed.

When I visited Mrs Henry's home I was again impressed by her calm and poise, her excellent care of and relationship with her son, and her ability to manage both a demanding career and discharge her child-care responsibilities in exemplary fashion, as well as dealing with the emotional upheaval of separation and divorce and her husband's angry campaign against her. Mrs Henry told me that Pierre's nervous tic still recurs briefly on occasions. When they were in Corsica this Christmas Pierre did show these symptoms briefly for a day or two after he had spoken to his father on the telephone. While they were in Corsica, Pierre rarely mentioned his father, other than to say of certain activities that he had also done with his father such as swimming.

. . . Pierre feels guilty that he is not with his father, and will tell his mother that it is 'not fair' that he spends more time with her. When I spoke to Pierre on his own at his father's he seemed stressed only when I asked about the time he spent with his father. Though he said he wanted to spend 'more time' with his father, his body language showed enormous tension, and I formed the view that he was reflecting his father's wishes rather than stating his own . . .

Onwards and upwards went the report. 'Putting his relationship with his child at risk.' That shook me. Mr Wheedle was threatening to take Pierre away from me altogether, that's how I read that. The final recommendation was for mid-week access to be stopped, and Sunday night access to be stopped. I was to get a bit extra of the holidays, but Marie-Sophie should be allowed to take him out of the jurisdiction (ie. England) for six weeks a year, me three weeks.

A wailing and a gnashing of teeth. The arrival of this report was probably the worst event of my life so far. I went off to the sports hall for football. I took the report and handed it to Michele. 'I need help, I need a witness. You've got to come to court with me. You've seen me. You've seen Pierre, you know Marie-Sophie, I need you to put the record straight.'

If she turned me down then the other person who could help my case would be Christa, but frankly I thought it would be unfair on her, a completely innocent third party caught in the cross-fire of a rather unpleasant divorce. She'd be bound to say no, but I might be able to persuade her if I offered to sub-poena her so that it looked as though she had come against her will.

I'd started with the idea of increasing contact and to get some certainty built into holiday arrangements. The recommendation was to reduce it sharply. I'd slightly begun to get cold feet about the hearing which is what made me write the 'Without Prejudice' offer. Now I had no choice but to go to court, I couldn't have withdrawn if I'd wanted to. It was about damage limitation.

<< >> << >>

THE big hearing was slated for Monday February 12 and, as luck would have it, I had Pierre for the weekend. Obviously my whole existence was geared around having Pierre to stay but this particular weekend I had a lot of sensitive stuff to prepare and would have preferred it if he'd been with his mother. I got Louise to take him off to the swings on Clapham Common with his new bike while I reread past statements and the new ones filed by Marie-Sophie, Tiffany et al. for this one. Michele also took him off my hands for an afternoon while I went round to see Hank. I'd rung up the court to find out who the judge would be and had been told it was one Judge Rampton.

Hank didn't know a vast amount about him beyond saying that he sometimes sat in the High Court and that he had a reputation as something of a 'muscular Christian', whatever that meant. Public school presumably, and church going; compassionate but firm and fair, one hoped.

<< >> << >>

ON Monday morning I decided that I was in no state to do the school run. I called Louise, 'I don't want to make you late for work, but I don't think I'm in any state to drive, you couldn't take Pierre to school for me could you?'

'Of course. Don't panic. I'll be round in twenty minutes, just leave it to me.'

Thank god for good women. And so to court.

Michele had been reluctant to be involved in the hearing to begin with as her experience of visiting Rachel had upset her. But, by the time she had read Mr Wheedle's report she agreed, a relief because it meant I would not have to subpoena Christa. Michele put the same conditions on me as she had on them when they had tried to recruit her as a witness. Her first condition had been that she would inform the other side of what she was doing so that they could have the opportunity to suggest things for her statement if they wanted. However, they turned this down.

Her second condition was that I make her say nothing at all bad about Marie-Sophie. I liked this condition: one of the things that had bothered me about Tiffany's evidence was that it lashed out at me gratuitously when she hardly knew anything about me. If I was to make an attempt to occupy the moral high ground I would have to avoid doing similar.

Marie-Sophie had also recruited a new witness, a playground superviser who I knew nothing about. His statement of evidence was pretty anodyne: apart from the usual stuff about Marie-Sophie being an incomparable mother it had one petty side-swipe at me – 'Pierre almost never mentions his father, except in an idealistic sort of way – Daddy is stronger than you, Daddy is bigger than you . . .' Pathetic stuff.

I'd also got my father to file a statement. Years serving abroad in the army made him expert at defusing angst-ridden officialdom. He would help dispel the idea that as a family the Henrys were a bunch of hate-filled Francophobes bordering on racists. His statement resisted a temptation to be rude about Marie-Sophie, limiting his comments on her to an expression of regret that she and my parents had never managed to become close. He'd also have no trouble if cross-examined by a whipper-snapper young barrister like Mr Crispe.

One of the things I'd learnt from Hank was that when representing myself at court I could take along a 'McKenzie friend'. The McKenzie friend's role is to keep your papers in order, mop your fevered brow, give quiet advice, and generally stop you from cracking up. I was warned that judges hate McKenzie friends – they take work away from lawyers – and so Hank provided me with a helpful piece of paper, the essence of which is 'Fuck off you toff, you can't stop me having a McKenzie friend'.

The paper looks like this:

A Friend In Court

At the hearing before Judge Bloggs on xxth February it is my intention to act in person and be accompanied by a friend.

Litigants in person are entitled to the presence of a friend (sometimes known as a McKenzie man) arising from the following:

- Rules of the Supreme Court, Order 35 rule 7/1.
- County Courts Act 1984, Section 60 (notes).
- McKenzie v McKenzie [1970] 3 WLR 472.

In order to avoid unnecessary delay on the day of the hearing, please will you place this letter before the court and confirm to me that there is no objection to my proposed course of action.

Signed

(Litigant in Person)

Background: The Court of Appeal ruling on McKenzie, which endorsed the precedent for a friend in court, did in fact relate to a divorce action where the judge had mistakenly debarred the 'friend' of a litigant.

The McKenzie ruling upheld that of Lord Tenterden in Collier v Hicks [7th July 1831] which stated that:
'Any person, whether he be a professional man or not, may attend as a friend of either party, may take notes, may quietly make suggestions, and give advice . . .'

I considered asking Hank to be my McKenzie friend but then I thought a woman would make a better impression, so

I persuaded my sister Katie. She knew all the ins and outs of the case, the history of the marriage, had provided a supportive shoulder upon each bulletin of the latest atrocity committed at the battle front. The idea terrified her – she thought I should be using lawyers – but nonetheless she agreed. A brother in need is a brother in deed. 'Of course I will if you think it will help you, but I won't have to speak will I?' she asked nervously.

'No, no, just keep me calm and on track so I don't crack up.' I said it half-jokingly but I knew I was going to need all the support I could get. I didn't inform the other side that I would be bringing my sister. The law seemed pretty unequivocal on the matter.

We arrived outside the court at the appointed hour to be greeted by Rachel Bonham-Lee and James de Vere Crispe, with Marie-Sophie hovering in the background. I'd told my witnesses to be on stand-by at home, but not to expect to be called until the afternoon, or more likely the next day.

As usual there was some waiting to be done outside court, and there was a point when unusually I found myself next to Marie-Sophie. She looked genuinely tired I noticed and rather vulnerable. I suddenly felt it was worth a final try for an understanding between us, a last attempt to spare us both more pain. 'Look, I'm sorry,' I said. 'Maybe I've fucked up. I'm messing you about. Just let's carry on the way we were, the same access. Just agree and I'll drop this. OK? Just say you won't try and take Pierre away for good without telling me. OK? Please!'

But she shook her head and said simply, 'I'm sorry Michael.' The sanctimonious expression on her face implied that she was fulfilling some awful duty, that she was being cruel to be kind.

There was nothing more to say so we sat there in silence looking at the wall opposite until Mr Wheedle arrived. He greeted Marie-Sophie like a long-lost friend while managing little more to me than an under-the-breath 'Good morning'. I'm sure court welfare officers develop instincts for self-preservation; in my case, if he'd been any more chatty I might well have nutted him.

James de Vere Crispe now approached me. 'Good morning, Mr Henry. I understand that you have your sister with you.'

'Yes. She's going to be my McKenzie friend.'

'I am bound to say that we will object to her presence. Children's cases are confidential, and it would be wrong for your sister to be here.'

Katie threw me a worried look, but I knew where I stood. 'I'm entitled to any McKenzie friend I want, I could win an appeal purely on the basis that my McKenzie friend was excluded. There are appeal court rulings to that effect, you know.'

'Mr Henry, you do not need to tell me the law. Could we perhaps go somewhere quieter? I think perhaps your, er, McKenzie friend should stay behind.'

Although I'd seen him in action plenty of times, this was the first time I'd ever spoken to Mr Crispe direct. It felt odd. Probably for that reason, I meekly agreed to his request and we moved out of the busy corridor running by the courts into the stairwell.

'My client instructs me that she is willing to settle on the basis of the court welfare officer's report. Alternate weekends through to Sunday night?'

And no mid-week contact, I thought.

'Well I'm not. I'll settle as before if I have to, but I'm not settling for that.'

'Mr Henry there is a very unequivocal report against you. I can tell you don't stand a cat's chance in hell of winning this case.'

A cat's chance in hell. I thought this assessment a little unkind, besides, I had nothing to lose now by carrying on with the hearing. Since Mr Wheedle's report the whole thing had become a damage-limitation exercise. If they weren't going to soften their position I had no choice but to slog things out in court.

'I don't agree,' I said. In fact I did agree, but there was nothing for it but to try and hang on to the access I had. 'That report is biased,' I continued. 'In fact it is so obviously biased, so filled with contradictions, that it will collapse under the weight of its own internal contradictions.' I found myself talking like Mr Crispe at his most sonorous.

'Very well, have your little day in court then,' was his parting shot.

My first impression of Judge Rampton was that he seemed forthright and decent, a bit brusque perhaps. His first words were, 'I see Judge Stern sat on this case last time. I think he should hear it again. Do you have any objection to that Mr Henry.'

I said 'No'. In fact I rather relished the opportunity to put him right: 'Where the evidence of Mr and Mrs Henry is in conflict, I prefer the evidence of Mr Henry.' But it was not to be. Judge Stern was part heard on another case and thus not free.

Judge Rampton seemed bit pissed off. 'How long do you think I will need to read these papers, Mr Crispe?'

'About an hour, Your Honour.'

'I will adjourn for an hour then.'

We went out while he read the papers. The suspense was hard to describe. Katie marched me into a coffee shop, but I could barely swallow I was so nervous. My mouth was all dry and tasted quite disgusting and there was that dreadful feeling you get in the stomach when you know that all bodily functions are in remission except vital ones for sustaining life.

When we went back in, Judge Rampton asked James de

Vere Crispe what the time estimate was for the case.

'Two days, Your Honour.'

'Well, having read the papers I am bound to say that this seems to me a very straightforward case. I can't see it taking anything like that length of time.

'Your Honour . . .'

'Yes Mr Crispe?'

'Mr Henry has come to court with his sister. I understand she is some sort of McKenzie friend. We believe that it would be inappropriate for Mr Henry's sister to be present during this hearing. Children's cases are held in private and for good reason. Part of our case will be to demonstrate the hostility experienced by my client for members of Mr Henry's family. Our client is anxious that with Mr Henry's unfortunate insistence on going ahead with this case she may feel constrained in what she feels she may, with regret, have to say when confronted with a member of the family. We do not think it right . . .'

I put up my hand to interrupt.

'Mr Henry, kindly allow Mr Crispe to finish . . .'

'We do not think it right, given the confidentiality in children's cases that a member of his family should be here.'

'Yes, Mr Henry?'

I had delved amongst my papers but failed to find the precedent of Tenterden v Hicks from 1831, or was it Collier v Tenterden, or Lord Hicks, or 1825 . . . I couldn't remember. 'There is a law which says you can have a McKenzie friend, Lord Hicks or something . . .' I rather assumed that the judge would know it. 'There is no worry about my sister hearing these proceedings. She's read all the papers already. There is nothing she doesn't know. What's more, once I get out of here, I'm bound to tell everyone in my family what happened. It wouldn't be human to try and keep that secret.'

'Mr Henry, I am bound to say that I think it would not be helpful to have your sister in court.'

'If my sister is excluded I will find myself alone in this court. My wife is supported by a solicitor, a barrister, his pupil, and frankly the court welfare officer. That's five against one. How will I cope?'

Crispe indicated a desire to speak.

'Yes, Mr Crispe?'

'Your Honour, Mr Henry will cope perfectly well. He has been planning his application for well over half a year. He has prepared detailed statements himself, entered into correspondence with my instructing solicitor. He has had ample time to prepare himself. He had a solicitor and counsel before, and now he has chosen to go it alone. I do not care to speculate why he has come to this decision. It may be that he did not like the advice that he was getting, namely that this application was very unwise.'

'It does seem most regrettable, Mr Henry, that you have chosen this course. You would be much better off with representation. Why, may I ask, did you decide to represent yourself?'

I thought this was none of his business, as indeed it wasn't. I was entitled to the same quality of justice whether represented or not. I didn't dare say so though. 'I just thought it would be better, Your Honour.'

'Mr Henry, I have made my decision, your sister must leave.'

'I want a judgment,' I said. Hank had told me that if the judge seemed about to err on any point, then insist on getting a judgment. That way he would know that I was considering an appeal. After all, the original Mr McKenzie had won his appeal on this very point.

'I don't think a judgment will be necessary. Your sister must leave now.'

'I insist on a judgment.'

'Very well, have your judgment.' His tone of voice was very similar to Mr Crispe's when he'd said 'Have your little day in court'.

Judge Rampton gave his reasons for excluding my sister, which were more or less those concerning confidentiality argued by James de Vere Crispe. My sister got up and left looking upset on my behalf. Round one to the enemy. Suddenly I felt very lonely. It seemed to me that it was not four against one, but five, the fifth man being Judge Rampton.

What with one thing and another time was getting on and Judge Rampton adjourned for lunch. 'Mr Henry,' he said, 'I think you should think things over before coming back but I will say this. Coming into court and conducting your own case, there is no magic to it. To me this seems to be a very clear-cut case. It is very rare that there are any rabbits to be pulled out of hats. It's not like Perry Mason you know.'

Condescending git, I thought.

Katie was waiting in the corridor for me. She was in tears. 'You'd better give up Michael,' she said.

'I think the judge just said something like that, too.'

We went out into the cold air in the courtyard of Somerset House. I was shivering and needed some warmth so we went off in search of a pub.

'Do you want me to stay, Michael?' Katie said.

'Don't worry, just hang around till I go back in again. I'm going to call my solicitor to see what she says.'

I rang Sally to see if she could see any way forward for me, but she wasn't there. I got her senior partner instead. 'Sounds like your case is going down the pan fast,' was all the comfort he could offer.

Perhaps the court welfare officer was right and I was wrong. Perhaps Pierre's best interests would be served by my involvement being reduced. Bollocks, I thought. Poor little chap. He'd be devastated without understanding why and she'd never explain it to him. I thought, no, I won't have this, I'm British. We think we have the best justice in the world, I'm not going to let myself be pushed around. (The thought did run through my head, though, that 'Be British' are said to be the last words of Captain Smith of the Titanic.)

With nothing to lose except everything, I said goodbye to Katie and headed back towards the small courtroom. 'Katie,' I called back. 'I'm going to mess these people about, I'm going to have fun . . .'

<< >> << >>

THE first thing I would do would be to ask for an adjournment while I got another McKenzie friend and if they wouldn't agree I'd conduct a guerilla war until they did.

Mr Rampton was late back from lunch, so the rest of us had to wait a little. The opposition were in buoyant mood. Mr Wheedle had taken a chair near them and was telling Marie-Sophie about the time he'd taken a holiday in Corsica. Crispe had been there too, although Rachel hadn't – she'd heard such good things about it from Marie-Sophie however that she was thinking about it for her next summer holiday. Mr Wheedle chipped in again with the merits of the beaches in the north-west as opposed to further down towards Ajaccio, '. . . and there's always Sardinia, parts of which are very beautiful and unspoilt.'

Suddenly, happy memories of summer holidays past got too much for me. 'Mr Wheedle, if you didn't spend so much of your time either ill or on holiday and did your job properly instead perhaps we wouldn't all be here now,' I said.

All smiles vanished instantly. 'You've all gone quiet

over there' as they sing on the football terraces. They really had gone silent. The court clerk, a nice grandmotherly lady seemed to be embarrassed on my behalf and gave me a kind smile when she thought no one was looking. I was amazed at the power of one not especially sharp comment. Imagine if I really got my oratory going.

'That shut you all up, didn't it,' I said. From jolly party it had gone to pin drop silence. I felt emboldened. 'I'm going to ask for an adjournment,' I said quietly to Crispe. Was it my imagination or did he turn a bit paler?

He turned round to Rachel and said with more urgency in his voice than the situation merited, 'He's going to ask for an adjournment.'

'Court rise,' said the usher. We stood as the judge came in.

'Well, Mr Henry, have you considered things?'

'Yes, I have.' I looked him in the eye. 'It's perfectly obvious that you've already made your mind up in this case. You've banished my McKenzie friend, you've put me under pressure to give up, and yet you haven't heard a word of evidence. You've made your mind up, and that's not fair. I want an adjournment so that I can go away and prepare myself differently.'

He looked me back in the eye. In fact we locked eyeballs. I'd never locked eyeballs with anyone in my life before – it's the kind of Mexican macho thing that gives the Latins a bad name. I made sure that I held my gaze longer than he did. He dropped his eyes and, sheepishly, it seemed to me, muttered, 'Well, I had come to a preliminary opinion, no more than that . . .'

It was a first minor victory. From then on he was at least polite; there were no more cracks about Perry Mason, or disparaging remarks about how regrettable it was that I had chosen to represent myself. But he didn't give me my adjournment.

He invited Mr Crispe to give a summary of the events leading up to the court case.

I said that as it was my application, it should be me who set out the background.

'Mr Henry,' he explained, 'Mr Crispe is used to the way in which we do things here, it will just be quicker that is all.' I could see that he was stuck between exasperation and appeasement. A nice place to have him.

Mr Crispe's style was to talk very fast. He began outlining the history of the case, but then also began to drop in elements of his own which he was not supposed to do at that point. 'You will have seen from the papers that this father's increasingly unusual behaviour . . .' (for which, in lawyer's language, read 'mad, bad and dangerous to know').

'Could you ask Mr Crispe to slow down please sir. I haven't got a McKenzie friend anymore, and I need to take down what he is saying.'

'Mr Crispe, could you slow down a little,' said Judge Rampton.

He paused then started off again at exactly the same speed.

'Your Honour, he is still going too fast.'

'Mr Crispe, please.'

'This father . . .' he started again. He had a peculiar way of making the word 'father' sound like a contagious disease. At first he spoke slowly, but soon gathered momentum, a spot of colour actually returned to his cheeks. I began to get a bit theatrical about how fast I was having to take my notes. I gave him a minute or two, then broke my pencil. I put up my hand.

'Please sir, I've broken my pencil. Does anyone here have a sharpener? Perhaps your clerk. No? Miss Bonham-Lee? I did have some spare pencils but I forgot to get my pencil case back from my McKenzie friend. I'm sorry.'

The judge said, 'Does anyone here have a spare pencil? Perhaps a biro would be better. Miss Bonham-Lee, perhaps you have one?' He eyed his own Montblanc protectively.

Miss Bonham-Lee did have a spare biro and passed it over. 'Can't seem to get it to work,' I said. 'Ahh there we go. Perhaps Mr Crispe would like to continue.'

James de Vere Crispe started again, but the intervening distraction had made him forget that he had to go slowly. My arm was only half-way up and the words 'Please sir' not even formed on my lips when the judge said, 'Really Mr Crispe, could you try to go a little more slowly.'

'Your Honour,' I said, now that I had his attention, 'This is not a situation of my making. This morning you excluded my McKenzie friend, I can't cope. It's five against one.'

'Five?'

'I'm sorry, four. Mr Crispe has a fully trained professional solicitor Miss Bonham-Lee, he has my wife, he has the court welfare officer. How am I supposed to cope?'

Judge Rampton looked at me and then he looked at James de Vere Crispe, before turning to Mr Wheedle. 'Mr Wheedle, perhaps Mr Henry could borrow a telephone to find himself a new McKenzie friend.'

I sensed an immediate reaction from James de Vere Crispe seated at my right. 'This father,' he began, 'is perfectly capable of running his own case without any assistance. He is highly intelligent, very able. A glance at his correspondence with my instructing solicitor will show that he is on top of every detail of this case. It is his own fault that he chose to bring his sister . . .' This was a change in tack. Hitherto I had been the devil incarnate, violent, racist, unloving, a hopeless father – now suddenly I was 'highly intelligent and able'. But Judge Rampton overruled Mr Crispe and adjourned the case while Mr Wheedle took me off to his office in search of a telephone and a new

McKenzie friend. The obvious person was Hank.

'Hank, it's Michael, stuck in court, I need a McKenzie friend, tomorrow, I know it's short notice, can you get someone to run the deli for you?'

He paused, thinking about it.

'It's urgent, Hank. I'm in deep shit, they're all ganging up against me. It was your idea this self-representation lark.'

'Alright, buddy calm down, I'll be there . . . but you'll have to pay the wages of the person standing in for me.'

'Done,' I said.

Back in court I told the judge that I had found a new McKenzie friend and that he could come tomorrow. Case adjourned until the next day.

<< >> << >>

THAT night I went round Hank's house and gave him my sister Katie's file of papers to peruse and we tried to map out a line of cross-examination. It was all a bit late in the day for Hank to be getting fully involved. I was expecting just to hand him the file and then disappear for some rest but he put me through the mill a bit.

'You can't go into court unprepared, Michael.' I was so tired, but he made me think of ways of conducting my questioning which would extract the information I wanted. 'The trick is to ask a series of questions which brings out uncontroversial information then hit them with the one which is important. If you've set it up right by then there is only one answer possible. Like, your cooking thing, you say to Marie-Sophie, "Am I a good cook?" and what does she reply . . .?'

'Last time she said, "If you call fish fingers and baked beans cooking".'

'So you don't ask that question. What you do is you ask

her about how much garlic you used to put in the cooking compared to her, how you used to fight about the amount of chilli, or get her to go on about that dispute you had over the brand of olive oil, or which coffee beans you buy, how runny the camembert, etc. It's your life, you can think of things. But by the time you come to the question about your ability to cook she's going to look stupid if she says all you do is frozen hamburgers.

'Never give the opposition the chance to deny something. Make them paint the picture. If you think she's going to deny you ever picked Pierre up from school, first get her to go on about how you were always late. She can't say you were late and deny you ever picked him up.'

It sounded good advice in theory, but I had the feeling it could get hopelessly complicated. It was certainly too late in the day to give it any practice.

<< >> << >>

DAY two in court, Tuesday February 13. Day one had seen nothing constructive achieved whatsoever beyond Judge Rampton reading the papers. I had thus given my witnesses the same instruction to be on stand-by, but not to expect to be called until the afternoon.

The opposition was already collected in the corridor when we arrived, as was Mr Wheedle, his former chattiness with the other side restored, although the conversation had moved on from holidays in Corsica. I could see James de Vere Crispe struggling to suppress surprise at the sight of the enormous black man I'd brought with me, and almost succeeding in affecting none whatsoever. Although he could have done with borrowing a bit of colour from Hank.

'Could you introduce me to your friend?' he asked with unusual politeness. You can say 'have your little day in court' to a litigant in person, in a sharply disparaging tone, but when confronted with a black man the dynamic is different. You express your haughter by being very polite. It must have been going through his mind that the racism part of his case against me was now looking just a touch dodgy.

'No,' I said. I didn't feel talking to him.

In court Judge Rampton too affected no surprise whatsoever. 'Mr Henry, ah, is this your McKenzie friend? Could you tell me who he is?'

'He's just a friend.' It ought to have been reasonably obvious that he wasn't a member of my family and thus a source of intimidation for Marie-Sophie.

'But who is he?'

'A friend.'

'But where have you got him from?'

It was another thing that I thought was none of his business but finally I said, 'Families Need Fathers', which seemed to satisfy him. I think the judge was probably genuinely puzzled by me. Here I was, son of a retired army officer, 'City' type of guy, putative member of the establishment, betraying it all by dispensing with lawyers to start with, then turning up with a black man. The case proper got under way. Mr Wheedle said he had commitments later in the day so he went in the box first. As a year before, I again had to watch the revolting spectacle of seeing him examined by Mr Crispe in the most flattering, unctuous, oleaginous way possible 'So, in your incomparable, monumental experience, and having applied your vast intellect and erudition to this case would you agree that Mrs Henry is the most wonderful mother you've ever witnessed?' That sort of thing.

'Yes, absolutely fabulous.' And so on.

'No further questions, Your Honour.' He hadn't asked many anyway, but he said this with a triumphalist flourish in the way that Perry Mason would have said 'I rest my case'. 'No further questions' was also code for 'This case is so cut and dried, as I think you already agree Your Honour, that we won't spin things out any more than we need.' Or as one of my prep schoolmasters might have said before administering a well-deserved beating, 'This is hurting me more than it is hurting you.'

So now it was my turn at Perry Masonry, at nailing the nasty court welfare officer (preferably by the bollocks to somewhere hard), at getting his report to 'collapse under the weight of its internal contradictions'.

'Mr Wheedle,' I began, 'one of the most far-reaching of your conclusions is that I am completely obsessed, and propelled only by the need to get back at my wife?'

'Yes, that's right.'

I shuffled my papers to find the right bit. Hank pointed it out for me. 'You've said "that it seems symptomatic of this father's highly obsessive attitudes that anyone who takes a different view to his own is considered by him to be guilty of bad faith, mendacity or incompetence. This appears to be his view, inter alia, of His Honour Judge Stern, myself and the mother's solicitors."

'Presumably you can see that there is a circularity to your logic? If I attempt to disagree with you in any way it tends to prove your point. It means you have to be right and I have to be wrong whatever I say. Do you ever make mistakes Mr Wheedle?'

It is a question to which there is only one honest answer, and unexpectedly he gave it. 'Well of course, I'm only human, I'm sure we all make mistakes.'

'So if you are only human, and you've made a mistake in this case, how am I supposed to prove it? If I disagree with you, immediately I'm in the position of obsessed madman who will do anything to get back at his wife. Can't you see that it is a sort of Catch 22?'

'What's wrong with that?' asked the judge smiling.

I made very little headway with the court welfare officer. It seemed to me that I backed him into cross-examinational corners several times in which he started stammering, caught out being inconsistent, but each time the judge would put on his supercilious voice and come charging to his rescue. For example, I read out to him what he had insisted, at the directions hearing, was the bare minimum he would need to investigate. Meetings at his office, together, severally, and in our homes, discussions with Pierre's teachers. In the end he'd got ill and limited himself to just visiting our homes. Depending on his mood it seemed that our case went from being the most complicated one since time started to the most straightforward. But this inconsistency didn't seem to strike him or bother the judge.

'Mr Wheedle,' I said, 'you have reported in your report that the petitioner has experienced hostility at the hands of my family on account of her origins . . .'

Mr Crispe suddenly interjected, 'We do not intend to make too much of this, Your Honour.'

Hank whispered to me in a stage-whisper so that everyone could hear, 'That's it, you've nailed the racism bit.'

'Would you please keep quiet,' said the judge.

I also had a go at Mr Wheedle about his qualifications. Most court welfare officers are probation officers by trade, trained in the handling of offenders. They can literally be a probation officer on Friday a court welfare officer on Monday then go back to being probation officer on Tuesday. There are no checks, standards or special training. They are instant experts.

'We do not normally discuss our qualifications in court.'

'Yes, Mr Henry,' said the judge, 'he is a very well qualified and experienced welfare officer. What is the relevance of his qualifications?'

'I'd have said they were very relevant.'

'Very well Mr Henry.' He smiled kindly at Wheedle and said,'Perhaps you might like to satisfy Mr Henry as to your qualifications.'

'Twenty-one years ago I passed my social work examinations part two and . . .' he trotted out a whole list of experience while the judge smiled and nodded encouragingly, ending by saying, '. . . and I have been seconded to the family division for five years in which time I have prepared reports in very many cases, many of them much less straightforward than this one.'

'Well,' said Judge Rampton, 'I think now might be the time to adjourn for lunch.'

'Well I haven't finished my examination of him,' I said. There was a whole host of questions I wanted to catch him out on.

'I will not be available after lunch,' said Mr Wheedle.

There then followed a little discussion in which I was insistent that I wanted to get him in the box again. The judge tried to indicate that he had heard enough of Mr Wheedle by now, but was stuck because it was my right to ask as many questions as I liked.

Suddenly it all got too much for me and I burst into tears. 'All I want is to see my son more, that's all. This man is so unfair, for some reason he can't stand the sight of me, why should I be having to go through this? It's such a simple thing I ask.'

'Mr Wheedle, are you available tomorrow?' asked the judge. He indicated that he was. 'Very well, I'd like you to come back in the morning and Mr Henry can complete his examination. Now I think it is time for us all to get some fresh air.' I had no doubt whatsoever that we would still be going strong into day three. I still had my two witnesses to call and she still had hers.

<< >> << >>

OVER lunch I discussed how things were going with Hank. 'I lost it a bit there, didn't I? Should have kept my self control.'

'Best bloody thing you did,' he said.

'I had the guy a few times, though didn't I?'

'You did, but each time the judge came to his rescue like a knight on a shining charger. They have to defend their own.'

'Their own?'

'Weird isn't it? Can you imagine any judge ever having a court welfare officer to dinner?'

We discussed how we should handle Marie-Sophie. I wasn't looking forward to cross-examining her at all. I didn't mind being cross-examined. I didn't find Crispe's style of advocacy even intimidating, he was too easy to fend off. But Marie-Sophie was a different kettle of fish. She knew me too well. I'd never catch her out. If I got close to winning a jousting point she'd throw it back in my face in some way, applying the correct spin to impress the judge – perhaps not actually lying but stretching the truth in the direction that the judge wanted it stretched anyway. Just as she had done before.

Hank said it was best to keep examination of her down to a minimum. 'You'll look petty in front of the judge if you succeed in humiliating her, plus she'll hate you for ever if you succeed. Better to avoid it if you can.'

With her witnesses and mine now gathered in the corridor outside court, the most urgent need for both Marie-Sophie and me was to get them processed so that they could go home. Hers were 'Aunt' Tiffany and the mystery playground operator. Mine were my father and Michele.

Michele said, 'Hey, you've got one fan.'

'Who?'

'The usher. When she came out she said what a pity it was, you seem such a nice guy. She's rooting for you. That guy there, who's he?'

'That's Mr Wheedle.' He was supposed to be too busy to appear this afternoon. It threw me off balance a bit because I wasn't ready for my rerun with him. I wondered what he was doing here.

'When I arrived there was this gaggle of people,' she said, 'including Marie-Sophie and him so I went over to say "Hi". Anyway that guy was saying something about having rung up Pierre's school and how when Pierre was dropped off yesterday Louise had said to the teacher in a loud voice, "Pierre's a bit funny today because it is the day his parents are in court." Louise wouldn't have said something like that would she? So I started telling him so. Then that guy,' she pointed at Crispe, 'came across and asked me who I was and who on earth I thought I was talking to. Very rude he was too. I see what you're up against.'

I caught Mr Wheedle's eye. 'Are we to have the pleasure again so soon? I thought you couldn't be here,' I asked in a self-confident voice, belying what I really felt.

'Just left something behind. I'll be here tomorrow,' he said as he scuttled off. I couldn't decide whether he was just being nosy or what.

When we went in it was decided that Marie-Sophie's witnesses should be seen first, I didn't quite follow why. Mr Crispe announced that little would be added by examining his client's witnesses. He evidently felt that he was cruising to a comfortable victory and that the best way to stay on the right side of the judge was to hurry things along as much as possible.

'Well I'd like to cross-examine them,' I told the judge. Judge Rampton didn't say so, but his tone suggested that he thought spoken evidence from Tiffany and Earle would not add to much to the current enquiry, so why couldn't I see it too? In a normal court without the litigant-in-person from hell running his case, the witnesses would be politely thanked and told they could go home.

First we had Tiffany.

It was Crispe's turn to question her first. She did her 'the whole truth and nothing but the truth' bit, then he started.

'Are you Tiffany Jones?'

'Yes.'

'And is your address 58 Acacia Avenue?'

'Yes.'

'No further questions, Your Honour,' he said in a rather over-dramatized voice.

So that was it? My turn. Time to give 'Aunt' Tiffany a roasting. Ha! At my mercy, I could grill her for as long as I wanted. First of all I thanked her very graciously for looking after Marie-Sophie and being supportive of her during what must have been a very difficult time – she would have needed all the help she could get from her friends. I really was most civil – the message was delivered with a smile and through teeth metaphorically clenched.

'Miss Jones,' I enjoyed addressing her as Miss, 'you are a great friend of my wife's?'

'Yes.'

'She is a colleague of yours at the TV station, is that correct?'

'Yes.'

'You say in your affidavit that "Mr Henry could be rude, and was not popular amongst Marie-Sophie's friends."'

'Yes.'

'Could it just be that you were one of the friends who didn't approve of me?'

'Well, er . . . sometimes you were quite nice.'

'I was perhaps not your favourite person on this planet, for which I do not blame you. Not every one likes me.' I smiled at the judge. 'You found me rude, and it was perhaps the reason why you rarely visited Marie-Sophie at our house. You tended to go out with her after work instead, is that not correct?'

'Well, it was more convenient,' she said defensively.

'You describe in your affidavit an incident where I was looking after Pierre. You use the words ". . . and this was the only time I ever saw Mr Henry acting as a father . . ." Could that just be because, as you've just said, you rarely came to our house, rarely saw me in the company of Pierre? In fact it really was the only time you saw me acting as a father. Literally.'

'Perhaps more than once.'

'Are you sure?'

'Perhaps. Twice, maybe three times, what does it matter?'

'The fact is that you have no idea whether or not I am a good father. All you know is what Marie-Sophie has told you.'

'Yes, I suppose so.'

'I repeat, thank you for all the support you have given my wife during a difficult time. I am sure she is very grateful. No further questions, Your Honour.'

Next was Earle Parker, the mystery witness from the playground. Again Mr Crispe insouciantly announced that he had no need to ask him any questions.

I had no need either really.

'This is the first time we have met, isn't it?' I began.

'Yes.'

'I just want to thank you for the support you have given Marie-Sophie during a difficult time.' He looked puzzled. 'No further questions, Your Honour.'

I was beginning to like the sound of this.

Mr Parker got up and went out. All keyed up for this then dismissed with no examination. A day wasted. I could see he had been disappointed. He'd been expecting a bit of a fight and I hadn't given him one. But I had had a purpose in bringing him. The way the witness box was oriented meant that his left ear faced the judge, and in his left ear were five earrings. Michele had pointed this out to me in the corridor. A judge like this one was never going to take a witness with five earrings in his left ear seriously.

So that was their witnesses finished with. Now for mine. Dad was Dad, so he could be kept waiting a little longer in the corridor, so we got Michele in first.

We went through the formalities of her name and where she lived. Then I began my masterly examination-in-chief.

'At the time that you knew me, who did you consider to be the primary carer of Pierre?'

'Why, you of course. You had a job which allowed you to do work at home, so mostly it was you. Sometimes I saw Marie-Sophie too, but mainly it was you I saw at the school.' Although she replied to me she addressed her remarks to the judge. She had a sort of forthright but feminine style of the kind that might go down well with a judge who fancies female barristers.

'What personal experience have you had of me in the father's role?' A slightly gauche question in the circumstances, but the delightful thing about Michele was that she was not of the 'hell hath no fury' brand of woman. Besides she seemed to be getting on very well indeed with Rupert. He had been asking me where he might take her in Paris for the weekend after Valentine's Day.

'Well it was quite an unusual situation. You are a caring father, you actually do things with the child, proper things, like organizing sport . . .'

'For example, in the last hearing it was suggested that I was an unsafe father. What would be your views on that?'

Judge Rampton interjected with a question for Mr Crispe: 'You are not pursuing that are you?' He seemed to be taking a bit of a shine to Michele and for the second time was picking on Mr Crispe rather than on me.

As far as Crispe was concerned the case was wrapped up, and it was just a question of going through the motions until I finished all my tedious questioning. The judge had indicated which way the land lay, his approach would be minimalist. 'Your Honour, it is not part of my case, we are not suggesting that.'

'That he is not safe?' continued Michele anyway. I think she sensed blood. Crispe's undead blood.

Hank did, too. He nudged me in the ribs. 'That's the safety thing knocked on the head, she's doing great, kid,' he said in his stage-whisper.

'I don't want to have to tell you again, keep quiet please,' said the judge.

'Completely safe in my opinion,' concluded Michele.

'Could you describe for us my Thursday afternoon football games?'

'Well every Thursday, even when Pierre is not there,' she turned to the judge and addressed him, 'it's a commitment Michael has made to all the families in the area. Michael takes Jake, that's my son, and quite a few of the children of that age off to a park, or in winter, like now, we book the local leisure centre and they race up and down playing football. Because they all go to the local state school, the one Pierre used to go to, they don't get much physical education like you do at a private school. I just wanted to stress that because it is really important to all of us and they thoroughly enjoy it. They talk about it and most of their stories at school are based around it.'

'How does Pierre fit in with that crowd of small children.'

'He is completely integrated with them. The weeks Pierre is not there, in fact I think that was last week if I remember rightly . . .' – she did, because it was the day I had received Mr Wheedle's report – ' . . . four or five children run up to Michael and say "Where is Pierre today, and why isn't he here?" So he is missed when he doesn't come, and indeed he has made new friends through the football that his father has arranged.'

'How would you describe the community in our part of Clapham?'

'Well it is unusual because in London most people do not exactly know who their neighbours are. But in our few streets it is a very tight-knit community ranging from QCs,' she paused and smiled at the judge, 'to painters who shampoo carpets to earn their bread and butter. A mixture of establishment and alternative types. And it all centres around the primary school, and the children are all in and out of each other's houses the whole time. It is very satisfactory for all concerned, and of course we miss Pierre when he is not there.'

'How would you describe Pierre these days, you have seen him both before and after the break up?'

'Mr Henry, how does this help you?' interjected the judge.

'She is a mother, very experienced, it might show that my influence has been a positive one.'

'Yes I know, but she speaks so well of you that there is no doubt of that. I mean she speaks extremely well about how good you are with other children as well.'

This was good. Judge being nice to me. Fancies Michele, I thought. It was lovely to watch. He beamed at her every time she said anything, just as Judge Stern had at Marie-Sophie.

'Marie-Sophie says in her statement that she only knows you by sight, the implication being that you know nothing of our situation. Would you say that was fair?'

'I don't quite know what she means by "sight". I mean she called me as a witness as a 'friend' and I've been invited to dinner at your house. And since you separated I bumped into her at a private view at Agnew's and she came up to me and introduced me to her companion as a "Pierre's best friend Jake's mother Michele". She knows more than just my name attached to my face, but we do not know for instance if the other has brothers or sisters.'

'Do you recall who used to take him to school more often?'

'I would say mostly it was you, because you worked from home a lot, and she worked full-time except between assignments.'

'It was more him?' asked the judge.

'Yes.'

'How would you describe my attitude to Marie-Sophie now?'

'Disappointed. Hurt as well, but certainly not hostile. Not horrible, just a sort of general disappointment at the way things have worked out, because you wanted to try to resolve things.'

'What to save the marriage?' asked the judge.

'Yes, Michael wanted to make the marriage work.'

'But what about the divorce?' I asked.

'I can only say what l have heard from you, but, but I think you have been disappointed with the way in which the whole thing has appeared like a tactical exercise from beginning to end.'

'I think you are aware who took Pierre to school on Monday morning.'

'Yes, it was your friend Louise.'

I was a bit worried that mention of the woman I had designs on would not go down too well but I felt the business of Mr Wheedle calling up the school to dig up more dirt on me should come out.

'There was an allegation made . . . '

The judge interrupted. He had reverted to his irritated manner. 'Do you mind this Mr Crispe, it is clearly hearsay on hearsay.'

'Your Honour, my own view is that it does not matter,' Crispe replied insouciantly.

'All right Mr Henry, you ask the lady,' said the judge.

I felt irritated that he needed to prompt Mr Crispe who was perfectly capable of objecting to anything on his own. It made me feel bullied, heckled, out-numbered again. Sod it, I can't be bothered anymore, why don't I just go home. 'No, I do not want to ask,' I said petulantly.

'Mr Henry, listen . . .'

'I do not have to ask questions if I don't want to.'

'You do not have to ask questions. But you started saying something about some allegation that something was said to Pierre on Monday. Well come on, ask about it. May I just say, Mr Henry, that technically Mr de Vere Crispe is entitled to object and I was just checking whether he wished to. Now go on,' he said to Michele.

'Can I say how I heard about this thing?' she asked.

'Yes.'

'I walked into the hall outside this court and I was completely lost. I saw a man with a great stack of files so guessed he must belong to this place and went over to him to ask him directions. Then I heard him saying, "And then the teacher said . . ." and he had a great big smile on his face as he was saying it, ". . . and then the teacher said to me Pierre had been clinging to her all day because some woman brought him in to school and explained to the teacher that Michael hadn't brought him in because he was uptight and emotional."

'Well I checked this out, and I rang up the school and got to talk to the teacher. She said she was completely misquoted and was horrified to think anything she'd said might be being used against either parent in court. Pierre was in the classroom way out of earshot, and she just said in her very soft voice, "You understand, today is the day of, you know, that they are in court."'

'She said this to the teacher?'

'To the teacher, " . . . today is the day they are in court, and Michael is a bit tired and emotional obviously, so I have brought Pierre in." In fact Pierre was very happy to have Louise bring him in. He wanted her to stay and look at his drawings. It turned out that the man who was telling this story so inaccurately was the court welfare officer, which I found quite extraordinary.'

'No further questions, Your Honour,' I said.

It was now Mr Crispe's turn. I think that probably he wouldn't have bothered cross-examining her, except that she had thrown out some awkwardness about the court welfare officer's attitude which needed countering.

'Of course,' he began, 'the difficulty we have is that you were not there at the school, were you?

'No of course not.'

'So we cannot establish what happened, but certainly Mr Wheedle is likely to give evidence to the effect that she spoke to the teacher about it and had it confirmed that these words were spoken in front of Pierre.'

'It is not the father's fault is it, Mr Crispe?' asked the judge.

Crispe paused. 'Your Honour, I do not pursue it. Mrs Stubbs, may I ask you this, how many of the papers in this case have you been able to look at?'

My heart gave a leap – with all that kerfuffle the day before about my sister not being allowed to witness confidential things, the fact that Michele had read the court welfare report could have seen me for the high jump.

'My own statement,' she said.

'What else have you looked at?'

'That is it.' Greater love hath no man or woman but to tell a white lie for a friend. I sighed with relief.

'You were discussing the case outside court with the

welfare officer?'

'The welfare officer? The man who turned out to be the welfare officer, the one who was making that statement about Pierre and the classroom as I walked through the door. I didn't know he was the welfare officer until you aggressively alerted me to the fact.'

Bullseye. The thing is that family law barristers are not supposed to be aggressive, they are supposed to be warm, conciliatory people. 'I told you it was improper for you to discuss it with the welfare officer,' he said defensively. It was nice to see Mr Crispe being defensive.

'I had no idea who the man was, as I told you.'

'All right. You met Marie-Sophie on, you think, two or three occasions?'

'No many more times than that.'

'Many more?'

'Yes, very many more.'

'But you have only spoken to her on two or three occasions?'

'No, we have exchanged niceties on many more occasions and she even asked me to be her witness. I think that she knows me quite well.'

'It may be that my note is wrong, but I got the impression from your evidence that you had only met at a dinner party and at a private view at Agnew's and otherwise scarcely at all.'

'I discussed things with her on those occasions, but I have met her and talked to her on many more occasions.'

'You say in your statement at page 193 in the bundle that "Michael Henry has asked me to prepare this statement . . . ".'

'Yes.'

'Then you say, "It is my considered opinion that Pierre's welfare would be best served living primarily with his father." Then you frankly admit that your opinion is based on observations with Michael in the role of carer because that is all you know. You do not know his mother's care at all do you?'

'I am sure it is perfectly wonderful. No, but I do not. She would only occasionally be seen with Pierre.' Another bullseye.

'I am just wondering how you are able to say you can give a considered opinion when . . .'

The judge had been observing this exchange with an increasingly angry look. 'Really Mr Crispe, Mrs Stubbs is doing her best.'

'Your Honour,' he said, 'I have no further questions.'

Michele left the courtroom, leaving Mr Crispe looking a little paler than usual, his lips bluer. Still, he could now restore his haemoglobin count with my dad.

Obviously there were several important things to establish while Dad was in the dock. One, to reaffirm what appeared to have been conceded, namely that as a family we were not a bunch of out-and-out racists. Two, that we were not all ganging up on Marie-Sophie.

He did the 'whole truth and nothing but the truth' bit and then I started my friendly examination. Former army officer, pleasant, decent old chap with white hair – the judge loved him, kept calling him 'grandpa', maintained a beatific smile of approbation, as I took my father over those parts of his army career that proved he was not a racist.

'Ah Malaysia, splendid chaps those Chinese. My wife and I went back last year and I must say that my chums put the boat out for us. Wouldn't let me put my hand in my pocket. And of course we played some more golf.'

'And you spent some time in Kenya too, I believe, before I was born.'

'Yes, commanded a regiment out there. Tremendous soldiers some of those men, I have great respect for them.'

The judge beamed. Mr Crispe must have been sickened.

Hank avoided the stage-whisper and pencilled me a note. 'Never seen the old school-tie work like it.' I could see that his American gob was being smacked by the whole bizarre experience, despite his own 80-plus court appearances.

Mr Crispe took his cross-examination far less insouciantly than he had with Michele. He tried to establish that my family had hated Marie-Sophie from the start, but my father had a very good answer for that, not one I had thought of before, or something that he had said to me.

'Yes my wife and I were opposed to the marriage, and we said so, but they were young and stubborn, and would not listen to what we had to say.'

I think Mr Crispe must have thought that he had drawn blood. Straight from the horses mouth, here was my father admitting that he and my mother had opposed the marriage.

'And so you concede that you were always hostile to Marie-Sophie?'

'It wasn't that. We could see instantly that Michael was far more in love with her than she was with he. She was very young, and pregnant, and confused, and we did not think she was ready for marriage. Although we accepted Marie-Sophie willingly once they had married, and although I believe she tried to reciprocate, I think she found it difficult, and so we have never managed to be close.'

My father is an emotional man. Like me he has feeble lachrymose glands, and as he added 'I just wish these two young people could sort things out between them . . .' he started crying.

Well that was two tearful Henrys. Three if we included Katie from the day before.

The judge said to my father, 'Well perhaps you could help them sort things out. I'm going to do something unusual. If Mr Crispe and your son have no objection I will adjourn for thirty minutes while you see if you can try to bring about a settlement.'

Neither Crispe nor I could really say much beyond 'I have no objection to that suggestion' and 'Neither have I' although to me it was pretty clear that Crispe was mightily pissed off.

The judge said he would come back in half an hour, 'But take your time, it would be so much better if you could find someway of agreeing things.' Rachel, Marie-Sophie, Hank and I left the courtroom to my father and Mr Crispe.

Marie-Sophie herself had sat fairly impassively throughout the proceedings. So far the judge had not had the opportunity even to hear her voice, so if this narrative gives the impression of ignoring her presence that is not far wrong. She might as well have not been there.Of course she was showing signs of strain like the rest of us, every now and again biting her lip or rubbing her eyes.

I felt the tide might be turning. Judge Rampton had liked Michele's evidence and also obviously liked my father.

When we got outside Michele was still there. I don't think she could bear to go home and was dying to know what was going to happen next. She'd loved being cross-examined by Crispe. 'Thanks Michele. You had him to lunch.'

'Hey, do you know whose case is going on in the next court?'

'No.'

'Bob Geldoff and Paula Yates. That's the hack from the *Sun* and that's the one from the *Mirror.* Apparently . . .' She began to tell me all sorts of interesting things which are probably severely bound by gagging injunctions. I'm not even sure of you can mention the name Fifi Trixibell. Ooops! I think it was one of the best days out Michele had ever had.

Half an hour or so later my father came out of the courtroom to announce that he had run up against a brick wall. They would agree to Pierre visiting me on a Thursday once a month, so there was some progress, a sop to the judge. But that was it.

Michele, my father, Hank and I grouped ourselves in our corner of the corridor wondering what to do. I thought that, for sure, the judge was not going to be best pleased about seeing us back in court to continue a continuation of a fight which was getting nastier by the minute.

Suddenly, I had an idea for forcing an end to the whole thing. 'What if . . .' and I explained my idea to Hank and Dad who both said, 'Go for it.'

We went back into court.

'Well?' asked Judge Rampton.

'I am afraid we tried, but there seemed to be no will for compromise,' said Mr Crispe.

I tried to interrupt, but the judge cut me short. 'Be quiet Mr Henry, you'll get your chance.' He was angry.

'I very much regret this . . .' said Mr Crispe.' Liar, hypocrite, I thought. '. . . because it will now be necessary to cross-examine this father extensively. This father, has brought this situation upon himself. Shortly after the first residence hearing almost a year ago our client was happy to agree to the arrangements outlined. The father declined to accept them and immediately afterwards, before we had left court even, he was trying to change them. This father has since conducted a campaign to undermine my client's loving care of their child. I will now have the regrettable duty of examining him in detail about his statement. Many hurtful things will emerge during this examination, and it must be regretted that this father has not found it within himself to come to the compromise that we have proposed to him.'

Judge Rampton listened with a very serious face, and it

seemed to me that if any of the blame for the failed negotiations was to stick I was really in the doghouse.

I waited for Crispe to end his tirade. 'Mr Rampton,' I began, 'the fact is that I was willing to compromise to something reasonable. I do not call one week day a month and two weekends reasonable. Your Honour, Mr Crispe knows that I am willing to compromise. I said so both to him and my wife yesterday morning and I wrote a letter offering to settle several weeks ago which you have all seen. I see no point in cross-examining my wife and I'm not going to offer any spoken evidence of my own. We've been here for two days, you've heard enough, I think it is time you made your mind up.'

Do your job, Judge – judge! Although I hadn't put it quite like that. It was a bit of a gamble. For once James de Vere Crispe was absolutely speechless. White as a shroud. Judge Rampton too, before saying, 'Mr Crispe, I would be in difficulty making a judgment now because if I did so, without having heard evidence in chief, we would run the risk of this case going to appeal.'

The judge and Mr Crispe batted the problem back and forth for a bit. I wasn't entirely sure where the risk of appeal arose. I rather hoped it meant that he was minded to give me some of what I wanted, that Mr Crispe and his client would be unhappy with this and that it would be they who would have to go to the appeal court. I didn't see how it could be me: if I opted out of the court process that was my look out, my grounds for appeal would be dead shaky. Unless I appealed on the basis that I had spent two days being bullied and had folded under the pressure. That wouldn't go down too well on the Judge Rampton CV if I could pull it off.

'Mr Crispe,' he was now saying, 'perhaps we should adjourn again. I think you should make a greater effort to come back with something acceptable to both parties.'

So we found ourselves back in the corridor again. There was nothing for me to do. 'What happened?' asked my father and Michele.

'The judge wants them to settle. I think we've done it.'

Nevertheless Mr Crispe, Rachel Bonham-Lee and Marie-Sophie were absent from our section of the corridor for a long time. Quarter of an hour, half an hour. Hank got out a pack of cards. It was like waiting for the puff of smoke from the Vatican to signify that the Cardinals had chosen a new Pope.

I think that Rachel and James de Vere Crispe had probably promised Marie-Sophie that I would be pulverized and were now having to explain to her why things had not worked out quite so well. Expectations should be lowered. Making her understand this was taking time. Boot on the other foot. About time I thought.

Three quarters of an hour. If we went back into court and they still hadn't come up with my extra afternoons of football, my reading of the situation was that the judge would be so annoyed with them I could end up with custody even.

An hour and they reappeared from their debating spot on the stairs. 'Mr Henry, mid-week access for football is agreed. One final thing. My client wants it to be Wednesday but not Thursday.'

They knew football was arranged for twenty children on a Thursday, so let's bugger Michael about and demand it changes to Wednesday. I could see no reason for this final bit of petulance beyond a hope that it would scupper the whole thing.

'Fine,' I said. I organized the football, I'd just have to change it, that's all. Nip down to the sports hall and rearrange our block booking. If the new time clashed with some of the children's piano lessons or something, it was sad, but out of my hands.

Judge Rampton was delighted as he put together the wording of the new order to replace the one made by Judge Stern. 'Residence remains with the petitioner mother, the father to have contact from Friday afternoon through to Sunday night on alternate weekends, and every Wednesday afternoon, after school to seven, ummh, and half-terms, now what have you agreed about half-terms?'

In all the toing and froing we had forgotten to negotiate at all about half-terms and holidays. 'Well I think contact should cover the football, don't you,' he said. 'So half-term contact to start on the Wednesday or end on the Wednesday but after football, Mr Crispe, don't you agree? And half the long holidays, don't you think Mr Crispe?'

'Er . . . yes,' said Crispe.

Well that was an improvement. For the last year I had had no control over half-term and although I'd won my case for the summer holiday, I'd had just that measly week at Christmas. Yielded by Crispe just like that? I was delighted. It would be my legal right to have Pierre, so no more wrangling with Rachel, no more angry answer phone messages with my wife – well I hoped. The best thing was that Pierre wouldn't be able to spend as much time in France. It made the whole horrible experience worthwhile.

'Perhaps you could draft the order for me and leave it with my clerk,' continued my good judge. 'Now costs.'

Costs? Not so good. Costs were another thing that we had clean forgotten to negotiate in the corridor. I had rather got the impression that they didn't award costs in children's cases, each side pays its own. Getting paid was obviously dear to Mr Crispe's heart. Mr Crispe had been a bit naughty not to have mentioned them to me there. The normal order would be 'No order as to costs'. Fair enough to pull a fast one on another barrister perhaps, but in a negotiation with a litigant-in-person, ethically, he really ought to have mentioned them, had a duty even. But not in this case. Mr Crispe launched into a tirade about how the whole case had been my fault. He said that the first hearing a year before (just one day) which should have settled everything had cost his client £20,000.

Twenty thousand pounds! I couldn't believe that, but barristers are under very strict rules about not lying so it must have been true. My costs that first time round had 'only' been around the five grand mark, so how could Marie-Sophie have run up four times the amount? This time around she was on legal aid so perhaps the two day hearing was another twenty grand? Forty grand in total. Plus my five. And we'd barely even started to argue about who owned the house. It brought real meaning to the words 'negative equity'. They are right when they say there are no winners in family law cases. (Actually there are winners. But not in the family.)

This whole costs thing took me utterly by surprise. My focus had been on contact. So I had to argue with the judge that I shouldn't have to pay costs. '. . . and what's more, Your Honour, it was not my fault that the case has taken two days. If my McKenzie friend of choice had not been excluded it would have taken one day. I don't see why I should be hit with the other side's costs.'

Judge Rampton did make me pay some of their costs. I suppose it was in return for two days of making fun of the legal profession. But he limited it to ' . . . a maximum of £4,000 pounds to be paid when all litigation, including over money, is finished,' and I sincerely hope that it will be much less than that. 'Mr Henry, I do consider that you have made concessions today, and that in bringing this case you did so entirely out of love for your son and not, I believe, out of a desire to get back at your wife.'

<< >> << >>

THE extent of my achievements still had not sunk in. Hank was full of enthusiasm for the result, and Michele and Dad were full of congratulations too. I think Dad's greatest relief was to see me out of the thing. He kept saying he couldn't thank Hank enough and gave him a cheque for £100 for Families Need Fathers and another for the extra wages of the guy Hank had had to pay to replace him at the deli.

Hank and I shared a taxi back. 'I thought you were done for, but you done great man. But watch yourself this next few weeks. You've spent a year building up to the most intense experience of your life and now it's over. It's like coming off a high. You're going to have a reaction. Even when you win sometimes you get depressed afterwards. Make sure you get out and about a bit over the next week or two. And whatever you do, this is a high you mustn't get addicted to, like I am. Stay out of court. Anyway, how are you getting on with the older women? Michele's sweet on you for sure.'

'Past tense Hank. Just very good friends, upped and offed with my lodger. In fact she's cooking us supper tonight, I'm sure you can come.'

'Thanks. But no, I'm taking Families Need Fathers tonight. I'll tell them your good news. So if not Michele, then who?'

'I'm into twenty-six-year-olds now. It would be nice to celebrate with her but she's off at a sales conference. Just my luck.'

I dropped off Hank then went round to Michele's. She was very excited by the whole day and couldn't stop talking, wanting to tell Rupert everything about her starring role. For my part I suddenly felt utterly spent and a little subdued. I was happy to collapse silently into my stew.

<< >> << >>

DESPITE being exhausted I didn't sleep well so I found myself out of bed nursing a piece of toast relatively early in the morning. The Today programme was on the radio and an item came up about 'National Marriage Week' and some plan to teach marriage guidance in schools. Enough to put you off your toast.

I heard items of mail fluttering to the front doormat. Good, that would be my paper. There was also a letter franked on the outside 'Lord Chancellor's Department'.

Oh fuck, I thought, not already. I decided I'd better grasp the nettle and open it to see what unpleasantness it contained. In it was an official looking piece of paper with the impression of various rubber stamps on it.

In the High Court Justice
Principal Registry of the Family Division

Referring to the decree made in this cause . . . whereby it was decreed that the marriage solemnised . . . between the petitioner and the respondent be dissolved unless sufficient cause be shown to the court within six weeks from the making thereof why the said decree should not be made absolute . . . *speak now or forever hold his peace*? (No, no, no it doesn't say that.) . . . no cause having been shown, it is hereby certified that the said decree was made final and absolute and that the said marriage was thereby dissolved.

Dated this . . . day etc.

It was my Decree Absolute.

So there it was.
I was a divorcee.
Back to my toast.
Then I spotted something bright and floral falling out of

my newspaper. It was heart shaped – junk-mail shaped – and I did a double take before I realized that, (a) it was addressed to me and, (b) the front was covered in smudged pink ink – hearts, arrows and the like. In it was a card which read 'Happy Valentine's Day for the Man of my Dreams'. It was signed with a question mark, again in smudged pink ink.

Valentine's Day. I'd forgotten all about it. This particular year it had been about as big on my calender as Chairman Mao's birthday. The year before it had seemed a bad idea. One year before that I had taken Marie-Sophie out for dinner at the Ritz, in a lavish attempt to shore up what was already a difficult marriage. It worked for that evening – what a wasted investment.

So I could be forgiven if I had a somewhat jaundiced view of Valentine's Day, except that this was in every sense the first day of the rest of my life – a new beginning, fresh fields and pastures new, a new man.

I rang up Louise to catch her before she went to work. 'Hey, I hadn't realized it was Valentine's Day, you realize I've been a bit preoccupied this last few weeks, it wasn't you, by any chance, who sent me that card was it?'

'Might have been.'

'What are you doing this evening?'

'Hoping I might be able to take you off your hands.'

'Right, my place at eight. Pierre's looking after his mum. Rupert is off for a hands-on date at Michele's so it'll be just you and me.'

I spent the day at Roger's office in the City, catching up on various half-finished translations I'd been doing for him at a ruinous hourly rate – his idea to go freelance – and agreeing the next couple of months work schedule. On the way back I dropped in at Leadenhall market and got some giant prawns, 'langoustines' the man told me, eight as a starter, and four quail. I had never done either langoustines or quail before but I thought I could cook up some way of basting them for the oven.

At 6.30 I had a bath in order to be at my freshest and not to look as though I had just got out of it when she arrived. By 7.30 I had tidied one corner of the sitting-room of strewn legal papers and puffed up the cushions on the sofa – with the hope we'd soon be flattening them again. At 7.45 the telephone rang. She was on her way. I hadn't even washed the spinach.

I started with the spuds. Straight new potatoes. Then the spinach. A nob of butter in the frying pan, a bit of olive oil, three crushed cloves of garlic, too much coarse black pepper (on purpose), a hint of Mrs M's Hot Jamaican Lime Pickle, in it all went. Pour on to langoustines – lay out in oven dish prepared earlier.

I had a look through the fridge and found some oyster mushrooms which must have belonged to Rupert. They looked like they had been there for a few days, but I hacked them about a bit, and turned them in the remaining oil in the frying pan. I reasoned she wouldn't notice. I then chucked the spinach on top and covered the pan with a lid to let the ensemble meld together without getting too dry.

I sat back exhausted on a kitchen stool and opened a can of lager. Half a can down and I was ready for the quails. The doorbell rang. Oh my God, she was here. I went to the door in my apron, greeted her lips first and ushered her in to the sitting-room. 'You'll have to sit here quietly for a few minutes while I apply a few finishing touches. Don't worry, it will be a masterpiece.'

I still wasn't quite satisfied that I had got my spinach and mushroom ensemble quite right so I had a look through the fridge again and found a half finished pint pot of cream which seemed fresh enough – under a week old, anyway. I took a gamble. We might not get as far as the pudding. The cream thus went on top of the spinach.

And it was a masterpiece, and we didn't get as far as the pudding in fact and although we ate all of the langoustines, the quails never made it out of the roasting tin. They smelt delicious but our minds were on other things. I don't have to specify what. 'Stop it, Michael, I like it,' she said at one point. And so to bed.

No more to add really. Consenting adults in private and all that. It was the date of the century. The boy done good, as they say . . . finally.

EPILOGUE

(A year and a bit on.)

READER, I didn't marry her. But by recent standards she lasted a long time, nearly a year, and certainly during the early part of the relationship I thought we were going to get married. Pierre liked her too. At one point he even said to me, 'You know I lit that candle for you in France?'

'Yes.'

'I think she's the one.'

Well, it wasn't to be. In retrospect it was far too early into my recovery. A shame really. It almost succeeded with Louise. I think I was nearly in love with her. Anyway, we're still good friends.

It hasn't quite worked out that way with Marcia. We'd said to each other, 'We'll go on being friends, won't we?' I'm sure we both meant it, but sad to say, it was one of those common situations where you break up and never see each other again. News reaches me on the wind from time to time, mainly through Michele. Apparently she has met the man of her dreams and, despite saying she'd never marry again, has done so. She is moving out into the countryside and is said to be genuinely happy. I hope so, because she deserves to be. I will always be grateful for her kindness and compassion and for picking me up at my lowest ebb and keeping me afloat. And some great sex.

Michele's 'thing' with Rupert is going well too. I reckon it could be wedding bells, we'll have to see. Rupert has got a steady job selling life assurance but is using his old army training to keep Jake and Charlotte in line. They appear to think he's great and Pierre tells me that Jake wants him to be his second dad. I hope it works out for all their sakes.

Roger I see less of these days because of working at home, but when I do see him he is just the same. He still maintains that he is an excellent source of attractive, intelligent women, even if most of them do see through him before it's too late. He was sorry to hear Louise and I broke up, but dealt with it in his usual light but philosophical style: 'Shame about her, I thought you were suited. Better than any old pork in a storm.'

My message to anyone contemplating a one-night stand with a perfect stranger in a far-off country is, Don't (capital D) do it. At times I think I may have to go ex-directory to stop Colette calling me up and offering me free tickets on Eurostar.

Hank won his case eventually, but not before getting beyond his hundredth court visit. He deserves a telegram from the Queen. His son Christopher started arriving on his doorstep. Attempts were made by the Official Solicitor's office to accuse him of abduction, but Hank would cover himself very skilfully each time Christopher arrived, informing everyone of what had happened including the local police. The Official Solicitor would say 'Bring him round to my office immediately or else', to which Hank would reply, not sweetly, 'Get lost, he came of his own accord. If you want him, come and get him.'

I was Hank's McKenzie friend when he was finally awarded his sole residence order. By chance Sally and Muriel were in the corridor outside court, a real team. 'My man's just won,' I told them.

'There are no winners in family cases,' they said, nearly in unison. I detected a note of irony. They had a point, because since he has gone to live with his father, Christopher's mother carried out a threat to blank him out of her life if he stayed with Hank. Emotional blackmail or what? A tragedy in itself.

Hank and I did an audit of his visits to court. He reckoned he'd had 30 High Court judges, and fifteen Appeal Court ones, including the Master of the Rolls on his case. It probably cost half a million in his wife's legal aid, a million if you add in the cost of court time. All that public money spent on keeping a decent dad from seeing his child.

Several Families Need Fathers members have cases like Hank's. The Lord Chancellor's Department say they know of no family cases costing over £50,000 in legal aid. The lawyers' scam works because in any one case they are adept at applying for separate legal aid certificates for each part of the case. The Lord Chancellor's Department apparently does no audit of this and has no idea of the total cost of each case.

I sat next to Hank during one of his appeals. There was a panel of three Appeal Court judges led by Lord Justice Butler-Sloss. Acting for the Official Solicitor was a case worker (a solictor), a barrister and a consultant child psychiatrist. For the mother was a solicitor and assistant, a barrister, and a Queen's Council. When QCs strut their stuff, the barrister has no discernible role beyond, as far as I can make out, acting as the QC's McKenzie friend. It's a real doubling of manpower of the kind the print unions were big on back in the late seventies. As Hank had told me, the law is the last big powerful closed shop. Hank and I are non-union labour. Lunatics-in-person, the lawyers like to call us.

Hank lost this appeal (court visit no. 95) although he did succeed in getting the Official Solicitor roundly bollocked by the good Lady Butler-Sloss. We liked her for that, but in turning down the appeal she said at one point, 'The father did not make a case that the mother was a bad mother . . .'

She is a former President of the Family Division and the message is clear: if you want to 'be successful' in a battle over a child, dish the dirt on your ex. In my view Hank was being heroic in resisting a near-overwhelming temptation to dish dirt. His argument was only that he was the more competent parent and above all that Christopher – age ten – wanted to live with him.

The year 1996 saw a change in the law, although it may not be until 2000 that it comes into force. Out goes 'unreasonable behaviour', in comes No Fault Divorce. I think the change will prove cosmetic at best. Unreasonable behaviour is a convenient sham. At worst, No Fault Divorce means automatic divorce. Under the new law one party simply has to express a desire to part from the other and, hey presto, one year later, you are divorced, like it or not. No defence. Marriage will have as much legal significance as a Christening; a nice event for all the family, an occasion for a party, but beyond that utterly meaningless. But the incentives for divorce will remain in place: if you're a woman, a bit fed up with your partner, and you know that you'll get the house, the kids and an income, why stay married?

A compulsory cooling-off period and the offer of mediation will be good things up to a point. The emphasis, though, will be on mediation rather than marriage guidance. The two, I have discovered, are very different things. Mediation is a form of litigation where the parties are guided to a divorce settlement. It will tend to be done by lawyers. Marriage guidance is about reconciliation and saving marriages. I spell this out because I wish I'd known that at the beginning.

There is a severe danger that the new system will lead to more acrimony not less. In a marriage where the couple really are at loggerheads there will be a premium on false allegations of domestic violence and sexual abuse in order to short-circuit the cooling-off process. I predict it will become a nice little nasty industry for guess which group of professionals.

Relations with Marie-Sophie are now cordial if not exactly friendly.

'Did you enjoy your weekend?' she asks.

'Yes, thank you, and you?'

'Ummh, not bad. That's a nice shirt your wearing.'

'Yes, it is, isn't it. It's from my rugby team. Bye, bye, Pierre, look after your mum.'

'Bye Dad. Kiss, kiss. Yuk!' We go through a kissing ritual involving both cheeks and tousling his hair. His mother tries to look enthusiastic.

'Well, Pierre, see you on Wednesday,' I say.

'Oh, Michael, could you make a special effort to bring Pierre back on time on Wednesday?'

'Yes, of course, I'll do my best, but the traffic is a little variable, you know how it is. Bye now . . .' The traffic is variable, it is true, but somehow it never makes me early.

So far Marie-Sophie hasn't moved back to France, and as far as I know the growth in her mother's head remains benign. My former wife doesn't bend court orders any more, so there are no longer any problems seeing Pierre. Nonetheless, I'd still feel reassured if she were to marry another Englishman. Jasper dropped out of Pierre's conversation for good some time ago and doesn't seem to have been replaced by anyone, so who knows what will happen. I'm cured of my passion for her but I have to admit she still looks beautiful, so some bloke is bound to lay seige to her at some stage.

Things got so civilized recently that we even managed to have a joint birthday party for Pierre. The three of us also sometimes go to restaurants together and Marie-Sophie and I sometimes do lunch when there any legal left-overs to tie up. It may or may not be a coincidence but this period of *détente* dates from when our financial affairs were resolved and Rachel Bonham-Lee disappeared back under her stone.

I think I finessed the whole financial thing rather nicely.

It showed signs of becoming a real Dickensian monster, with me demanding all Marie-Sophie's bank statements and bills virtually back to the year of her birth and she, or rather Rachel, while complaining that my demands were 'oppresive' (they were), was demanding the same of me. It would have taken forever. Finally I wrote saying, 'Broadly speaking this is what I am worth and what I earn, but if you don't believe me ask any question you like to my accountant, my bank and the Inland Revenue. I enclose the appropriate authorizations.' They never did which just goes to show they didn't want the information in the first place.

Shortly afterwards I met Marie-Sophie and said, 'If I pay any capital to you, you won't get any because its first port of call is to pay back the Legal Aid Board. I'll give extra maintenance for Pierre instead and you can go and spend it on dresses.' I think she was as battle-weary as I was and the offer was accepted.

Pierre still wants a brother or a sister although he now says that they might be a pain and break his toys. His nervous tic makes cameo appearances from time to time but has largely subsided. He likes to tell people that 'Dad has nice girlfriends but he can't get married'. I have even heard him say it to his mother. Occasionally he tries a divide-and-rule trick with his parents. He'll say 'I want to go back to Mum's house'. I'm supposed to panic and go out and buy him a new box of Lego Technics. Instead I just say 'Fine, ring her up and tell her we're coming, and then I'll drive you over'. I find that shuts him up immediately. He seems to have got the hang of divorce now.

And as for me . . . I'm holding a dinner party tonight, and Roger's not coming.